FAITH ALIVE

A STUDY COMPANION
TO THE CATECHISM

Edited by
REV. KEVIN MICHAEL LAUGHERY, J.C.L.

LIGUORI
PUBLICATIONS

One Liguori Drive
Liguori, Missouri 63057-9999
(314) 464-2500

NIHIL OBSTAT:
The Reverend Michael Evans, M.Th.

IMPRIMATUR:
The Right Reverend Monsignor John Hine, Ph. L.

ISBN 0-89243-832-0
Library of Congress Catalog Card Number: 95-76178

Excerpts from *The New Jerusalem Bible*, copyright © 1985 by Darton, Longman & Todd, Ltd. and Doubleday, a division of Bantam Doubleday Dell Publishing Group, Inc. Reprinted by permission.

Originally published in the United Kingdom 1994
by Hodder & Stoughton Ltd.

U.K. edition by Rowanne Pasco
and John Redford

Text design by Information Design Unit,
Newport Pagnell, England

Copyright © 1995, Liguori Publications
Printed in the United States of America
3 5 7 9 8 6 4 2
First Printing

Contents

PART IV – CHRISTIAN PRAYER

PART V – APPENDICES

Forewords

Foreword to the original edition by Cardinal Hume, Archbishop of Westminster

I warmly commend *Faith Alive* as an inspiring presentation of the Catholic faith for adults and congratulate the many people from all walks of life who have contributed to it.

I pray that it will lead many Catholics to a deeper understanding of the riches of our tradition and give many Christians of other denominations and people of other faiths enlightenment in their spiritual journey.

Foreword to the original edition by Thomas J.Winning, Archbishop of Glasgow

The great need today for adult formation in the faith is rivaled only by the hunger in people for that very kind of formation. Both need and hunger can be satisfied in many different ways. One of these is by *Faith Alive*.

Foreword to the new edition by George Carey, Archbishop of Canterbury

Few things are more important to Christian growth than a willingness to wrestle with the deep truths of the faith. As a contributor to *Faith Alive* I am delighted that it gives to the reader an opportunity to look afresh at the core of our faith. May it prove a point of growth for many.

Preface

The need for commandments

I hope that, in reading this new edition of *Faith Alive*, the reasons for the emphasis on the Commandments will become clear. But I would like to begin with a simple story which illustrates, for me, the importance of commandments in Christian life. Any precious gift, including the most precious of all, the life of God in us, can be abused, even lost, unless we understand and obey the "dos and don'ts" that govern its correct operation. Otherwise, the gift can be the prelude to disaster rather than to happiness.

I vividly remember receiving my first bicycle, at about the age of ten. I came home from school on a Thursday afternoon – it must have been Thursday, because my mother closed her grocery store early on Thursdays, and that was her only free afternoon – and turned the corner to go down our street.

I could see my mother, standing there with a radiant smile on her face, holding my new bicycle. The spokes, rims, and handlebars gleamed in the sun. I say "new," but of course the bike was second-hand, bought from a huge man with hands always black with grease whom my mother called "Mr. Dale," and who ran a one-man bicycle selling and repair business. I think she paid him £5 for it, the equivalent of about £50 today I suppose. But no millionaire surveying his gold-plated new Rolls Royce was ever more proud of his vehicle than I was of mine.

Then, I had to start riding it, which of course I tried to do immediately. I had an audience, because our street was one where mothers and children would stand in their doorway and make everyone else's business their own. As I struggled along, with my mother holding firmly on to the handlebars, then releasing them briefly to see whether I could ride the bike even for a few yards on my own, advice was not lacking. "Don't look down, John, look straight ahead, that's a good lad. Don't be frightened, push down hard with your left foot, then with your right. That's better, John."

As time went on, those rules became second nature, obeyed unconsciously as I cycled around our streets. Then, only after some long time, I was allowed on what we called the "main road." Cars were rare in the side-streets where we lived during the forties, and children could play in the street with safety; but traffic was beginning to increase on the arterial roads through towns and from town to town (the "A" roads, as we call them now).

First, I was not allowed to go on to those roads on my own, but only with older and more experienced children. Then, I was taught very important rules, in order to preserve my own life and limb. I was taught to stop my bike and look behind to see if anything was coming, then to move into the center of the road to make a right again. Then, to turn right into the main road, I was taught to look right, then left, then right again. Only then was I to turn right into the main road. I must never, never cycle into that main road without stopping to see whether a car was coming.

My mother had given me a beautiful present, which I could enjoy using for years, and which also was part of my growing up and maturing. But that present was also a potentially lethal weapon. My mother fully realized that the joy of my new possession could turn into family grief and tragedy if I did not obey the rules of the road, the *Highway Code*, the commandments.

It is remarkable that in every area of life people expect rules and regulations, except in religion. This is perhaps part of our conditioning in the Western world of seeing religion as purely a private and personal affair. No one else is going to tell me how to worship my God. But the Catholic Church, for nearly two thousand years, has insisted that Christ our Lord left commandments for us to follow, rules whereby the precious gift of his own grace and life which he has left us may be preserved and grow in us. Ignore those rules, or disobey them, and we risk greater disasters than neglecting the rules of the *Highway Code* when riding a bicycle. Follow those rules, and they will help us grow in the supreme law, the law of charity, which is God himself.

But we begin in *Faith Alive*, not with the Commandments, but with the Gift, which is God himself, revealed to us in Jesus Christ through the Spirit in the Church.

John Redford

Acknowledgments

First of all, we would like to renew our thanks to the many people who helped us produce the original edition of *Faith Alive* with their encouragement and contributions. It is hard to single out any individual, but we would like especially to mention Gerald McGuinness who, as managing director of *The Universe* when the series *Faith Alive* appeared in that paper, shared our confidence that the project would succeed. Also, Anne White, editorial assistant for the series, who took such trouble with the details and the illustrations.

We also want to thank Emma Sealey at Hodder Headline plc for her encouragement in preparing this new edition of *Faith Alive*.

Finally, we would like to record our gratitude to our mothers, from whom we first learned the Good News.

Rowanne Pasco
John Redford

Introduction

Faith Alive began as a series of supplements in the weekly *Universe* newspaper in Great Britain. It was then made into a book which has met a widespread need for a straightforward and clear presentation of the Church's teaching. Now, we are using the new official Catechism, itself only launched by the Pope in Rome in October 1992, to further update and improve *Faith Alive*, for the needs of the end of the twentieth century and the beginning of the twenty-first.

The compilers of the new Catechism of the Catholic Church wish their work to be used in a particular way. The Catechism of the Catholic Church is not like the old Baltimore Catechism, which Catholics used for many generations. Instead of being brief the new Catechism is over six hundred pages long. It is a Catechism first and foremost for those who teach the faith rather than for those who are beginners in it; although everyone is encouraged to read it, and we would be delighted if your reading *Faith Alive* stimulates you to read the new Catechism itself.

The new Catechism, however, is mainly a sourcebook for teaching the Catholic Faith. It quotes the Synod of Bishops in Rome in 1985, which requested such a Catechism. The bishops wanted a book to serve as a point of reference for catechisms or compendia which are composed in different countries (*CCC 11*).

The new Catechism is published to help us in our work of producing local expressions of our faith, like *Faith Alive*. No one book, however carefully prepared by how many experts, can express our faith in every local situation. The new Catechism has been published as a source book to stimulate local catechisms.

This new edition of *Faith Alive* is intended as an adaptation of the new Catechism for North American readers.

Faith Alive follows broadly the structure of the new Catechism. After introducing the subject of our search for God and the need for faith, we explore the CREED, the ancient expression of our faith. Then, we look at our WORSHIP, particularly the sacraments. Then follows the MORAL section, which contains a great deal of new material including a full analysis of the Ten Commandments. Finally, we end our new edition of *Faith Alive* with a section on PRAYER, the heart of our Christian life.

We have injected ideas from the new Catechism throughout the book. We have decided not to quote the new Catechism directly, but rather to paraphrase it in our own words. This decision partly arose from the fact that the English translation was delayed in publication, and we had to use the official French version (*Catéchisme de l'Eglise Catholique*, Paris, Mame-Librairie Editrice Vaticane, 1992). But, more importantly, we found that we could express the ideas of the new Catechism better in our own way; which again, the new Catechism encourages us to do.

The new Catechism constantly refers to its own sources: the Scriptures, the early Fathers of the Church, great theologians and saints, and the Councils, especially the Second Vatican Council, which met in 1962-65 to renew the whole life of the Church. In using the new Catechism, therefore, we have quoted from these sources, and enriched *Faith Alive* by key references to great writings in the two-thousand-year tradition of teaching in the Catholic Church.

Faith Alive now contains a much expanded moral section, which follows the new Catechism in its third part entitled "Life in Christ." In the new Catechism this takes up nearly 200 pages of text, more than one-quarter of the whole. With the challenge of moral problems today, the compilers of the new Catechism saw clearly the importace of tackling in depth the whole question of the moral teaching of the Church.

In the long process of consultation worldwide, which preceded the publication of the new Catechism, the moral section was itself a focus of controversy. The first draft of the Catechism was sent to every diocese in the world, and some theologians thought that there was too much emphasis upon the Commandments, leading to legalism, a law-based rather than a freedom-based approach to Christian morals.

Because of this, in the final edition of the new Catechism, the section introducing morality has been much deepened, emphasizing the grace of God which has set us free in Christ. Also, the Christian context of the Ten Commandments has been emphasized, basing our obedience to the Commandments on the twofold law of love of God and love of neighbor, as Christ himself taught.

However, the compilers of the Catechism have not budged from their original conviction that it is vital to deal with the Ten Commandments in detail when teaching Christian morality.

The section on the Commandments occupies nearly 100 pages of the new Catechism – more than one-fifth of its length. In our new edition of *Faith Alive*, therefore, we have devoted one chapter to each of the Ten Commandments.

Rowanne Pasco
John Redford

North American Editor's Note

The authors call attention to the fact that there are numerous references to early Church writings, such as the works of those who are known as the "Fathers of the Church." The Catechism gives the titles of these works in their original languages. I have striven to provide an English title in all cases. The cited works include such renowned books as the *Confessions* of St. Augustine and some obscure writings, many of which may not exist in English. English titles will at least encourage the thorough student or teacher to research boldly and persistently.

The Reverend Kevin Michael Laughery, J.C.L.

Farmersville, Illinois

1 The desire for God

The Church's essential teaching is not new: it is only expressed in a new way for every age of the human race. There is no clearer example of this than the first section of the new Catechism, which tells us that the desire for God is written into the heart of the whole of the human race throughout history. Why? Because, says the new Catechism, we are created by God and for God. We have within ourselves an attraction towards him, and, says the new Catechism, it is only in God that human beings will find the truth and the happiness for which we never cease to search (*CCC 27*).

Of course, these thoughts are not new. They take up the words of one of the greatest Christian saints and brilliant theologians, St. Augustine of Hippo (*A.D. 354–430*), who had a checkered career. Although brought up as a Christian, Augustine was a wild young man, living with a mistress for fifteen years, and being attracted to a strange religion called Manicheanism, not dissimilar to some of the weird sects today. Augustine was following an academic career as a rhetorician, and, while lecturing in Milan, he met the great Bishop Ambrose, and was convinced by his arguments for Christianity.

One barrier remained, that of his own chastity. One day he was reading the Scriptures and opened the page at random (*Rm 13:13–14*) which reads:

> Let us live decently, as in the light of day; with no orgies or drunkenness, no promiscuity or licentiousness, and no wrangling or jealousy. Let your armor be the Lord Jesus Christ, and stop worrying about how your disordered natural inclinations may be fulfilled.

Augustine returned to the authentic Christian faith, founded his own monastic community, was soon made a bishop, and wrote some of the greatest books in the history of the Western world. One of those books was his *Confessions*, statements of his own faith and love of God.

That truth discovered so dramatically by St. Augustine sixteen hundred years ago has been found by billions of people all down the centuries. Yet we

---

First issued in 1885, the old Catechism that many of us learned as Catholics, called the Baltimore Catechism, asked right at the beginning:

Q Who made the world?

A God made the world.

Q Why did God make you?

A God made me to know him, to love him, and to serve him in this world, and to be happy with him for ever in heaven.

Why do so many people remember those questions so well? It is because they are so fundamental that we cannot understand our own existence unless we first understand that truth: that God is the only reason for our existence. Our supreme and only true happiness lies in him.

> You are great, Lord, and highly to be praised: great is your power and your wisdom has no measure. And we humans, a small part of your creation, dare to praise you, precisely we who, being reduced to our mortal condition, carry in ourselves the testimony of our sin and the testimony that you resist the proud. In spite of everything, we humans wish to praise you. You yourself move us to do this, in so making us find our delight in praising you, because you have made us for yourself and our heart is restless until it finds its rest in you.
> (St. Augustine, *Confessions 1,1,1; CCC 30*)

humans are always attempting to run away from it, and to find our happiness in other things than God. Each age produces its own forms of temptation. The modern age is secularist: that is to say, many people find it quite easy to live without any expressed need for God. Our technology, the marvels of modern science, give us the impression that we humans are omnipotent, and can run our own world our own way. Even if something like two-thirds of the world claim to believe in some kind of God, in the Western world many have become what Vatican II calls "practical atheists," living their lives without seeing the need for developing any kind of relationship with God.

People do try to find happiness in other things, and forget God. We are able to do this, because we have free will, and can choose the object of our happiness. It is possible to choose to find happiness in money, power, sex, or popularity. It is also possible just to live from day to day, taking life's joys and sorrows as they come, without any special hope of future life or of any meaning to life beyond the next meal. Our eyes are meant for light; but like coal miners we can spend so long in the dark that we become accustomed to living in the darkness, so much so that coming up to the daylight can be painful.

But all of us know that it is unnatural to live in the darkness; and none of us would choose to do so unless it was necessary to make a living, or for some very special reason. To choose God is to choose the Light, because, as John tells us, God is Light and in him is no darkness at all.

Even Christians pressurized by secularization will try to emphasize the importance of human relationships rather than their relationship with God.

Genuine Christian faith will resist such attempts to remove the transcendent from our faith. Of course, our faith has moral implications. Jesus himself rejected those who called him Lord but did not come to the aid of those in need. But human relationships, however important, are not the be-all and end-all of our lives. Perhaps one reason why in the Western world we are making such a mess of human relationships, particularly of marriage, is that many people are leaving God out.

Forgetting God is not new. Two and a half thousand years ago, the prophets had to reprimand the people of Israel in the same terms: "The ox knows its owner and the donkey its master's crib. But Israel does not know, my people do not consider" (*Is 1:3*).

If God is our aim, then our love is directed first to him. This becomes the purpose of our whole being. If that is the case, then the purpose of our human

St. Augustine of Hippo, one of the greatest Christian saints and a brilliant theologian.

relationships is to help each other relate to the ultimate source of our lives and of our love, God himself. Then not only does our relationship with God come right, but also our relationship with other people.

The new Catechism sets out to show not only that God is our only true ultimate desire, but also that he has given us the means whereby this desire is fulfilled beyond our wildest dreams. We are capable of knowing the existence of a personal God (*CCC* 35). God has shown us himself by creating us in his own image. He has also sent his only begotten Son to show us the way back to the Father, he has left his Spirit as his permanent gift in our hearts, and he has left his Church to nurture our faith and form us into a community as a sign of that final happiness with him which is our privileged destiny.

God is always present to us. Sometimes we experience that presence and sometimes he seems to be far away. But he is always there.

Many religions agree with this but disagree about how God is present. Christian faith is that we actually share in the inner life of God, the Father, the Son, and the Spirit. Jesus taught his disciples to call God "Abba" – Father, because through his coming we really have been made the children of God.

St. Paul expresses this beautifully in the Letter to the Romans.

> All who are guided by the Spirit of God are sons of God; for what you received was not the spirit of slavery to bring you back into fear; you received the spirit of adoption, enabling us to cry, "Abba, Father!" The Spirit himself joins with our spirit to bear witness that we are children of God (*Rm 8:14–16*).

It is the Holy Spirit who brings about this change. When Jesus was leaving his disciples he promised that he would come with the Father and that they would make their home in us. In the Gospel of John we find this promise fulfilled when Jesus is raised from the dead. He stands among his disciples and he says to them: "Peace be with you." Then he breathes on them and says, "Receive the Holy Spirit. For those whose sins you forgive, they are forgiven" (*Jn 20:22–23*).

We live by the Spirit of Jesus.

> It is no longer I, but Christ living in me (*Ga 2:20*).

We are so identified with Christ that the love the Father has for us is the love he has for Christ. So it is, that we can pray in the name of Jesus.

> Anything you ask from the Father he will grant in my name (*Jn 16:23*).

Our Christian faith is founded in our relationship with God: the Father who created us out of love and to whom we are infinitely lovable; the Son who made that love visible in his life and death; the Spirit, the love of Father and Son, who confirms us in the power to live in faith and love.

Our natural life is a mystery to us. How much more true is it of God's life in us. God is known by us in the way someone who is loved knows the one who loves. When we love we enter into the world of the one we love. God, in Jesus, enters into our world and our lives because he loves us unconditionally.

But we are challenged also to do our utmost to remain in and develop this relationship. Without it I cannot be fully myself.

Pilgrim people

Christian faith is a journey through this world to the promised land of eternal happiness with God in heaven. None of us is perfect. We are on the way to perfection.

Every human being is born a child of God. Christians believe that because of original sin, our relationship with God is damaged. Baptism restores that relationship and through the gift of the Holy Spirit given to us in the death and resurrection of Christ we share the divine life.

But each of us must make our own response in faith. This is conversion. We commit ourselves to live in right relationship with God, following the example of his Son, Jesus Christ. We acknowledge the gift that enables us to do this, the Spirit of God. The theological term is justification (making righteous). We are set free to be what we are.

Our commitment brings us into the community of the Church, but there always remains a tension between the Holy Spirit in us and the inherent tendency toward sin.

The work of the Holy Spirit is to form Christ in us and us in Christ. Gradually and sometimes painfully his grace defeats the tendency to evil in us. This, in theological language, is sanctification: making us holy, or whole.

Holiness means not just freedom from sin, and good in the religious sense of the word, but also whole and integrated human beings in a relationship of love with God. We are becoming what we are.

Not until we die will this tension between the tendency to sin and the divine life in us be resolved. Faith will give way to the sight of God and we will become perfectly what God wants us to be, in communion with him and with each other.

It is impossible to imagine what this will be like except that it will be marvelous.

Christian faith is a journey through this world ...

Questions

1 Why do you think that so many people seem to find it difficult to relate to God today?

2 Is there real happiness without God?

2 God's plan

The first book of the Bible, the Book of Genesis, teaches us that God wished from the beginning to invite human beings to friendship with him. The new Catechism relates how the sin of our first parents Adam and Eve did not destroy God's plan. It (*CCC* 55) quotes Vatican II on Revelation as a magnificent expression of God's plan for salvation from the beginning:

> God, who creates and conserves all things by his Word (*Jn 1:3*), provides men with constant evidence of himself in created realities (*Rm 1:19–20*). And furthermore, wishing to open up the way to heavenly salvation, he manifested himself to our first parents from the very beginning. After the fall, he buoyed them up with the hope of salvation, by promising redemption (*Gn 3:15*); and he has never ceased to take care of the human race. For he wishes to give eternal life to all those who seek salvation by patience in well-doing (*Rm 2:6–7*). In his own time God called Abraham, and made him into a great nation (*Gn 12:2*). After the era of the patriarchs, he taught this nation, by Moses and the prophets, to recognize him as the only living and true God, as a provident Father and just judge. He taught them, too, to look for the promised Savior. And so, throughout the ages, he prepared the way for the Gospel (*Divine Revelation, no. 3*).

Genesis 1–11 is the story of our rejection of God's command from the beginning of human history. Adam and Eve, Cain and Abel, the Tower of Babel, all tell of human disobedience, pride and hatred – a not unfamiliar story today. But God refuses to use our sin as an excuse to destroy the world. Rather, God decided to save the human race, in spite of our failures (*Gn 6–9*).

Biblical scholars dispute how much history is contained in the story of Noah and the Flood. But the story tells us that God, through chosen people who follow his way, will save the world from disaster.

The start of the plan: Abraham and sons

God wished to gather together a people of faith who would follow his way. So first he called Abraham from his own country, from his own family and relations (*Gn 12:1*). Abraham and his people lived a nomadic life, wandering round the "fertile crescent," rearing sheep and cattle, and trading in the cities. But God had other intentions: he was to make of this man "the father of a multitude of nations" (*Gn 17:5*). To Christians he is "our father in faith." He was the first person to recognize and worship the one true God. God said that in this man Abraham, he would bless all the nations of the earth, including you and me (*Gn 12:3*). At God's command, Abraham settled in the land of Canaan, south of Jerusalem at Hebron.

The new Catechism (*CCC 65*) quotes a key text:

> At many moments in the past and by many means, God spoke to our ancestors through the prophets; but in our time, the final days, he has spoken to us in the person of his Son ... (*Heb 1:1–2*).

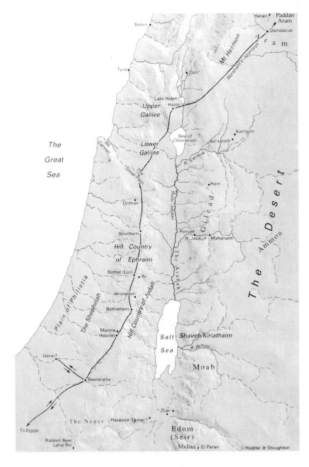

Yahweh said to Abram, "Leave your country, your kindred and your father's house for a country which I shall show you" (*Gn 12:1*).

The Christian economy, therefore, since it is the new and definitive covenant, will never pass away; and no new public revelation is to be expected before the glorious manifestation of our Lord, Jesus Christ (*Divine Revelation, no.4*).

This does not mean that the Church does not grow in understanding of the revelation of Christ, as indeed must we all as individuals. But it does mean that new revelations, and in particular those that contradict the revelation of Christ, are to be rejected because God has spoken his last Word in Jesus. Thus, for instance, the new revelations of the Mormons and the Jehovah's Witnesses are not acceptable, because they proclaim a new revelation.

God's plan handed on

We believe that God's revelation has been handed on in Scripture and Tradition. Scripture is the Word of God contained in the writings of the Old and New Testaments. Tradition is the Word of God handed on in the life of the Apostolic Church.

We believe, with the writer of this early letter to Jewish Christians, that Jesus is the fullness of God's revelation, as God's only Son, true God and truly human, the Word become Flesh.

Later, we shall consider the person and the work of Jesus. In a sense, this book is all about Jesus. Everything relates to him, and to the fact that God's plan came to fruition in his life, death and resurrection.

For the same reason, we believe that revelation was completed with Jesus. Vatican II in its *Constitution on Divine Revelation* put it this way:

Our faith is not only a religion of a book, even of a most holy and inspired book, the Bible. It is a religion of the living Word of God, which came first to people – prophets, kings, writers – and then was written down in a body of writings which we call the Bible or the "Scriptures." "Tradition" does not mean musty clothes and old documents, but the living Word of God handed on in the Church in teaching and in the celebration of the sacraments in union with the bishops and with the successor of Peter, the Bishop of Rome, the Pope.

The Word of God, the message that Jesus Christ is risen from the dead and that all must be baptized and have their sins forgiven in his name, was first preached by the apostles on the day of Pentecost. Later, these same apostles, together with the dynamic St. Paul, put the Word of God into writing, in the form of letters, called the Epistles, and eventually as the "Gospels," collections of sayings and deeds of Jesus.

It was the apostles who, under the inspiration of the Holy Spirit, put that message into writing and also testified to its authenticity. The Church tells us which books constitute the sacred and authentic list of inspired writings – what we call the "Canon" or "Rule" of Scripture. That same Apostolic Church explains the meaning of Scripture.

At the time of the Reformation, in the sixteenth century, Protestants disputed that Tradition was a valid source of revelation, and the cry was "Sola Scriptura," "Scripture Alone" for salvation. But the logic of revelation, as we have just described it, tells us that the Scriptures are themselves part of the living tradition (the word *traditio* in Latin means "handing on"), and can only be rightly understood within the community of the Church.

The new Catechism (*CCC 82*) quotes the teaching of the Second Vatican Council on Scripture and Tradition:

Sacred Scripture is the speech of God as it is put down in writing under the breath of the Holy Spirit. And Tradition transmits in its entirety the Word of God which has been entrusted to the apostles by Christ the Lord and the Holy Spirit ... Thus it comes about that the Church does not draw her certainty about all revealed truths from the holy Scriptures alone. Hence, both Scripture and Tradition must be accepted and honored with equal feelings of devotion and reverence (*Divine Revelation, no. 9*).

Questions

1 How does God speak to us today?

2 Which are the most common ways our society rejects God?

3 God's word in Scripture

At Sunday Mass, we usually have three readings from the Scriptures. The first is usually from the Old Testament, to which we respond with a psalm. The second is usually from the Epistles or the Acts of the Apostles. The last and most important reading is from the Gospels.

The Old Testament

The Bible is a library of works by different authors, written during many centuries. They wrote poetry, prose, prayers and songs, fact and fiction. In all there are sixty-six books written over 1,000 years.

One thing binds them all together. They are the Word of God. God speaks his truth to us. We call this revelation. He does so through human writers. We call this inspiration.

The Old Testament is the foundation for God's self-revelation in the living Word made Flesh, Jesus Christ.

The Bible is the world's best-selling book. It has been translated, in whole or part, into 2,000 languages and dialects.

The first "books" of the Bible were scrolls, hand-written in Hebrew. In 1947, in a dry desert cave in Palestine, near the Dead Sea, a remarkable collection of scrolls was found. They were probably the records and writings of a religious sect called the Essenes. Among them was the complete text of the prophet Isaiah. It is, to date, the oldest surviving Old Testament manuscript.

The first complete translation of the Old Testament, into Greek, was begun in the third century B.C. It was called the Septuagint because 70 scholars are supposed to have worked on it (Greek septuagint = seventy).

The new Catechism quotes Vatican II on the Old Testament:

Christians should accept with veneration these writings which give expression to a lively sense of God, which are a storehouse of sublime teaching on God and of sound wisdom on human life, as well as a wonderful treasury of prayers; in them, too, the mystery of our salvation is present in a hidden way (*Divine Revelation, no. 15*).

The Psalms

At the Last Supper Jesus as a Jew sang psalms with his apostles before he went to his death (*Mt 26:30*). He was brought up on the psalms and sang them regularly in the synagogue.

Virtually every religious service in the Jewish calendar, every life-cycle event, is marked by the recital of entire psalms or particular verses.

Christians and others have sung the psalms because they find in them varied moods which relate to their needs at different times, and, of course, our roots are in the Jewish tradition.

We seem to have become more aware of psalms over the past few years. At one time they were just part of another book of the Old Testament. Now they are a feature of every Mass as the responsorial psalm and, indeed, of every full celebration of any of the sacraments. The Liturgy of the Hours – the official prayer of the Church, said daily by all clergy and religious and by an increasing number of lay people – uses the psalms as its basic form of prayer.

Psalms can also be used as entrance chants, at the preparation of the gifts and at Communion, and they are often included in the celebration of other sacraments.

The psalms are important to the liturgy because they are prayers inspired by the Holy Spirit.

The Holy Spirit is always present with his grace to those believing Christians who with good intention sing and recite these songs.

We were born with this book in our very bones. A small book; 150 poems; 150 steps between death and life; 150 mirrors of our rebellions and our loyalties, of our agonies and our resurrections. More than a book, it is a living being who speaks, who suffers, groans and dies, who rises again and speaks on the threshold of eternity; who seizes one, bears one away, oneself and all the ages of time, from the beginning to the end (*A. Chouraqi in the Introduction to the Grail translation of the Psalms*).

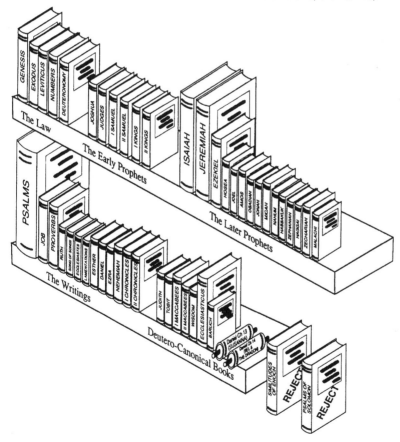

The Old Testament Canon (= Rule) of books accepted by the Catholic Church as sacred Scripture. This list differs from the Protestant and Jewish Canons by the addition of the "Deutero-Canonical" books displayed above.

The Gospels

The Church gives priority within the Scriptures to the Gospels. At a Solemn Mass, the Gospel will be greeted with incense as a sign of special reverence, and the priest will kiss the Gospel as a sign that Christ comes to us in the reading of the Gospels. The reason for this special place is obvious, as Vatican II explains:

> It is common knowledge that among all the inspired writings, even among those of the New Testament, the Gospels have a special place, and rightly so, because they are our principal source for the life and teaching of the Incarnate Word, our Savior (*Divine Revelation, no. 18*).

What is a Gospel?

The word "Gospel" means "Good News" – from the Anglo-Saxon God-spell. The Good News is that Jesus Christ is risen from the dead.

It is very likely that from the earliest times the sayings of Jesus, and stories about him, were memorized and handed down to the first Christians by Peter and the other apostles in their teaching (see *Ac 2:42*). Jesus was acknowledged in his day as a rabbi (teacher). He would often sum up a lengthy instruction in a sentence which could be easily memorized, such as

> Many are called, but few are chosen.

In the first ten or twenty years after the Church began, the words of Jesus were handed on mostly if not entirely by word of mouth. These sayings were treated with great reverence, because Jesus himself was "the Lord," governing his people on earth from his place in heaven "at the right hand of the Father."

Christians then began to collect the sayings of "the Lord" and to write them down. Many scholars think that the teachings of Jesus were put into collections, some time before the Gospels as we know them were written. Some have even thought that these collections can be identified, from a scientific examination of the Gospel text. They have called one of these early collections "Q" (from the German *Quelle*, "Source"). This Source Q contained Jesus' sermons, such as the "Sermon on the Mount" (*Mt 5-7; Lk 6:20-49*), and many of his parables.

The Second Vatican Council commits us to affirming the "apostolic origin of the four Gospels" (*Dogmatic Constitution on Divine Revelation, no. 18*). This means that there is a real link between the four Gospels and the original apostolic witnesses of Christ.

This link is affirmed most clearly at the beginning of Luke's Gospel:

> Seeing that many others have undertaken to draw up accounts of the events that have reached their fulfillment among us, as these were handed down to us by those who from the outset were eyewitnesses and ministers of the word, I in my turn, after carefully going over the whole story from the beginning, have decided to write an ordered account for you ... (*1:1–3*).

The link with eyewitnesses is confirmed by modern scholarship. The four Gospels were all written before the close of the first century A.D., within the possible lifetime of eyewitnesses, and certainly within the lifetime of those who knew those first apostles.

Although the Gospels are not a verbatim account of what Jesus said, they are an accurate record

The four Gospel makers

The writing of the Gospels

Christian tradition has associated the four Gospels with the names of:

Matthew, one of the Twelve chosen by Jesus (*Mt 10:3*), a tax collector.

Mark, the John Mark mentioned in the Acts of the Apostles, a companion of Paul (*Ac 12:12*). He may have been the young man who fled naked at the arrest of Jesus (*Mk 14:51–52*). Mark, according to tradition, used Peter the apostle as the main source of his Gospel.

Luke, the physician and friend of Paul the apostle (*Col 4:14; 2 Tm 4:11; Phm 24*).

John, son of Zebedee – with his brother James and Simon Peter, one of the three closest to Jesus among the Twelve (*Mt 17:1*). John was also the "beloved disciple" who at the Last Supper reclined on his master's breast (*Jn 13:23*).

The dates of the New Testament books

30	Death and resurrection of Christ. The Christians preach the Good News.
30-50	The sayings of Jesus handed on mainly by word of mouth.
50-64	Collections of the sayings of Jesus.
64	Gospel of Mark.
70	Gospels of Matthew and Luke.
90	Gospel of John.

11

of the sense of his teaching. To guarantee this, we have the inspiration of the Holy Spirit, who, Jesus said, would teach his disciples everything, and remind them of what he had said (*Jn 14:26*).

Scholars consider that, from A.D. 60 to the close of the first century, the Gospels of Matthew, Mark, Luke and John were put together in the form in which we know them today. Most experts consider that Mark's Gospel was first, followed by Matthew, Luke and John. The writers believed in Jesus as the Son of God and wrote so that others might come to faith.

Although the four Gospels are not biographies of Jesus, they are

The new Catechism (*CCC 126*) speaks of a three-stage process in the writing of the four Gospels: The life and teaching of Jesus, oral tradition, and the written Gospels.

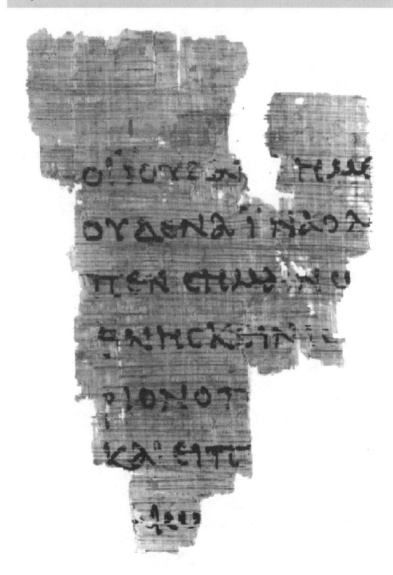

A precious scrap of paper. The world's oldest New Testament manuscript fragment P52

historical, in that they tell of a person who really existed, and give us genuine historical information about him.

Symbols

The symbols associated with the four Gospel writers are based on the description of the four living figures in Ezekiel's vision (*Ezk 1:5–12*). Each had four faces, a human, a lion, a calf and an eagle. In the Book of Revelation four similar figures appear (*Rv 4:6–8*).

The early Church found these figures, who "went where the Spirit urged them," a good symbol for the writers who produced the Gospels under the guidance of the Spirit.

Matthew is the human face because his Gospel begins with the family tree of Jesus the man. Written for Jews, it stresses Jesus the Messiah.

Mark's Gospel, which is based on the experience of the apostle Peter, begins in the desert, the home of wild beasts, so his symbol is the lion. Jesus, in Mark, overcomes the devil, who in early Christian symbolism figures as a lion. For example,

> your enemy the devil is on the prowl like a roaring lion
> (*1 P 5:8*).

Luke wrote for Gentile Christians. His emblem is the calf, a symbol of sacrifice. His Gospel opens with the story of Zechariah taking his turn to offer sacrifice in the temple. Jesus, in Luke, is the Good Samaritan and Healer, laying down his life for all people.

The eagle fits John's Gospel which begins in the highest heaven with the Word who was in the beginning. Jesus in this Gospel is Christ the King, Son of God and Lord of all. John had written to deepen the faith of Christians when the first witnesses were dying and to make them realize that Christ had sent his Spirit to be with them at all times.

The Epistles

It is remarkable that the earliest Christian documents we possess are not theological treatises, or manuals of church discipline, or even words of Jesus. They are letters, the earliest written by Paul to the newly-founded church at Thessalonica, barely twenty years after the death and resurrection of Christ.

It seems that these letters would first have been read out in the Christian community to which they were addressed, much like letters that are read out in the family.

Paul and the Christian leaders who wrote these letters sometimes had serious messages. There is deep theology, pastoral counseling, and even serious admonition. But the personal element is never far away. Paul wants to know how Syntyche and Priscilla are getting on. He wants them to know that he will come and see them as soon as possible. And, above all, don't forget the collection!

There are twenty-one epistles, or letters, in the New Testament. Of these, fourteen are attributed to St. Paul, three to St. John, two to St. Peter and one each to St. Jude and St. James.

The second reading at Mass is always either from one of the Epistles or from the Acts of the Apostles or the Book of Revelation.

Paul's letters were written to Christian communities in towns such as Philippi or Corinth; or to individual Christians, such as Timothy, Titus or Philemon.

The other letters – from Peter, John, Jude and James – are usually called the Catholic Epistles, because they were written to all Christians (*kath-holos* is Greek for "according to the whole"), rather than to specific local churches, or to individuals, as were the epistles of Paul.

All the letters in the New Testament come from the early Christian community. None is dated by scholars later than the first decade of the second century A.D., well within a century after Pentecost.

When we consider the authorship of the Epistles, or of any New Testament book, we must remember that the ancient world had a concept of authorship different from ours. In those days, the apostle – Paul, Peter, John – could be called author, *even if he had not actually written the work*. If a disciple of Paul, for instance, had written one of his epistles, and Paul had directed the work, even from a distance, the finished product would have been attributed to Paul as its authority and inspiration.

The Acts

Most of what we know of the first twenty years of the church is to be found in the book called "The Acts of the Apostles."

Acts tells the wonderful story of how the Good News spread after the Day of Pentecost from Jerusalem, through Samaria, and then throughout the known world. It focuses on Peter, who founded the church in Jerusalem, and then on Paul, who took Christ's message to the Gentiles. The story ends with Paul's arrest in Jerusalem, his appeal to Caesar, and his eventful journey to Rome, on which he miraculously escaped shipwreck.

Acts reads like an exciting novel, but it must be taken seriously as history.

The author of Acts is the same as the author of Luke's Gospel, and takes up the story where that Gospel leaves off, with the ascension of Jesus. Tradition has it that the author of the Third Gospel and of the Acts was Luke the physician and companion of Paul. There are good reasons advanced for this tradition – but it is difficult to prove. It is not a question central to faith. In any case, Acts is a very early Christian apostolic document, dated at the latest towards the close of the first century A.D.

Although Acts finishes with Paul arriving safely in Rome, the story seems incomplete. What happened to Paul after he arrived in Rome? Acts does not tell us. Some scholars think that that is because Paul had only just arrived in Rome when Acts was written (A.D. 61), so there was no more to tell. But it may be also because the author of Acts wants us to realize that the story IS incomplete. The Acts of the Apostles is still being written, by the Church through the ages – and by you and me.

The Acts of the Apostles and the letters to the young churches (Epistles) give us many of the early hints and instructions on prayer.

The work of the Spirit in prayer is a recurring theme with St. Paul. Harking back to Christ's prayer he writes:

> [We] cry out, "Abba, Father!" The Spirit himself joins with our spirit to bear witness that we are the children of God (*Rm 8:15-16*).

A little further on, he gives great hope to those of us who find praying difficult:

> The Spirit comes to help us in our weakness, for, when we do not know how to pray properly, then the Spirit personally makes our petitions for us in groans that cannot be put into words; and he who can see into all hearts knows what the Spirit means because the prayers that the Spirit makes for God's holy people are always in accordance with the mind of God (*Rm 8:26-27*).

If you want to know when to pray, turn to Paul again:

> Always be joyful; pray constantly; and for all things give thanks; this is the will of God for you in Christ Jesus (*1 Th 5:16-18*).

Prayer

This, then, is what I pray, kneeling before the Father, from whom every fatherhood, in heaven or on earth, takes its name. In the abundance of his glory may he, through the Spirit, enable you to grow firm in power with regard to your inner self, so that Christ may live in your hearts through faith, and then, planted in love and built on love, with all God's holy people you will have the strength to grasp the breadth and the length, the height and the depth; so that, knowing the love of Christ, which is beyond knowledge, you may be filled with the utter fullness of God (*Ep 3:14-19*).

Questions

1 Jesus probably wrote nothing down. Has this been good or bad for Christianity?

2 Choose one of the parables and retell it in a modern setting.

4 Faith

I believe

The new Catechism (*CCC 142–143*) tells us that by his revelation the invisible God addresses us in his love, and calls us to be his friends, to enter into communion and conversation with him. The only proper response to this invitation is faith. By faith, we submit completely our mind and our will to the God who reveals. This assent of faith holy Scripture calls the "obedience of faith" (*Rm 1:5*).

Faith, then, for Christians, is not just a "shot in the dark," a vague opinion and forlorn hope that someone might be up there to rescue us from our misery. Nor is it just a vague experience or feeling of the divine presence, although experience is involved. It is rather an act of obedience to God who has already spoken to us, in the prophets and finally in Jesus Christ, a response in which we use all our powers of mind and will to say yes to God.

The new Catechism (*CCC 145*) quotes the Epistle to the Hebrews 11:8, which praises the faith of Abraham who, in about the eighteenth century B.C.,

> obeyed the call to set out for a country that was the inheritance given to him and his descendants, and ... set out without knowing where he was going.

The whole of Abraham's life as recorded in Genesis was one of faith, wandering in a land unknown to him (*Gn 23:4*). His wife Sarah conceived a child in her old age after the divine promise (*Gn 17:19*); and Abraham had to decide if he should offer his son Isaac in obedience to God (*Gn 22:1–14*), this being a test to prove that Abraham would choose God even above his own family. Of course, God would not let Abraham actually sacrifice his son, but gave him a ram in his son's place (*Gn 22:13*). Thus Abraham became the father of all those who believe.

The faith of Mary

The new Catechism (*CCC 148*) proposes Mary as the perfect example of faith. She was obedient to God when the angel came to her to tell her that, although she was a virgin, she would give birth to a Son who would be the Savior of the world. Mary believed the angel and that "nothing is impossible to God" (*Lk 1:37*). Mary, the Catechism explains, still believed even when Jesus suffered his excruciating death on the cross (*CCC 149*). Because of this faith, all generations will call Mary blessed (*Lk 1:48*). Incidentally, Martin Luther, the architect of the Reformation, had great devotion to Mary, based upon this fundamental idea: that she was the example of faith for all generations.

The new Catechism then goes on to speak of the object of our faith, the one in whom we believe: in God alone as one who reveals to us the truth; in Jesus Christ the Son of God whom the Father has sent into the world. We can believe in Jesus Christ because he is himself God, the

Word made Flesh. And finally, we believe in the Holy Spirit, who penetrates our heart by faith, and who enables us to understand the deep things of God.

> The Church never ceases to confess its faith in one only God, Father, Son and Holy Spirit (*CCC 152*).

The characteristics of faith

The Catechism teaches that faith is a gift of God (*CCC 153*). Peter the apostle was told by Jesus, after Peter had confessed Jesus as Son of God, that "it was no human agency that revealed this to you but my Father in heaven" (*Mt 16:17*). Vatican II says:

> Before this faith can be exercised, man must have the grace of God to move and assist him; he must have the interior helps of the Holy Spirit, who moves the heart and converts it to God, who opens the eyes of the mind and "makes it easy for all to accept and believe the truth" (*Divine Revelation, no. 5*).

The fact that the grace of God is necessary in the act of faith does not make it any less a free act of the human person (*CCC 154*). It is in no way contrary to human freedom for us to put our confidence in God and the truths he reveals to us.

We believe first and foremost, says the new Catechism (*CCC 156*), "on the authority of God himself who reveals, and who can neither deceive nor be deceived." The act of faith in the revealing God goes beyond the powers of reason, into trust in God himself the Revealer.

However, this act of faith is not contrary to reason, nor is it blind. God has given us external proofs of his revelation: miracles and prophecies, and in particular the life, death and resurrection of Jesus. These "are certain signs of revelation, adapted to the intelligence of all," called "motives of credibility" which show that the assent of faith is not an irrational movement of the Spirit (*CCC 156*).

Thus, says the Catechism (*CCC 157*), faith is certain, because it is founded on the Word of God which cannot be untrue. Secondly, faith seeks to understand. Faith is always searching to understand and believe more (*CCC 158*). Finally, faith, while beyond reason, is never contrary to science (*CCC 159*). One of the tasks of theology is to show the conformity between faith and reason, to the mutual benefit of both science and theology.

No one, says the new Catechism (*CCC 160*), must be compelled to faith. Faith must be a free human act. The Church repents of those times in its history when it has not allowed people freedom of faith, but has either encouraged or connived at religious persecution aimed at imposing the Catholic faith on

Mary ... treasured all these things (*Lk 2:19*)

the population. The development of faith in the Church is evidenced by this clearer consciousness of the freedom of the act of faith emphasized in the Second Vatican Council.

The Scriptures and the Church teach that faith is necessary in order to please God and to come to eternal life (*CCC 161–162*). Since God has made us for communion with himself, and faith is the only adequate response to God's revelation, then it follows that faith is absolutely necessary for salvation.

It is also possible to lose faith, the gift of God, by our own decision or actions. Some extreme evangelical views hold that faith, once given, can never be lost. But Scripture tells us that we must be careful that no one snatch away our crown of life (*Rv 3:11*). Those who are faithful to the end will be given the crown of life (*Rv 2:10*), and only those (*CCC 162*).

But for those who sincerely follow Christ to the end, faith is even now the foretaste of eternal life. St. Basil describes faith in terms of a mirror: in this life we receive the blessings of faith in part only, as when we see someone only partly in a mirror's reflection. One day the full reality will be revealed.

Thus we receive encouragement from the clouds of witnesses of faith: Abraham, Mary, and also a great company, more than can be numbered, of those who have been faithful to death, and so have received the crown of life (*Heb 12:1–2; CCC 165*).

We believe

The new Catechism, while insisting that faith is a personal act (*CCC 166*), also states that it is not an isolated act. Each believer, the Catechism says, is part of a "chain" of believers. "We believe" is a statement of the community of faith, in conferences of bishops, in liturgical assemblies.

The Catechism is clear that we must distinguish between the Church and revelation. God, not the Church, is the author of our salvation (*CCC 169*). The Church is our mother, the educator of our faith. As Augustine puts it, no one can have God as his Father without the Church as his mother. The Church is the pillar and ground of the truth (*1 Tm 3:15; CCC 171*), which guards faithfully the deposit of revelation. This makes the Church's message one throughout the ages.

How do I come to faith?

Because faith is a "gift of God," we cannot come to it simply by our own intellectual efforts. To believe in God, we need his help.

Because, if there are different languages throughout the world, the content of the Tradition is one and the same. So, neither the churches established in Germany have any other faith or any other Tradition, nor those who are in Spain, nor those who are with the Celts, not those of the East, of Egypt, or Libya, nor those which are established in the center of the world ... The message of the Church is therefore true and solid, because there is but one and only one path of salvation which has been revealed across the whole world (Irenaeus, *Against Heresies, 1, 10, 1–2*).

That is why it is most important to pray for the gift of faith, even if we are not even sure that God exists. In the Gospels, a father who wanted his boy cured was challenged by Jesus saying "Everything is possible for one who has faith"; to which the man replied, "I have faith. Help my lack of faith" (*Mk 9:24*). This paradox of belief and unbelief is in all of us to some extent.

But this does not mean that all that we can do to come to faith is to pray. Jesus did say, "Seek and you will find, knock and it will be open to you." Work and commitment are involved on our part, even if, as Paul says, in that process it is still "God who is working in us."

Questions

1 What do you believe in?

2 Who has influenced your faith most?

3 How has your faith been tested?

5 The Creed – Introduction

Our creeds are very ancient, dating back to the early centuries of the Church, when the General Councils of the Church were concerned to define the true nature of Jesus Christ as God and man.

When we express our faith, we need to use words, and words to express a mystery, the mystery of God, which is beyond words. But we believe that the Holy Spirit guides the Catholic Church to keep the truth, and never to err in matters of faith.

Apostles' Creed

This creed dates back to at least A.D. 390, although its title "Apostles' Creed" indicates that there was a tradition that it goes back to the twelve apostles themselves. This cannot be proved, still less the legend that each of the twelve articles was written by one of the twelve apostles. The core of truth in this story is that the Apostles' Creed is itself based upon an even earlier statement of faith now called the Old Roman Creed, which was the official baptismal creed of the Church of Rome at least from the end of the second century onwards. We are then not too far on from the apostolic age itself. At least, there is no reason to believe that the statement of faith required by the twelve apostles was very much different from this Apostles' Creed, although it would probably have been shorter.

> **The Apostles' Creed**
>
> I believe in God, the Father almighty,
> creator of heaven and earth.
>
> I believe in Jesus Christ, his only Son, our Lord.
> He was conceived by the power of the Holy Spirit
> and born of the Virgin Mary.
> He suffered under Pontius Pilate,
> was crucified, died, and was buried.
> He descended to the dead.
> On the third day he rose again.
> He ascended into heaven,
> and is seated at the right hand of the Father.
> He will come again to judge the living and the dead.
>
> I believe in the Holy Spirit,
> the holy catholic Church,
> the communion of the saints,
> the forgiveness of sins,
> the resurrection of the body,
> and the life everlasting.
>
> *Amen.*

Nicene Creed

This creed, longer than the Apostles' Creed, is also later in its origin, its earliest use at Mass being A.D. 476, at Antioch in modern Syria. It is called "The Nicene Creed" because it is linked with a Creed produced at the Council of Nicea in A.D. 325. This Council was preoccupied with opposing the Arians, who did not believe in the doctrine of the full divinity of Christ. That is why the Nicene Creed includes the statement – not in the Apostles' Creed because it was not necessary at an earlier age – that Jesus is "of one being" or "substance" (*homoousios*) with the Father.

The new Catechism used this text for its teaching on Catholic belief.

The Nicene Creed

We believe in one God, the Father, the Almighty,
maker of heaven and earth,
of all that is seen and unseen.

We believe in one Lord, Jesus Christ,
the only Son of God,
eternally begotten of the Father,
God from God, Light from Light,
true God from true God,
begotten, not made, one in Being with the Father.
Through him all things were made.

For us men and our salvation
he came down from heaven:
by the power of the Holy Spirit
he was born of the Virgin Mary and became man.
For our sake he was crucified under Pontius Pilate;
he suffered, died, and was buried.

On the third day he rose again
in fulfillment of the Scriptures;
he ascended into heaven
and is seated at the right hand of the Father.
He will come again in glory to judge the living and the dead,
and his kingdom will have no end.

We believe in the Holy Spirit, the Lord, the giver of life
who proceeds from the Father and the Son.
With the Father and the Son he is worshiped and glorified.
He has spoken through the Prophets.
We believe in one holy catholic and apostolic Church.
We acknowledge one baptism for the forgiveness of sins.
We look for the resurrection of the dead,
and the life of the world to come.

Amen.

6

God the Father and creator

The good news for the human person, for society, and for the world is that there is Someone who loves us and is able to provide for all our needs.

Christian revelation names this Someone as God and goes on to say that God is Trinity. Another way of saying that is that God is community. The Father, the Son and the Holy Spirit are in a perfect communion of love. Their relationship is the model for the community of believers – the Church.

The Trinity (Latin for "threefold unity") is a mystery. The revelation of God in Scripture and in the Church invites us to know God through our relationship with the Father, through the Son, in the power of the Spirit.

How do we experience God?

When Moses came down from the mountain, his face was shining from his personal encounter with God. God, for Moses, was not a boring Sunday chore. God inspired and enriched his life and also his relationships with others.

There is only one God

The three major religions in the world, Judaism, Christianity and Islam, believe that there is only one God. Independently of these beliefs, however, the Greek philosophers Plato and Aristole in the fifth century B.C. came to the same conclusion. It was ridiculous to think that there were many gods; there could only be one God, one ultimate cause of all things.

> "You have made us for yourself, O God, and our heart is restless until it finds its rest in you" (St. Augustine).

St. Thomas Aquinas argued that God must be one, because God is infinite in all perfections. If another god existed, that god would have a perfection which God does not have; which would make God not God at all, since God would then lack that perfection. God therefore must be One, and there can be no other God. We will consider the oneness of God, and what that means in terms of our lives, later when we deal with the first commandment, to love God and our neighbor. At this point, we are considering our faith in God revealed as One to his people throughout history.

Nothing comes from nothing

The arguments for God's existence have been presented by the greatest minds: Anselm, Kant, Newman, Berkeley, and above all in the Five Ways of St. Thomas Aquinas. Philosophers dispute the validity of these proofs, and indeed no one can come to love God just as a result of logic. The gift of faith is needed. But all these proofs have their use in demonstrating that nothing comes from nothing. Either the world as we know it comes from nothing, and so everything is absurd, or there is an infinite creator, the cause of all things.

God's mysterious name

It is easy to have a false picture of God, as an old man with a beard. This is especially so when we emphasize as Christians that God is our Father. Before we think of God as Father, therefore, it is important to realize that God is not like any picture we might paint of him. He is the unseen and unknown God. St. Thomas Aquinas again stated that we do not know what God is, only what he is not. We know that God must exist, because creation can have no other explanation than that of an Uncaused Cause. But the identity of this unseen cause, whom we call God, is a mystery, beyond our understanding.

The Israelites, in the early days, thought that God had some kind of physical shape. Moses yearned to see God, but all that Moses ever saw on the holy mountain was the "glory" of Yahweh, the fire and the cloud which hid God from Moses. Moses saw a bush burning without being consumed, and heard a voice speaking to him. God was revealing his name.

The new Catechism (*CCC 205*) quotes:

> Moses then said to God, "Look, if I go to the Israelites and say to them, 'The God of your ancestors has sent me to you,' and they say to me, 'What is his name?' what am I to tell them?" God said to Moses, "I AM HE WHO IS." And he said, "This is what you are to say to the Israelites, 'I AM has sent me to you.'" God further said to Moses, "You are to tell the Israelites, 'Yahweh, the God of your ancestors, the God of Abraham, the God of Isaac and the God of Jacob, has sent me to you.' This is my name for all time, and thus I am to be invoked for all generations to come" (*Ex 3:13–15*).

The Jews, long before Christ, understood the revelation of this name to be that God was always with them, always present with them to save them; and that his name was mysterious. Christians

Murillo's "The Two Trinities"

The new Catechism quotes the famous text from Deuteronomy (*CCC 201*):

Listen, Israel: Yahweh our God is the one, the only Yahweh. You must love Yahweh your God with all your heart, with all your soul, with all your strength. Let the words I enjoin on you today stay in your heart. You shall tell them to your children, and keep on telling them, when you are sitting at home, when you are out and about, when you are lying down and when you are standing up; you must fasten them on your hand as a sign and on your forehead as a headband; you must write them on the doorposts of your house and on your gates (*Dt 6:4–9*).

later believed that this holy name referred to the infinite being and the existence of God.

The Christian religion is unique in calling God simply "love" (*1 Jn 4:8, 16*). This remarkable statement of John is the climax of an idea present throughout the Old Testament, that God loved his people, even though they were so often unfaithful to him (*CCC 218*). God promises his people that his love for them is eternal (*Jr 31:3*), like a father for his son (*Hos 11:1*) and a woman for her child.

God is Father, Son and Spirit

The doctrine of the Trinity is that God is three equal persons, Father, Son and Spirit, in One God, and that those three persons are not three gods, but One God. It links naturally with the doctrine that God is love, since love implies both unity and relationships, infinite in God.

The Trinity does seem incomprehensible. But any thought about God implies mystery, for instance that he created us, and yet gave us free will. The new Catechism states (*CCC 234*) that the Trinity is the most central doctrine of our faith, the most essential in the hierarchy of truths. It is not against reason. Three infinities, Father, Son and Spirit, all infinite God, do not make three infinities (three gods) but one. You cannot multiply infinity, or add or subtract it. But, if the doctrine of the Trinity is not illogical, it is still mysterious, open only to the eyes of faith (*CCC 237*), revealed only by the Son of God, Jesus Christ, God from God and Light from Light.

The Father revealed by the Son

God occasionally is called the "Father" of the people of Israel in the Old Testament, with Israel being his first-born son (*Ex 4:22; CCC 238*). It is very clear that, in the Old Testament, the term "Father" for God has no sexual connotation, which it had in some Near Eastern religions, where the gods mated to produce the human race.

The term "Father" for God in the Old Testament simply refers to God's authority over all the world. He is the origin of all things, and, above all, he has tender love for his creatures, and especially his chosen people Israel, just as a human father has love for his children (*CCC 239*). As we have seen above, the Old Testament also introduces maternal imagery to describe God (*Is 66:13*). God is like a mother as well as like a father; but as God, he transcends the human father and the human mother. He is God (*CCC 239*).

Liturgy: the sign of the cross

Catholics begin and end their prayers with the sign of the cross and the words: "In the name of the Father, and of the Son, and of the Holy Spirit. *Amen.*"

The sign of the cross on the forehead, breast and shoulders is coupled, not with a reference to Calvary, but to the Blessed Trinity. This is because the cross is much more than an emblem of suffering – it is shorthand for the whole Christian reality of salvation.

We say "In the name of the Father, and of the Son, and of the Holy Spirit." We are calling on the power of the Trinity which has been manifested in history to us. We call on the creating love of the Father, the redeeming love of the Son, and the liberating love of the Spirit.

For this reason, some Christians, influenced particularly by the movement for women's liberation, do not wish to use the word "Father" for God too frequently. Since in a sense, God is Father and Mother, and transcends all human parenthood as the Cause of All Things, should we not drop the too-frequent use of the term "Father" for God, which image will only serve to reinforce male domination?

In this case, however, we are surely bound to the basic imagery for God handed on to us in Scripture and in Tradition. In particular, we have the indisputable fact that Jesus called God his Father, and commanded us to call God our Father in the Holy Spirit, as in the Lord's Prayer. Jesus called God his Father, "my Father," and Mary his mother. Thus, in Christian tradition, the feminine has always been the symbol of created being, responsive to the creative power of God's Word, the place where God finds his home.

We call God our Father; and with reason.

The image for all our ideas of God is Jesus Christ himself, God made man, called in Scripture the "image of the unseen God" (Col 1:15).

> He is the reflection of God's glory and bears the impress of God's own being ... (Heb 1:3; CCC 241).

Our knowledge of God ultimately does not come from our own rational reflection, although that is important. Our knowledge of God comes through Jesus Christ revealed as the Son of the Eternal Father. The Son, the Second Person of the Blessed Trinity, is eternally begotten by the Father, the First Person of the Trinity.

The Spirit

As the new Catechism states (CCC 245), it was the Council of Constantinople in A.D. 381 which defined that:

> We believe in the Holy Spirit, who is Lord and who gives life; he proceeds from the Father.

Just as the Son of the Father was revealed to us when Jesus Christ was born, so the Spirit was revealed to us at the day of Pentecost, when the apostles were filled with the Spirit (Ac 2). The Spirit, the Third Person of the Trinity, is with us to reveal the Son to us and enable us to live the life of God, given to us at our baptism and at our confirmation. This Spirit is with us always, teaching us the truth of God (Jn 16:13). This Spirit is the animator of the Church, the Body of Christ.

Ultimately, our destiny is to be filled with the life of the Trinity, a life which has already begun, but which awaits its perfection in the future, when God calls us finally to himself.

God the creator

The new Catechism (CCC 279) quotes the very first verse of the Bible:

> In the beginning, God created heaven and earth (Gn 1:1).

The creation, from nothing, was the beginning of the whole of God's plan of salvation. The Catechism states that the two questions are inseparable:

> From where do we come?
>
> To where do we go and where does everything go that exists?

It is because God has made us and set us in a world in which he has written his plan, that we know where we are going and where everything which exists is going: back to God himself our ultimate happiness.

The new Catechism insists on the importance of the Christian doctrine that God has created everything out of nothing. There is no question of any preexistent matter existing before God (CCC 296). Again, there is no question of dualism, the idea that there are two opposing forces at the origin of the world, God and the devil, Good versus Evil. On the contrary, God created the whole world and all that he made was good (Gn 1). The devil is a created being who rebelled against God, saying "I will not serve."

God is the Master of the world and of history (CCC 314) precisely because he created everything out of nothing. But, as the Catechism says, the paths of his providence are often obscure; and many of our questions will only be finally answered when we meet our Creator "face to face" (1 Co 13:12). Until then, we have to be content with looking at reality through a dirty and cracked mirror, trusting that God is guiding us even if we cannot always see the way. The Way, after all, is Jesus Christ himself, who has already gone before us to heaven to prepare a place for us.

The good angels

God created both the visible world, of which we are part, and also a world of invisible spirits, whom we call angels (messengers). The Church also believes, with the testimony of Scripture, that these invisible spirits can help us personally in our lives.

Scripture is mysterious about angels. In the early books of the Old Testament, God himself seems to take a human shape. In the book of Genesis, "Yahweh appeared to Abraham" in the form of three men standing before him (*Gn 18:1–2*). The "angels" in this case are simply the human shape of God.

It was not until the later Old Testament period (after the Exile, 597 B.C.) that the angels, as messengers of God, began to work overtime. Post-exile Jews thought of God as more distant, and angels functioned as intermediaries, dispensing God's message. It is here that we encounter the famous names of angels, such as "Raphael" (healing of God), "Gabriel" (God's might), and "Michael" (who is like God?).

Scripture is less interested in describing who the angel is, and more interested in describing the function of angels, as spirits whose work is service (*Heb 1:14*). They still perform that function for us. The idea of guardian angels, taught to Catholic children down the ages, goes back even before Christian times.

There is the story of Tobit, a loyal Jew who falls into misfortune, and who is helped by the angel Raphael, who comes disguised as a man looking for work (*Tb 5:7*). Eventually, the angel tells him who he really is.

> I am Raphael, one of the seven angels who stand ever ready to enter the presence of the glory of the Lord (*Tb 12:15*).

Angels often appear in very heavy disguises.

Experiencing God – in prayer

The God of Christians is a hidden God. Though we can and should go a long way in seeking God through reason, God is "beyond" reason. St. Paul writes:

> Now we see only reflections in a mirror, mere riddles (*1 Co 13:12*).

and:

> we are guided by faith and not yet by sight (*2 Co 5:7*).

"We believe in one God, Son and Holy Spirit, creator of things visible – such as this world in which our brief life runs its course – and of things invisible – such as the pure spirits which are also called angels – " (*Profession of Faith of Pope Paul VI*, 1968).

A little boy was once asked, "Who are guardian angels?" He thought for a moment, and then replied, "Guardian angels are people who help you." This is not a complete theological description; but Tobit would say that there is at least a measure of truth in what the boy said.

In the observable world causes are found to be ordered in series; we never observe, nor ever could, something causing itself, for this would mean it preceded itself, and this is not possible ... One is therefore forced to suppose some first cause, to which everyone gives the name God (Thomas Aquinas, *Summa Theologiae*, 1, q.2, a3).

Praying because we simply believe is essential. It does not deny but supplements the use of reason. For prayer experience we need Scriptural study, the use of theological insights, shared experience of Christian living, and practical involvement in loving God, self and neighbor.

In the Old Testament, God is so holy that his name is not to be used. *Adonai* was substituted. God is distant, the smiter of enemies, the judge. People reading and even teaching the Old Testament can miss the trust shown by Abraham in prayer, the close contact of Jacob wrestling with the angel, the forgiveness of David, the immense patience of God as he reclaims Israel again and again from idolatry.

Yet God is also portrayed more gently:

I have loved you with an everlasting love (*Jr 31:3*);

As a mother comforts a child, so I shall comfort you (*Is 66:13*).

Patriarchs, prophets and writers of the psalms experienced his tenderness and closeness.

The new Catechism (*CCC 344*) quotes the famous song of creation by Francis of Assisi:

Praise be to you, Lord, in all your creatures,
Especially for brother Sun
by whom you give light to the day;
it is beautiful, shining out from a great splendor,
and of you, the Most High, it offers us the sign ...
Praise be to you, my Lord, for sister Water
who is most useful and most humble,
precious and chaste ...
Praise be to you, my Lord, for our sister Mother Earth
who bears us and nourishes us,
who produces the diversity of fruits
with various flowers and herbs ...
Praise and bless my Lord,
Render him grace and serve him
with all humility.

Questions

1 Which proof of God's existence, if any, do YOU find convincing? Or do you have your own reasons?

2 What is the strongest evidence to you of God in your own life and experience?

7 The human person

The new Catechism (*CCC 355*) summarizes its teaching on the human person. First, God created us in his own image and likeness (*Gn 1:27*). The human race holds a special place within creation. Second, as human beings, we unite within ourselves both the world of spirits and the material world. We are created male and female. Third, God has established us in his own friendship.

Some people try to put a price on another human being in terms of how much that person can earn, or benefit other people. For the Christian, no limit can be set on the worth of any person.

God loves us just as we are. He made us in his own image and likeness. Alone among living creatures, we can be aware of ourselves – to know that we know – and of a power which we call "God" greater than ourselves, an infinite spirit.

God created us for a loving relationship with himself and with each other. But this image has been tarnished by what we call "sin."

One effect of this is that we tend to develop a low opinion of ourselves. When we do not experience the love of other people, we feel that God does not love us either. We think he can only love us if we are good and successful. This is particularly true when we experience misfortune.

But God the Father sent Jesus his Son to show us the way to become really ourselves again: to show us how to love with God's own love, and to realize to the full our human dignity.

The challenge for the Church and for each Christian is to find a way to proclaim this Good News: to love and not to be afraid to show it. This is how the early Christian community attracted so many people.

> "God saw all he had made, and indeed it was very good" (*Gn 1:31*).

God does not make junk!

Christians believe that God created all human beings in love, and calls us to be his children, brothers and sisters in one human family.

It is important to remember that we are essentially good, since God creates us, calls us by name, and makes us holy. God does not make junk. People can become so obsessed with their own sin and failure that they grow blind to the goodness of God which is in them.

Christian faith is meant to heal us and set us free. Faith gives us a profound knowledge and experience that "God is love" (*1 Jn 4:8*). This reality is shown in our creation and our redemption. It makes us believe in ourselves no matter what happens. Every person has value and dignity, and these qualities make them lovable.

> ... if God loved us so much, we too should love each other (*1 Jn 4:11*).

Human dignity is not always easy to recognize, particularly among the outcasts of society.

Human nature has a flip side

God does not make junk. But good products can be
spoiled. Christian faith teaches that the human race
is tarnished by sin. From the beginning people have
disobeyed God. This does not mean that the human
person has less value; but it does mean that we are
weak in our resistance to sin. We must always
remember that the spirit is willing but the flesh is
weak.

How wonderful it would be to become
wise (see *Gn 3:6*).

What is sin?

Many people think of "sin" as "naughty but nice";
God, like a miserable father who cannot bear us
enjoying ourselves, gives us rules just to make us
unhappy. In reality, sin is a stunting of our human
growth, a loss of our dignity as human beings. Adam
and Eve, after eating of the forbidden fruit, are
ashamed of their own bodies, and have to cover
themselves up. They cannot bear to look at each
other. This is a powerful image of the loss of dignity
and pride in ourselves as made in God's image.

What was this sin? The Book of Genesis says it
was eating from the fruit of a tree which God told
Adam and Eve not to touch. The Bible does not say
that it was an "apple" (*Gn 3:2*). We do not know
what the "original sin" actually was, except that
this was a deliberate act of disobedience against
God.

The important thing about the story of Adam and
Eve is that it is a parable of human history. We are
constantly making choices, and often tend to make
the wrong ones.

But, just as the Christian believes that paradise
was lost by the folly of the first humans, so we
believe that it was regained for us by the perfect life
and love and sacrificial death of Jesus Christ, God's
divine Son made man.

Through this, God has redeemed human nature,
offering it forgiveness and a new life. We can accept
or reject this.

Baptism into the Christian community signifies
our acceptance and frees us from original sin; but,
like a sick patient who is cured from an illness, we
are still weak. We need the daily strength of the
Holy Spirit to conquer that weakness, and the support of each other. That is one important reason why
we need to belong to the Church, the community of
believers.

This story of the fall of the human
family is recounted in Genesis,
chapter 3. This is a popular story,
and is not intended to be an
accurate history in detail. But the
Catholic Church teaches that the
human race disobeyed God from the
beginning, and that the effect of this
has been passed on to the whole of
the human race. Thereby, Man and
Woman (Adam and Eve in the
biblical story) lost their perfect
happiness, for they could not have
such happiness without God.

Questions

1 Jesus said, "Love your neighbor as
yourself" (*Mk 12:31*). What does
loving yourself mean in Christian
terms?

2 Which people have been "images
of God" for you? (They could be
people you know personally or
people you know about.)

8 Jesus Christ our Lord

Christian faith is founded upon a historical fact: Jesus of Nazareth lived and died and rose again in Palestine in the first thirty years of the first century A.D.

Jesus means "savior" and he is the center of our religion. The world has never been the same. The first Christians, who were all loyal Jews, had a powerful faith in the One God Yahweh. But, if Jesus was truly Lord, one with his Father in heaven, then how could faith in the One God be preserved? Were there not two Gods now, Father and Son? And what about the Spirit, who came upon Jesus at his baptism, and upon the disciples at Pentecost?

Were there three Gods? Or perhaps there was one God, with three different ways of showing himself?

After six centuries of controversy, the fully developed doctrine of the Trinity emerged.

There was a second question, equally important. If Jesus was God, then how could he be human? The Greeks could understand that the gods walked the earth. Such an idea was often described in their mythologies. But they could not understand how God could so lower himself to become human.

The earliest heresy in the first century A.D. was not the denial

The Trinity (Tri-Unity) is the Christian faith that the One God is Father, Son and Spirit. Not three Gods, but One. And Father, Son and Spirit are not three aspects of God, but three persons in one God. It is because Christian faith is in Jesus as God made man, who sent his Spirit upon all believers, that the question of the Trinity emerged.

Glory to God in the highest
And peace to his people on earth ...

Those who denied the humanity of Christ were called "Docetists," because they believed that Jesus only seemed (Greek *dokeo*, appear) to be human. God could not die, they supposed. Therefore, Jesus could not have died on the cross. Simon of Cyrene, who the Gospel of Luke tells us was made to carry Jesus' cross (*Lk 23:26*) in reality was put to death in his place, said some Docetists.

of Jesus as God, but the denial that he was really human.

That is why we find such a strong affirmation of the true humanity of Christ in the Gospel and Epistles of John, written towards the close of the first century A.D. "The word became flesh," says the Gospel of John, "he lived among us" (*Jn 1:14*). And the First Epistle of John is even stronger, making belief in the humanity of Jesus a touchstone of faith (*1 Jn 3:2–3*).

This belief became known as the doctrine of the Incarnation – that in Jesus God the Son has become flesh (incarnatus), that is, human.

It became important for early Christians to provide a balance between the divinity and humanity of Christ, and to express both.

The human mind of Jesus was finite, created. Nevertheless, in the Middle Ages it was insisted that the human mind of Christ "knew all things in the Word" (Thomas Aquinas).

But what do we mean by "all things"? Do we mean that the infant Jesus, in his mother's arms, was aware of Einstein's mathematics and the Second World War?

Modern theologians have interpreted "all things" as being "all things relevant to his divine mission"; and known by Jesus in a human way. This knowledge came from his unique awareness of God as his Father.

There is an opposite danger in modern theology, that the divinity of Christ will be underplayed. This radical view is linked very much with the rise of modern Biblical criticism, and the question of the "historical Jesus."

If Christ is to be our Savior, he must not just be God for us, but God with us, the true Emmanuel (*Is 7:14*). This is the teaching of the New Testament, expressing the basic meaning of Christian worship.

Unless we believe that Jesus the man is also truly God, we cannot expect him to be our Savior and lead us to God.

The new Catechism (*CCC 426*) claims that Christ is the center of all catechesis, that is all Christian teaching. The point of all catechesis is

to put us into communion with Jesus Christ: He alone can lead us to the love of the Father in the Spirit and can cause us to participate in the life of the Holy Trinity (*Pope John Paul II, Catechesi Tradendæ, no. 4*).

Our concentrating here on the life of Jesus, therefore, is not just from a historical viewpoint. By his life, death and resurrection, Christ draws us into the life of God.

Incarnation and life

Through the Incarnation God has become one of mankind, he has flesh. All human reality, all material things, have been made holy by the mystery of God's descent into matter.

All reality is incarnational; all creation can disclose to us the love of God. This means that in the midst of the affairs of our daily life we can encounter God.

To foster and maintain this vision we need an "incarnational spirituality," which enables us to seek and find the kingdom of God in the midst of daily life. Because of the Incarnation there can be no split between religion and life, between faith and work, between social life and spiritual life. Such a split, as the Second Vatican Council says, must be recognized as "[o]ne of the gravest errors of our time" (*Church in the Modern World, no.43*).

So often this split between religion and life occurs because religion remains in the intellectual realms and does not touch on experience.

Incarnational spirituality is experiential because it seeks, in the words of St. Ignatius, "to find God in all things." It is experiential on a threefold level. On a personal level it is becoming aware of

Christ among you, your hope of glory (*Col 1:27*);

on a social level it is awareness that

by his Incarnation the Son of God in a certain way united himself with each person (*Modern World, no. 22*);

on a political and economic level it is realization that we seek the kingdom of God

by engaging in temporal affairs (*Church, no. 31*).

The Incarnation sheds a completely new light on the whole of human existence and thus "fully reveals man to himself." As the Council says,

it is only in the mystery of the Word made flesh that the mystery of man truly becomes clear (*Modern World, no. 22*)

– the mystery being, Christ in us, Christ in our neighbor, Christ's kingdom in the world.

But we must not confuse *thinking* about the spiritual life with the life *itself*. Because Mary was open to the Holy Spirit, Jesus became incarnate in her womb. As we open our whole lives to that same Holy Spirit, Christ is formed in us and, in the most encouraging words of St. Paul,

Christ Jesus ... for us was made wisdom from God, and saving justice and holiness and redemption (*1 Co 1:30*).

Because of the Incarnation the whole of creation discloses to us the glory and love of God. We live out

> The Second Vatican Council says:
>
> ... [B]y reason of their special vocation it belongs to the laity to seek the Kingdom of God by engaging in temporal affairs and directing them according to God's will (*Church, no. 31*).

Jesus shared our human life.

> For so many marvels I thank you; a wonder am I, and all your works are wonders (*Ps 139:14*).

this great mystery in our own lives when we praise God for the wonders of his creation and, most of all, when we praise him for the wonder of ourselves.

As we pray in this way, thanking God for the wonder of our being, we become aware of that Original Blessing of creation and we hear again the words

> God saw ... and indeed it was very good (Gn 1:31).

Jesus – the evidence

Christians believe that Jesus is God and man. This is a matter of faith, and cannot be answered entirely by examining the historical evidence. But it is important for us to demonstrate that Jesus really existed, and that we have historical evidence about his life on earth. Otherwise, our faith that he was the most important person who lived would be unreasonable.

If, in Jesus, God actually became man, it is essential to try to know something about his historical situation.

Most of our historical information about the life of Jesus is in the Gospels of Matthew, Mark, Luke and John. But is this information, written by believing Christians, confirmed by other sources?

The most reliable evidence outside the Gospels is that of Tacitus, the Roman historian, writing in A.D. 115. He is no friend of Christianity. But referring to the Great Fire of Rome in A.D. 64, and to the Emperor Nero fixing the blame on Christians, Tacitus traces the name "Christian" back to "Christus":

> who was executed by sentence of the procurator Pontius Pilate when Tiberius was emperor. That checked the pernicious superstition for a short time, but it broke out afresh – not only in Judaea, where the plague first arose, but in Rome itself, where all the horrible and shameful things in the world collect and find a home (Annals, xv, 44).

The younger Pliny, while governor of Bithynia in Asia Minor, wrote to the Emperor Trajan about A.D. 112, asking what to do about the problems caused by the remarkable spread of Christianity in the province. Pliny writes:

> they would meet on a fixed day before dawn and sing responsively a hymn to Christ as to a god, and to bind themselves by oath, not to some crime, but not to commit fraud, theft, or adultery, not to falsify their trust, nor to refuse to return a trust when called upon to do so. When this was over, it was

"It was at that time that a man appeared – if 'man' is the right word – who had all the attributes of a man but seemed to be something greater. His actions, certainly, were superhuman, for he worked such wonderful and amazing miracles that I for one cannot regard him as a man; yet in view of his likeness to ourselves I cannot regard him as an angel either. Everything that some hidden power enabled him to do he did by an authoritative word.

"Many of the common people flocked after him and followed his teaching. There was a wave of excited expectation that he would enable the Jewish tribes to throw off the Roman yoke. As a rule he was to be found opposite the City on the Mount of Olives, where also he healed the sick. He gathered round him 150 assistants and masses of followers. When they saw his ability to do whatever he wished by a word, they told him that they wanted him to enter the City, destroy the Roman troops, and make himself king; but he took no notice" (Josephus, The Jewish War, about A.D. 77).

their custom to depart and to assemble again to partake of food, ordinary and innocent food. Even this, they affirmed, they had ceased to do after my edict by which, in accordance with your instructions, I had forbidden political associations. Accordingly, I judged it all the more necessary to find out what the truth was by torturing two female slaves who were called deaconesses. But I discovered nothing else but depraved, excessive superstition.

Josephus, the Jewish historian, who completed his *Antiquities of the Jews* in Rome during the reign of Domitian (A.D. 81–91), twice mentions Jesus. He refers to the stoning of James, "the brother of Jesus the so-called Christ," in A.D. 62. The second mentions Jesus, who

drew to himself many Jews and many of the Greek race ... Pilate at the instance of the foremost men among us sentenced him to be crucified ... and even now the tribe of Christians named after him is not extinct.

Jewish tradition accepts the existence of Jesus as historical fact. This tradition, collected in the body of writings known as the Talmud, taught that Jesus was a practicer of magic (referring to his controversies with the rabbis of his day), and was hanged on Passover Eve for heresy and for misleading the people.

The fact that the enemies of Christianity accept the fact of the existence of Jesus is a most powerful argument for its being an indisputable truth of history.

It was not for over 500 years that anyone thought of using the birth of Christ as the starting point of a new era. And then the monk who worked it out, Dionysius Exiguus, got it wrong. He interpreted the "about 30 years old" of Jesus in Luke 3:23 as though it meant exactly 30 years old.

If we take the historical data of the infancy stories seriously, Jesus must have been born before 5 B.C. King Herod died in 4 B.C., and Jesus must surely have been a year old if Herod ordered the boy children up to the age of two to be killed.

But why December 25? Nobody knew the day or the season of Jesus' birth. But a couple of days after the winter solstice, the longest night and shortest day of the year, the Romans had a feast of the birth of the new sun. As the symbolism of Christ as "the rising Sun ... come from on high to visit us" (*Lk 1:78*) became more popular – and there is a memorable wall painting of it in the catacombs below St. Peter's – this feast day seemed eminently suitable. In the Eastern Church the Epiphany receives more

The Gospel Accounts

Matthew and Luke present the birth of Jesus from different perspectives. Matthew recounts the annunciation to Joseph (*Mt 1:18–25*); whereas Luke recounts the annunciation of the angel Gabriel to Mary (*Lk 1:26–38*).

Clearly, different traditions are at work. It is all the more remarkable that Matthew and Luke both record the following facts:

1 The principal characters were Jesus, Mary and Joseph.

2 These events happened in the days of Herod the King (*Mt 2:1; Lk 1:5*).

3 Mary, a virgin, was betrothed – a formal engagement – to Joseph (*Mt 1:18; Lk 1:27, 2:5*).

4 Joseph was descended from David (*Mt 1:16; Lk 1:27, 2:4*).

5 Jesus was conceived in Mary's womb without intercourse with a male (*Mt 1:18, 20; Lk 2:7*).

6 Jesus was born of Mary in Bethlehem (*Mt 1:25; Lk 2:7*).

7 The name Jesus was given prior to his birth (*Mt 1:21; Lk 1:31*).

8 Jesus was descended from David (*Mt 1:1; Lk 1:32*).

9 The family settled finally in Nazareth (*Mt 2:23; Lk 2:51*).

Jesus Christ: who was he?

He was born in an obscure village, the child of a peasant woman.

He worked in a carpenter's shop until he was thirty, and then for three years he was an itinerant preacher.

He never wrote a book.

He never held an office.

He never owned a home.

He did none of those things we usually associate with greatness.

He had no credentials but himself.

While he was still a young man, the tide of public opinion turned against him.

His friends ran away.

He was turned over to his enemies.

He went through the mockery of a trial.

He was nailed to a cross between two thieves.

While he was dying, his executioners gambled for the only piece of property he had on earth, and that was his coat.

When he was dead, he was laid in a borrowed tomb through the pity of a friend.

Nineteen centuries have passed, and today he is the central figure of the human race.

All the armies that ever marched, all the navies that ever sailed, all the parliaments that ever sat, all the kings that ever reigned, put together, have not affected the life of man upon this earth as has that one solitary life.

Why?

prominence than the Nativity. This seems to date from the fourth century, when the feast spread to counter the still lively Alexandrian festival of the birth of the divine "Eternity" on January 6.

Born of the virgin Mary

Matthew and Luke both testify that Mary did not have intercourse with her husband Joseph, or with any other man, before Jesus was born (*Lk 1:34–36; Mt 1:18–25*).

This belief has always been part of Catholic faith. Ignatius of Antioch (A.D. 117) and Irenaeus of Lyons (A.D. 180) are early witnesses among the Fathers of the Church. And the perpetual virginity of Mary was defined by the General Council of the Lateran (A.D. 649).

From early on, the doctrine of the virginal conception of Jesus was ridiculed.

But Christian faith refused to be put off. Ignatius argued that the virginity of Mary was a sign

The Holy Family.

of the new beginning in Christ. Adam and Eve communicated sin and death to the human race, said Irenaeus. The virginity of Mary, the new Eve, was a sign of this new beginning.

The virginal conception of Jesus is a sign, not only of this new beginning, but also of the fact that Jesus is both God – because only God is his Father – and man, because he shared in the flesh of Mary his mother. The virginal conception is one of the greatest safeguards of the true doctrine of Christ, as God and man.

The miracle of the virginal conception does not mean that Jesus did not share our human condition. He learned, worked, slept, prayed, suffered and died as we all do. The way of his coming into the world is extraordinary because God becoming man was extraordinary.

Prayer of St. Richard of Chichester

Thanks be to you, my Lord Jesus Christ, for all the benefits and blessings which you have given me, for the pains and insults which you have borne for me. O most merciful Redeemer, Friend and Brother, may I know thee more clearly, love thee more dearly, and follow thee more nearly.

Questions

1 Make a list of stories, incidents or sayings from the life of Jesus which emphasize:

a) his humanity

b) his divinity.

2 Choose three stories from the New Testament which show individuals coming to faith in Jesus as the Son of God. What do they have in common? What lessons do they teach us about how to help people in their search for God?

9 Ministry of Jesus

The contemporaries of Jesus knew him as one who healed the sick, opened the eyes of the blind, preached the good news to the poor, and challenged the establishment (*Lk 4:16–19*).

That was the difference between Jesus and any prophet before. The prophets were excellent at telling people what they must, and must not, do, in the name of the Lord. What made Jesus different was that as God and Savior he brought salvation. He was not just the messenger.

He came to die in a way no one else could, to save the whole of humanity. He came to show us, in word and action, that God loves us. He also showed us what God is like.

> Anyone who has seen me has seen the Father (*Jn 14:9*).

Jesus is the Way to God.

Jesus' mission was one of love and forgiveness. But it was also a challenge to the faith of his hearers. His claims were simply too much for many; and some who flocked to hear him and see him perform miracles went away when they heard what they considered blasphemy (*Jn 6:66*). But Peter in the name of the Twelve expressed faith in Jesus:

> Lord, to whom shall we go? You have the message of eternal life, and we believe; we have come to know that you are the Holy One of God (*Jn 6:68–69*).

Christian faith affirms that in Jesus of Nazareth the eternal Word of God became man for our salvation. He was born at a particular time, in a particular place, into a particular family and nation, and lived in a particular historical situation. He became a figure of national significance during his lifetime but his ministry was limited to his own people, the Jews. His international significance increased phenomenally after his death and resurrection. Within a few years his followers began to proclaim him as Lord and Savior throughout the Gentile world.

Hints of the mission to non-Jews appear very early. St. John tells us, for example, that the inscription placed above Jesus on the cross, announcing his identity and the charge on which he was sentenced to death, was written in Hebrew, Latin and Greek. The Hebrew needs no explanation; he lived and died in the land of Israel.

But why Latin? Because the land of Israel was at that time under Roman domination; the judge who pronounced the death sentence was the Roman governor of Judea. And why Greek? Because Greek was the lingua franca of the Near and Middle East at that time. The empire which Alexander the Great had conquered for himself over three centuries before did not long outlast his death as a political unit, but as a cultural unit it endured for a thousand years.

To this cultural unit Jewish Palestine belonged, sharing its Greek language and (in some degree) its Greek way of life, although some of its population, following the precedent of the Maccabees, resisted these alien

Capernaum, where Jesus taught in the synagogue.

influences vigorously. It was to these latter elements in the population that Jesus belonged; he shared the traditional Jewish heritage. He spoke and taught, for the most part, in Aramaic, but the Gospels were written in Greek, because they were intended not for one nation only, but for all.

Apart from the historical Jesus, the Christ of faith might be a figment of our imagination; as it is, we know whom we believe in because he lived on earth, he shared our human lot, he died and rose again, he is always present when we need him. He is the risen Lord, the Savior of the world, the Builder of his Church, the coming King.

The good news of the kingdom

All four Gospels link the beginning of Jesus' ministry to that of John the Baptist. Jesus' message was very similar to John's, and possibly was even inspired by him. They both called for repentance because the kingdom of heaven is close at hand (*Mt 3:2, 4:17*). John's personal appearance, asceticism and preaching all proclaimed an inevitable, imminent judgment that men and women would escape if they underwent a baptism of repentance and radically changed their lives. But Jesus' prophetic message proclaimed that the kingdom had arrived.

The reign of God is not so much God's violent intervention, but the revelation of God's identity and love in all its fullness. Jesus' ministry is one of making this good news known.

Jesus' message of God's nearness in mercy was offered to all of Israel, not just an elect few. And Jesus did not only say God was merciful. His actions *showed* it.

The new Catechism (*CCC 561*) quotes a Church document on catechesis focusing on the meaning of the whole life of Christ, including his ministry:

The whole life of Christ was a continual testimony: his silences, his miracles, his actions, his prayer, his love of people, his love of the little ones and of the poor, his acceptance of the cross for redemption of the world, his resurrection, are all the putting into actuality his word and the accomplishment of revelation (*Pope John Paul II, Catechesi Tradendœ, no. 9*).

His parables express this from several different angles. The parables of the sower (*Mt 13:4–9*), the mustard seed and the leaven (*Mt 13:31–33*) speak about the inevitability of God's full and final manifestation. The parable of the unmerciful servant (*Mt 18:23–35*) speaks dramatically of the human response of forgiving others – not as a condition of God's love but as a consequence of it. The parable of the good Samaritan, besides answering the question "Who is my neighbor," is another lesson in undeserved, even extravagant response to someone in need. These and other parables point to the God whom Jesus describes with a special word: "abba" which means "father."

Some religious groups in Jesus' day tended to separate themselves from ordinary people and especially from those considered "unclean" or sinners. Anyone suffering from a disease, for instance, or from what was considered a demonic possession, was considered unworthy of the coming deliverance of Israel. Anyone who collaborated with the Roman occupation forces, and in particular the tax collectors or "publicans," were without hope. Women of easy virtue were also excluded, as well as other marginalized individuals in Jewish culture like half-Jewish Samaritans, non-Jews or the poor.

But Jesus offered the gift of God's graciousness to all – and this was a large part of his Good News. Only those who stubbornly refused to accept this offer – or who refused to accept that it was offered to all – would go unforgiven and unreconciled. In Matthew 12:31 Jesus is reported to have said that any sin could be forgiven except this obstinate refusal, which was "blasphemy against the Spirit."

It was this indiscriminate generosity and reconciling love that was seen in all Jesus' healings. It was God's fatherly/motherly care that was revealed in Jesus' association – particularly in the intimate gesture of sharing meals – with outcasts and sinners, rich and poor, male and female, religious elite, or religiously excluded, with men like Zacchaeus the tax collector and Simon the Pharisee and women like Mary of Magdala.

The task of the Church is to continue Jesus' ministry of proclaiming the reign of God. We do this in our faithful teaching of the message of God's indiscriminate, lavish love, and in our own actions on behalf of men and women of all nationalities, all races, and all degrees of brokenness.

> Jesus' parables of the wicked tenants (*Mk 12:1–12*), of the wedding feast (*Mt 22:1–10*) and the great parable of the final judgment (*Mt 25:31–46*) all illustrate his conviction that God's kingdom is intended for all, and that now is the time for a joyful but radical change of the heart.

Who do you say I am?

From the beginning of the public ministry of Jesus people were wondering about his identity, remarking:

> He gives orders even to unclean spirits and they obey him (*Mk 1:27*).

Jesus was reluctant at first to encourage speculation as to his true identity (*Mk 3:12*). This may have been either because the people would have followed him for sensationalist reasons rather than for his message; or because they would have expected him to lead a revolt against the Romans if he gained the reputation of being the Messiah (*Jn 6:15*).

He wanted to be known as the one who brought the kingdom of God (*Lk 11:20*), conquering the power of the kingdom of Satan by his healing miracles and by his exorcisms, the healing power of God in action.

But he could not stop people wondering. He challenged his own disciples to answer, "Who do you say I am?" (*Mt 16:15*). Peter's response of faith, "You are the Christ ... " drew the response from Jesus that human beings had not revealed this to him, but God the Father.

As time went on, Jesus began to make statements which seemed to be blasphemous to his Jewish hearers. "Who can forgive sins but God?" said the by-standers angrily after Jesus had said to a sick man, "Your sins are forgiven you" (*Mk 2:1–12*).

But it was when he went to Jerusalem that the real "offense" occurred as the Gospel of John recounts (chapters 7-10). Jesus became more forthcoming about his own identity. "Before Abraham ever was, I AM" (*Jn 8:58*), he said, linking his identity back to the Yahweh God of the Old Testament (*Ex 3:14*). The Gospel tells us that the Jews took up stones then to kill him for blasphemy, but Jesus escaped and left the Temple (*Jn 8:59*).

Following Jesus

What was expected of the first disciples? In the first place, renunciation. Theirs would be no easy road. Jesus may not have been technically a vagrant, but after the beginning of his public ministry there is no mention of his having a permanent home. His disciples were expected to take the barest necessities as they set out to preach the Good News.

Alongside this capacity for renunciation, and forming part of it, was singleness of purpose:

> No one can be the slave of two masters: he will either hate the first and love the second, or be attached to the first and despise the second (*Mt 6:24*).

"... I ... taught in ... the temple" (*Jn 18:20*). The outer wall of the platform on which stood the Temple in Jerusalem.

The disciples of Jesus had to expect to be persecuted simply because they acted like the Master and in his name:

> Blessed are you when people abuse you and persecute you and speak all kinds of calumny against you falsely on my account (*Mt 5:11*).

On the other hand Jesus expected different types of commitment from different people. He did not require everyone to take the road and follow him literally. For instance, the man who had been cured of a legion of devils begged to stay with Jesus, but the Master said no.

> Go home to your people and tell them all that the Lord in his mercy has done for you (*Mk 5:19*).

This man, like many others, was to follow his vocation at home.

The disciples also played different roles within the Jesus group. He chose the Twelve, who were to be the leaders of his community; and one of those, Peter, was to be the leader. Christ called Simon "Peter" (Rock), "and on this rock I will build my community" (*Mt 16:18*).

Christ did not expect his disciples to be only in a movement

"Foxes have holes and the birds of the air have nests, but the Son of man has nowhere to lay his head" (*Lk 9:58*).

"Leave the dead to bury the dead." In his wholehearted commitment to his Master, the disciple of Jesus was required to surrender even this sacred duty for which generations of his countrymen had risked their lives.

Questions

1 The Gospels portray Jesus as sometimes going against the customs of his day: against the traditions of the elders, against the current interpretation of the Law, and in being the friend of outcasts and sinners. How far should we oppose the trends of today in following him?

2 How is the ministry of Jesus continued in the Church?

which would finish when he died, but to build a church (Hebrew *qahal*, assembly), which would last until the end of time.

Much of what applied to the disciples can be applied to us. We can expect persecution if we truly follow Christ, especially if we renounce materialistic values. We can expect ridicule if we accept the teaching of Christ, not least if we affirm faith in the Real Presence of his Body and Blood. In Jesus' own day, we are told, many of his followers could not take this teaching.

Above all, we are called to be disciples of Christ by loving one another. Christ said,

> It is by your love for one another, that everyone will recognize you as my disciples (*Jn 13:35*).

The harvest is plentiful. An army of disciples is urgently needed to go out and gather it in.

We can be disciples in any situation.

10 Miracles of Jesus

Jesus was renowned as a miracle worker. His healing the sick, raising the dead, casting out demons, made the crowds wonder whether he was the Messiah, the chosen one of God who was to come and save his people.

Even his enemies had to acknowledge that Jesus had extraordinary power. He could not do the wonderful things that he did unless something supernatural was working through him.

His enemies explained this power as being the devil in Jesus, or "Beelzebub" as the devil was then called, the Babylonian evil deity "The Lord of the Flies" (*Mt 12:24*). Jesus retorted that this idea was completely absurd. How could the prince of the devils be casting out his own army?

Many people, even some Christians, prefer to play down the miraculous element in the life of Jesus. Perhaps the "devils" he cast out were psychological illnesses which his peaceful presence cured? Perhaps the girl he raised from the dead was not dead (*Mk 5:41*), but only asleep? Perhaps he did not walk on the water, but only on the shore, the mist on the Sea of Galilee at the time, causing the disciples to make a mistake?

Two thousand years after the events, it is impossible to verify whether individual miraculous events associated with the life of Jesus occurred. It is difficult enough when a miracle occurs in our own time to get at "the facts."

What we can do is to discuss whether miracles are possible, in what conditions they occur, and how they can help us come to faith.

The teaching of the Church

The First Vatican Council, which was called by Pope Pius IX in 1869, dealt specifically with one question of the miraculous, in the light of attacks on the Christian faith by rationalists. The Council states both that miracles are possible, and that they are a sure sign of divine revelation.

> In order that our faith might amount to a "submission in accordance with reason" (*Rm 12:1*), God wished to link external arguments of his revelations to the internal helps of the Holy Spirit. These external arguments are divine happenings, and especially miracles and prophecies which, since they clearly demonstrate God's omnipotence and infinite knowledge, are certain signs of divine revelation and suited to every intelligence.

The Council put what it had to say on the subject in more forceful language, in one of the "canons" (*no. 4*).

> If anyone asserts that miracles cannot happen and that consequently all accounts of them, even those contained in the sacred Scriptures, belong to the realm of fable and myth: or that it is never possible to establish with certainty that a miracle has taken place; and if anyone asserts that miracles do not prove the divine origin of the Christian religion, let him or her be anathema. (That is, excommunicated.)

43

"We read of the apostles: and they went forth and preached everywhere, while the Lord worked with them and confirmed the message by the signs that attended it (*Mk 16:20*) and again it was written: and we have the prophetic word made sure. You will do well to pay attention to it as to a lamp shining in a dark place" (*2 P 1:19*). (*Vatican I Session III Ch 3: Faith*)

The new Catechism (*CCC 547*) affirms that Jesus' teaching was accompanied by "miracles and portents and signs" (*Ac 2:22*). These testify that Jesus was the Son of God. But they can also be the "cause of falling" (*Mt 11:6*), if they are seen simply to satisfy curiosity or fulfill a desire for magical powers. Jesus' miracles, for the eyes of faith, are most of all a confirmation that he is the Son of God, and also that the power of Satan has been conquered (*CCC 550*).

These strong words of Vatican I are confirmed by the effect the miracles of Jesus had in his own day. Many people saw Jesus just as a superstar, and did not grasp the deeper meaning of his miracles; yet others, like the man born blind who was cured by the Lord, were helped to come to faith by the extraordinary healing power of Jesus. As the First Vatican Council says, these miracles were signs "accommodated to the intelligence of all."

Miracles are not a magic way in which we can come suddenly to believe. They are only short steps along the road to faith. Above all, they help us come to faith only in conjunction with a growing personal relationship with Christ. This is made clear by the Second Vatican Council.

Vatican II's Dogmatic Constitution on the Church says of the miracles of Christ that they "demonstrate that the kingdom has already come on earth," but it makes it clear that this is a role which they share with his word, his works and his presence. In fact, it says that the kingdom is revealed principally in the person of Christ himself, Son of God and Son of Man, who came to serve and to give his life as a ransom for many (*Mk 10:45*) (*no. 5*).

The Dogmatic Constitution on Divine Revelation (*no. 4*) puts the role and importance of miracles in the life of Christ in similar perspective. It says that Christ completed and perfected revelation

> by the total fact of his presence and self-manifestation – by words and works, signs and miracles, but above all by his death and glorious resurrection from the dead, and finally by sending the Spirit of truth.

In his "Evangelization Today" Pope Paul VI lists Christ's miracles among the

> innumerable signs which arouse the wonder of the multitudes and at the same time draw them to him in their desire to hear him and to be transformed by his works.

The Pope points out, however, that for Christ there was "one sign in particular" which "stood out" among all those to which he attributed a special importance: the weak and the poor were evangelized.

This is also made clear in the Gospel stories of miracles. The writers are leading us away from the wonder as such towards a personal love of our Lord. In the story of the transfiguration, for instance, Jesus appeared miraculously to his disciples on the holy mountain, together with Moses and Elijah, two Old Testament figures. But finally, the vision went and "when they looked round, they saw no one with them any more but only Jesus" (*Mk 9:8*).

"Our friend Lazarus is at rest; I [Jesus] am going to wake him" (*Jn 11:11*).

Lourdes – the facts

One of the best-known sites of miracles is Lourdes, in France, where our Lady appeared to Saint Bernadette in 1858. Since the opening of the famous shrine, 6,000 cures have been certified. From 1946 to 1965, 64 miracles were officially recognized.

- 1,300 cures have seemed sufficiently serious to be the object of a file.
- 57 have been passed on by the Medical Office to the Committees (national or international).
- 19 only have been conceded as miracles by the diocesan bishop.

Meditation

"Ask, and it will be given to you; search, and you will find; knock, and the door will be opened to you. Everyone who asks receives; everyone who searches finds; everyone who knocks will have the door opened.

"Is there anyone among you who would hand his son a stone when he asked for bread? Or would hand him a snake when he asked for a fish?" (*Mt 7:7-10*).

Questions

1 Christ saw sickness as an evil – the "bondage of Satan" (*Lk 13:16*). Yet those whom he cured had to die. What sign was he giving in healing the sick?

2 Many people expect God to work miracles constantly. They ask, "Why did he allow this earthquake, this plane crash, the death of a child?" Should a believer expect such interventions? Is it a sign of childlike faith or credulity?

On most occasions when Jesus performs a miracle he is reacting to an intercession.

They have no wine.

Lord, that I may see.

Lord, my servant is sick.

But always, Jesus couples his willingness to do what is asked with the faith of the asker or receiver.

All prayer of intercession must be made in faith. It is quite right to pray for healing of body, mind and soul – for ourselves and others.

By praying in faith, our faith is tested and strengthened, because we have to be still, to wait, perhaps not to get an immediate answer. We must continue trusting, praying in faith. Patience in prayer will heal us, giving an inner peace and making us more able to listen to others and help them.

11 Teaching of Jesus

Jesus seems to have taught by word of mouth, not by writing. His teachings are only to be found in the writings of the Christian community which preached his resurrection from the dead.

How much, then, of this teaching recorded in the Gospels is actually Jesus' own words, and how much is put into his mouth by the writers of the Gospels? This is a controversial question, and scholars differ among themselves.

Christians believe that the Bible is the inspired Word of God.

But this does not necessarily imply that everything recorded in the Gospel as our Lord's words has to be exactly as he said it. God, in inspiring the Gospel writers, used their human talents and the normal means of communication.

It is acceptable today in some circumstances to report the speech of a person not in actual words but in the words of the reporter. It was the same in our Lord's day also. The Gospels frequently report what Jesus said rather than the way in which he said it.

The Mount of Beatitudes, Sea of Galilee

The inspiration of the Holy Spirit enabled the writers of the Gospels to be faithful to what Jesus said, and indeed to what he was saying in the Spirit after the resurrection to the Christian community of that time, and to us.

The substance of Jesus' teaching is in the first three Gospels, Matthew, Mark and Luke – called the "synoptic" Gospels (from the Greek syn-opsis, "seeing together"). "Seen together," these Gospels seem to present evidence that the teaching of Jesus was put into collections before the Gospels as we have them today were compiled. Christians wanted to remember the Lord's words.

The best proof that these synoptic Gospels are substantially reliable records of the teaching of Jesus is that they "ring true" when read. A teacher of great genius is behind them, not a community or committee. Matthew tells us that our Lord taught the people "with authority" (*Mt 7:29*). This authority permeates the Gospels.

Fulfilling the law

Sometimes the teaching of Jesus seems incomplete, even fragmented. This is because he did not set out to provide a complete set of morals for every occasion.

Jesus never considered that he had to give the whole of God's teaching to his disciples. He believed that God's Torah (usually translated "Law," but better translated "Teaching") already existed, in what we call the Old Testament. There was plenty of moral teaching already there.

Jesus said clearly,

> Do not imagine that I have come to abolish the Law or the Prophets. I have come not to abolish but to complete them (*Mt 5:17*).

Traditions

Jesus' attitude to the Torah seemed revolutionary to his contemporaries, and understandably so. By the time of Jesus, a long tradition of interpretation of the Torah had grown up, particularly within the Pharisaic party.

The real difficulty was sorting out the important commands within the Torah from the less important. The five Books of Moses contained legislation for every part of life down to the size of Temple pillars. Out of these hundreds of commands, all given by God, a scribe asks him "Which is the first?" (*Mk 12:28*).

An example of how Jesus reinforced the law is the attitude he took to the precept, part of the Ten Commandments, "You shall not commit adultery" (*Ex 20:14*). Jesus actually made this command much stricter, by covering internal desires as well as external infidelities:

"But I say this to you, if a man looks at a woman lustfully, he has already committed adultery with her in his heart" (Mt 5:27–28). It was in a case of adultery that Jesus also showed the great forgiveness of God. He said to the woman who was about to be stoned for this crime, "Neither do I condemn you. Go away, and from this moment sin no more" (*Jn 8:11*).

Jesus' answer says nothing new. He quotes two texts from the Torah, the first from Deuteronomy:

> ... you must love Yahweh your God with all your heart ... (6:5)

and the second from Leviticus:

> You ... will love your neighbor as yourself (19:18).

Jesus' moral strategy was to lead people back to the Torah and then to explain its teachings in a new and refreshing way.

His complaint was that some teachers of the Torah had obscured the Scriptures by their traditions. People could even avoid the implications of the command "Honor your father and mother" by offering money to the Temple, thereby relieving them of the obligation to help their parents in their old age (Mk 7:8–13).

But Jesus was even more radical in his interpretations of other parts of the Torah.

He taught that some commandments within the Torah of Moses should give way to a more important command. He taught that the law of Sabbath rest, imposed in the Books of Moses on pain of death (Nb 15:32–36), could be broken in order to heal a person.

> The Son of man is master of the Sabbath (Lk 6:5)

he said to his shocked hearers.

Jesus could even cancel some precepts of the Torah in order to go back to what he saw as a more primitive dispensation. The Books of Moses allowed divorce, provided that the man gave a writ of dismissal to his wife. This was to protect the wife from being reclaimed by her husband, leaving her permanently free to marry another man, and so find some source of livelihood (Dt 24:1). Note that the wife could not divorce her husband.

Jesus went right back to Genesis 2:24, and nullified the Deuteronomic Code.

> It was because you were so hard hearted that he [Moses] wrote this commandment for you. But from the beginning of creation [God] made them male and female ... So then, what God has united, human beings must not divide (Mk 10:5,8).

Follow God's law as described from the beginning, says Jesus, and you will not divorce at all.

Jesus' teaching was shocking. Even his own disciples did not always understand him. But it had an inner consistency. Matthew says:

> His teaching made a deep impression on the people because he taught them with authority, unlike their own scribes (Mt 7:28–29).

His teaching was as effective as his miracles in drawing crowds and making disciples. A man who could treat the Torah with such apparent arrogance, and yet make such obvious sense of it, must be special.

Jesus' moral package is unbelievably demanding. He wants us to love our enemies. After a lifetime of service of God, we are to say, "We deserve nothing. We are unprofitable servants." When we fast, we cannot even have the satisfaction of looking miserable. We have to pretend to be happy.

Yet Jesus insisted: "My yoke is easy and my burden light" (Mt 11:30). There certainly was a feeling of liberation about it, as one began to acquire Jesus' own view of the Torah. But what really must have made the burden light was the fact that Jesus did not see the Torah just as a series of precepts to be learned off by heart.

Rather, Jesus actually lived his own love of God and his neighbor.

The sayings of Jesus seem very difficult, even impossible to put into practice. He tells us to "turn the other cheek" (*Mt 5:39*) rather than resist evil. And he told a rich young ruler that, if he wanted to be happy, he would have to sell all he had and give to the poor (*Mk 10:21*).

How can we apply such ideas to everyday living? Throughout the history of the Church, people have distinguished between "counsels" (advice given by Jesus e.g. to the rich young ruler) and "commands" (precepts for all, like the Ten Commandments).

This distinction was particularly active in the Middle Ages, and it created a two-tier Christianity, one for clergy and religious, and another tier (lower) for lay people. The bulk of the teaching of Jesus is contained in the Sermon on the Mount (*Mt 5-7*), which begins with the Beatitudes.

The Beatitudes

"How blessed are the poor in spirit:
The kingdom of heaven is theirs.

Blessed are the gentle:
they shall have the earth as inheritance.

Blessed are those who mourn:
they shall be comforted.

Blessed are those who hunger and thirst for uprightness:
they shall have their fill.

Blessed are the merciful:
they shall have mercy shown them.

Blessed are the pure in heart:
they shall see God.

Blessed are the peacemakers:
they shall be recognized as children of God.

Blessed are those who are persecuted in the cause of uprightness:
the kingdom of heaven is theirs.

Blessed are you when people persecute you and speak all kinds of calumny against you falsely on my account.

Rejoice and be glad, for your reward will be great in heaven; this is how they persecuted the prophets before you" (*Mt 5:3-12*).

The Beatitudes

The core of Christ's teaching is in the Beatitudes. This teaching can be understood only when we try to start living according to Jesus. Otherwise it appears quite illogical, as we can see from the list.

The Latin word for "blessed" is "*beatus.*" *Beatitudo* means "blessedness" or "happiness." And so we have the English word "beatitude."

In these Beatitudes, the "Magna Carta," as they have been called, of Christianity, Jesus is telling us of joys and rewards beyond the joys and rewards of this world.

Jesus knows our hearts. He made them himself, for himself. He designed them in such a fashion that they could never be satisfied but by himself.

Although he had many friends in this world these were not the source of his joy. This lay in his union with his Father and the Holy Spirit.

The Beatitudes tell us that basic human happiness, not only in the next life but also in this, has its roots in our union with God.

We are all sinners. Only Mary was without sin. But if we keep trying to model our lives along the lines of the Beatitudes – if we keep trying to be more detached from this world, if we try to have true sorrow for our sins, if we try to spread peace, to be chaste and keep our hearts intent on God, thirsting for him, if we try always to forgive others and put up with the wrongs done to us – then even in this life we shall experience something of the joys of heaven.

The Beatitudes tell us where true joy may be found. By implication, they tell us too where deep misery lies.

For years we can struggle against God. We try to bargain with him, hoping he may reduce his demands, hoping he may let us keep all we have and still have him. We are afraid of finding ourselves stripped. Yet this is what God requires before he will fill us with himself, which alone can make us happy. And so, for fear of being unhappy in this world, we run the risk of being unhappy for ever.

The new Catechism (*CCC 543–546*) focuses the teaching of Jesus on the kingdom of God, to which we are all summoned to enter, and to which Jesus called the people of Israel from the beginning of his public ministry.

> If we let ourselves be influenced by some current thinking, we can come to think that the worst suffering is to be without food or shelter or liberty.
>
> This is not so. The worst suffering in this life is to be without God. Without God, the whole world cannot make us happy.

Living the Beatitudes

The greatest danger in Christian life is to become too good at religion. We keep the rules, do spiritual exercises, think we have it sewn up. The Beatitudes turn all that upside down. "How happy are the poor in spirit" says that the Gospel is for those who are not very good at religion, or anything else for that matter.

"Blessed" gives the idea that, whatever our situation in life, happy or sad, we are in a position which makes for ultimate happiness. We are blessed if we are walking the way we should be, the way in which God made us to act.

The Beatitudes may seem foolish. "How can we be peacemakers? We have to look out for number one." Then, in a sense, we are beginning to live the Beatitudes. We are beginning to realize that we are not worthy of God. They turn everything upside down. When we think we are not living them, then we begin to realize that perhaps in a strange way we are!

The Church is a church of sinners. God forgive us if cowards, prostitutes, wealthy stockbrokers, and gamblers feel out of place in the Church.

The Beatitudes do not say "Happy are those who achieve righteousness," but "those who hunger" for it. Even if we cannot achieve something good, we can yearn for it. Prayer is a most positive way of yearning. We can yearn for our own fulfillment, we can yearn for the hungry to be fed, we can yearn for love in broken marriages. That does not absolve us from doing something about it if we can. But sometimes we are helpless to do anything.

People who are helpless and weak can be doing more in the eyes of God than those who are strong.

> One of the earliest heresies was that of the Donatists, who believed that only faithful Christians should be allowed to remain in the Church.

Questions

1 Choose any one or two of the social or moral concerns of the present day and explain what application of the teaching of Jesus you would make to resolve the issues.

2 Are the Beatitudes a practical guide for the Christian life today? Present a case for and against.

3 How would you have reacted to the teaching of Jesus had you lived in Galilee then and heard his teaching?

4 Why is Jesus' teaching popular even among people who do not totally accept him as the Son of God?

But the Beatitudes do not encourage us to wallow in our helplessness, to feel sorry for ourselves! The Beatitudes teach us to yearn for something better and try to achieve it.

They tell our parishes, for example, that we are not following Christ necessarily because we have a marvelous parish council, a well-organized liturgy, excellent parish organizations, and have paid off the parish debt. The greatest danger is always to think, "I have arrived." That was the sin of the Pharisee, who recounted all his good deeds before God, while the tax collector simply beat his breast and said,

God, be merciful to me, a sinner (Lk 18:13).

12 Death and resurrection of Christ

Why did God do this to me? Perhaps most of us have said this in a time of great stress. A child dies, a family breaks up, a business collapses. As far as we can tell, we have done nothing to deserve it. Then why does God apparently reward with evil the good that we have tried to do?

This question is most of all to be asked about Jesus of Nazareth. He was loved by the common people, one who cast out evil, healed the sick, an inspiring leader, a prophet of God, the Son of God. Yet he was put to death in the most excruciating way invented by man: suspended on a cross.

Why did God allow this to happen to his own Son? The answer must be historical and theological. The death of Jesus happened historically, as a result of a number of religious and political factors. But Christian faith is that this death of Jesus was part of a plan, the plan of God for the salvation of the world. And if Jesus' death has a meaning, then no suffering of any person on earth is without meaning anymore, because we can all share in the death of Christ, taking up our cross with him.

What happened?

According to the synoptic Gospels, it took only one week for Jesus to antagonize the Jerusalem leaders so thoroughly that they determined on his death. In Galilee the opposition had come from the Pharisees and their inability to stomach his attitude toward legal observance and his re-interpreta-

tion of the Law. But now the clash was with the Sadducees, the custodians of the Temple, over the issue of Jesus' authority. After Jesus had solemnly entered the city and taken possession of the Temple on Palm Sunday, the challenge to their authority meant that this unorthodox leader from Galilee had to be removed before he disturbed the delicate equilibrium which left government under the imperial eye of Rome in the hands of the rich high-priestly aristocracy.

So whether it was after questioning by Annas, the godfather figure behind several high priests, or after a formal interrogation presided over by Caiaphas, the high priest, the charge adopted was political, that of being a messiah, at that time the synonym of a rebel leader. Jesus had not fully accepted this role and preferred to preach the realization of the kingship of God, his Father.

The Roman procurator Pontius Pilate, trained in Roman law and used to feuding factions, was obviously uneasy. Three times he tried to throw out the charge. When the Jewish leaders still pressed it, he tried to persuade them to accept this presumably popular figure as the beneficiary of the Passover amnesty. But the Galilean held no interest for the Jerusalem mob: they wanted one of their own, the rebel Barabbas, released. Still Pilate hesitated till the Jewish elders played their trump card: if you release this man you are not a "friend of Caesar." If Pilate lost this status by being reported to Rome for releasing a possible rebel leader, he might well lose his job, and even his head.

John represents this scene before Pilate as being the final denial by the Jewish leaders of the kingship of God.

The theme of judgment by encounter with Jesus is a thread which runs through the fourth Gospel. The climax comes when Jesus, still robed as King of the Jews, is brought out and rejected. In rejecting him they condemn themselves finally and explicitly as Jesus is seated on the Chair of Judgment (Jn 19:13) and the chief priests proclaim, "We have no king except Caesar." If God is not king of Israel, Israel ceases to be as a holy nation.

Jesus said, "I am thirsty" (Jn 19:28).

The At-one-ment

The death of Jesus is central to the New Testament. Without it there is no Gospel, no sacraments and no Church. Yet after two thousand years it remains a mystery. "Why did Jesus have to die? Why couldn't God let bygones be bygones?" There have been a number of theories and each adds something to our understanding.

One of the earliest explanations was that Jesus' death was a ransom offered to defeat the powers of evil. The early Church delighted in the idea of God's conquest of the devil and the triumph of the kingdom of God over the kingdom of darkness.

Another theory attractive to the medieval period was Peter Abelard's idea of the death of Jesus as a moral influence. A 12th century scholar, he brilliantly anticipated modern ideas concerning the power of love. As he saw it the death of Jesus did not influence God because how could God need reconciling. After all, it was he who was in Christ. No. Jesus' death draws us to him. As we see that love which drove him to a cruel cross, our hearts and wills melt before the greatness of that example and we are led back to God.

Another set of theories concentrates upon the notion of Christ dying for each one of us. One of them sees Jesus as our representative who as perfect man takes our despair and sin to the cross and dies for us. As the perfect and best he is able to represent us before the Father and open the way to eternal life. This idea is very Biblical and accords with he sentiment in Cardinal Newman's hymn: "A second Adam to the fight and to the rescue came."

The similar theory of substitution goes a little further and says Jesus is my substitute, dying a death that I deserve. This theory also finds Biblical warrant in Paul's language of "Christ being made sin" (2 Co 5:21; Ga 3:13).

But the death of Jesus should not be separated from his earthly life. His death is the culmination of his Incarnation. He came to save us all from all that stops us being the people that God longs for us to be. He comes to reconcile humankind to God, to heal the brokenhearted and to make all things new. The angel said to Joseph,

> You must name him Jesus, because he is the one who is to save his people from their sins (*Mt 1:21*).

His death was his triumph. According to John's Gospel it is his moment of glory.

> It is fulfilled (*Jn 19:30*)

is the splendid cry from the man on the cross.

The resurrection is the vindication of Christ's ministry in life and death; without the resurrection the death has no power or hope.

There is something compelling and beautiful about the idea of Christ dying for you and me.

Sacrifice and victory

Even today the language of sacrifice is perfectly understandable. If I am poor and starving and someone offers me food which they desperately need, I can understand how that sacrifice can save me. In a deeper way I can see that if our condition is as serious as the Bible declares, salvation can come only from God. Here then is the basic theology of the Mass. Christ's "one for all" sacrifice becomes the basis for our celebration.

Cross of glory

Crucifixion was the most shameful execution, used for slaves. Even in Christian liturgy and art it was not until the fourth century that the cross became a widely-used and acceptable symbol. The crucifix with a tortured body became common only in the thirteenth century. Early

representations portrayed the victory of Christ rather than the suffering and pain.

The Jews

The new Catechism (*CCC 597*) makes the important point that the Jews as a race are not to be held collectively responsible for the death of Jesus. Rather, as the old Roman Catechism stated,

> sinners themselves were the authors and instruments of all the pains which the divine Redeemer endured (*Roman Catechism, 1:5, 11 cf. Heb 12:3*).

Rather, Christ offered his life, and his death, for our sins (*CCC 606*).

Descent into hell

The Church has always rejected Calvin's view that Christ actually went to hell for our sins. This is never stated in Scripture, and is against any kind of logic; since Christ could not preach the Good News to those who were totally hardened against God. Rather, Christ preached to those who were waiting for him. The new Catechism (*CCC 633*) once more quotes the Roman Catechism concerning those who were dead, and to whom Christ announced the Good News after his death:

> It is precisely these holy souls, who awaited their Liberator in the bosom of Abraham, whom Jesus Christ delivered when he descended into Hades (*Roman Catechism, 1, 6, 3*).

He is risen!

The death of Jesus, without the resurrection, would just have been the end of a beautiful dream. Yet another good man, even perhaps the best man on earth, was put to death by foolish and cruel authorities.

Many skeptics down the centuries have imagined that the resurrection was wishful thinking on the part of the disciples.

But what is strangest of all about their faith in the resurrection is that it took everyone, including themselves, completely by surprise; so much so, that the only adequate explanation of this extraordinary faith is that what they said was true. The risen Jesus had appeared to them.

The evidence from 1 Co 15:3–8, the Book of Acts and elsewhere in the New Testament establishes that the preaching of the resurrection went back to the very origins of Christianity.

Both then and now Christian faith stands or falls with the resurrection of Jesus from the dead.

Resurrection in the Old Testament

By the time of Jesus, most Jews had come to believe that, at the end of the world, there would be a general resurrection from the dead. But this faith itself had taken a long time to develop.

What was not expected at all was that the Messiah, when he came, would die and rise again, appearing to his disciples. Some believed that the Messiah, like Elijah, would be assumed into heaven in a fiery chariot. This would be the ascension of Christ. But not his actual suffering, death, and bodily resurrection. This was totally unexpected.

There were prophecies in the Old Testament about the Servant of God being vindicated by rising from the dead after suffering (Is 53). But this was such a vague idea that it was not until after Jesus had appeared to them that the disciples were able to understand what those scriptures meant (Lk 24:26).

The appearances

But why should we today believe that the crucified Jesus rose from the dead?

First, we have testimony from some of the men and women who launched Christianity. Jesus ended his earthly life in slow agony nailed on a cross. But some time afterwards, he appeared gloriously alive to different individuals and groups – several hundred in all. St. Paul lists many of these witnesses. He adds his own testimony as a persecutor turned believer:

In the end he appeared also to me (1 Co 15:8).

Luke and John also draw attention to the way the risen Lord has been changed and transformed. Closed doors are no obstacle to him (Jn 20:19, 26).

Believing in the risen Christ is more than merely accepting the testimony of others to a unique event which took place nearly 2,000 years ago. Easter faith means experiencing the difference the living Jesus can make in our lives now. We experience his powerful presence in the Scriptures and above all in the Eucharist, and in a thousand other ways. He comes to us in prayer, behind the faces of those who suffer and need our help, in the joys and pains of daily life.

He appears and disappears at will (*Lk 24:31–36*). People who had known him in his earthly existence fail, at least initially, to identify him. On the road to Emmaus the two disciples recognize him only in the moment of his disappearance (*Lk 24:31*). Mary Magdalene at first supposes him to be a gardener (*Jn 20:14*). Jesus has risen bodily from the dead, but he has become "gloriously" different.

The empty tomb

Closely tied up with the nature of the bodily resurrection is the question of the empty tomb. Some allege that faith in the risen Jesus does not need to affirm his empty tomb. He is risen from the dead but his earthly corpse decayed in the grave. Against this is the evidence from the Gospels that Mary Magdalene (all four Gospels) with one or more female companion(s) (Matthew, Mark and Luke), visited Jesus' grave and found that it was open and that the corpse had mysteriously disappeared.

There is a reasonable case to be made in support of the claim that Jesus' grave was found empty. Naturally the opponents of the Christian movement explained the missing body as theft (*Mt 28:11–15*). But we have no evidence that anyone, either Christian or non-Christian, alleged that Jesus' tomb contained his remains. Furthermore, it would have been impossible in Jerusalem for the disciples to start proclaiming his resurrection if his grave had not been empty. Their enemies could at once have produced his corpse.

Sign

But what does the empty tomb mean? It powerfully symbolizes that redemption is much more than a mere escape from suffering and death. Rather it means the transformation of this material world with all its history of sin and suffering.

The first Easter began the work of bringing our universe to its ultimate destiny. The empty tomb is God's radical sign that redemption is not a mere escape

"He is not here, for he has risen" (*Mt 28:5*).

The new Catechism (*CCC 638*) sums up the teaching of the Church on the resurrection in a beautiful quotation from the Byzantine Liturgy:

Christ has risen from the dead!
By his death he has vanquished death;
To the dead he has given life.
   (*Troparion of Easter*)

Light from the Council

"As an innocent lamb he merited life for us by his blood which he freely shed. In him God reconciled us to himself and to one another, freeing us from the bondage of the devil and of sin, so that each one of us could say with the apostle: the Son of God 'loved me and gave himself for me'" (*Pastoral Constitution on the Church in the Modern World, no. 22*).

Questions

1   Some say if the bones of Jesus were found today, their faith would remain the same. What would you say to this?

2   Point to some examples of Christ's agony in today's world. A display (e.g. using newspaper clippings) could be prepared for your church. This could help a parish celebration of the liturgy of Good Friday to link up with everyday life.

3   What do you understand by the Christian teaching that "Christ died for our sins"?

to a better world but an extraordinary transformation of this world.

Early Christians knew that if they were wrong about Jesus' rising from the dead, they would be the "most pitiable" of all people (*1 Co 15:19*). But they were not wrong. At Mass we continue to cry out with joy:

Dying you destroyed our death, rising you restored our life. Lord Jesus, come in glory.

Through the risen presence of Jesus we know that our story will not end in the empty silence of annihilation. The world to which we go is no grey haunt of ghosts, but a richly satisfying existence in which we shall know all our dear ones.

After the resurrection, Christians were constantly being challenged to give an account of how they saw their Lord. Their immediate reaction was not to say that he was God.

In Jewish-Christian circles, they turned automatically to the Old Testament. Paul certainly does. He pictures the risen Christ in Biblical imagery. He is the Lord who will come again on the clouds to judge the world and take his faithful followers with him in his triumphal procession (*1 Th 4:16*).

Later he had to explain the contrast between the old and the new covenants. He describes Christ as the second Adam, the founder and leader of a renewed humanity. He is now the model and exemplar of humanity. He is the Son of God in whom all others can become adopted sons and call God intimately "Father."

At about the same time, confronted with the divisions within the Christian community at Corinth, Paul sees the Church as the body of Christ, the indivisible Christian community. Its members make up the total body of Christ and live with his life.

Paul expresses this faith of the early Christian community most strongly in his use of the word "Lord" (*Kyrios*) – Jesus is the Lord. It also refers back to the Old Testament use of "Yahweh" as the name for God. Jesus is given this title by the Father because he was the obedient son.

The final stage in the development of understanding was the vision in St. John's Gospel of Christ as the "Word made flesh." This idea of the Word of God links back to the creation story in Genesis where God created all things by his word. Christ is revealed as the Son of God.

13 The Holy Spirit

There would not be a Church without the Holy Spirit. The Spirit brings believers into the community (the Church), is the appointed means by which God saves the world, and continues the redemptive work of Christ.

Many people if you say "church" think of a building. But if all the church buildings were destroyed there would still be a Church. It is the "koinonia," the community of believers, which is the Church, the temple of the Holy Spirit and the sign of salvation for the world.

In the same way the body of bishops led by the Pope is the gift of the Holy Spirit to the Church. They continue the mission of the apostles. The Pope is the center of visible unity of the universal (catholic) Church.

This unity of hierarchy and people is the new family, brought to life by the Holy Spirit, brothers and sisters of Christ.

Within this family the Spirit's gifts are for everyone (1Co 12:4). To be "charismatic" simply means to acknowledge that our gifts come from God, and to use them.

The Spirit is at work even when we are not aware of it. Sometimes we can only discern his presence with hindsight. But we have Christ's promise that the Spirit will be with us always to guide us into the truth.

> For, when we do not know how to pray properly, then the Spirit personally petitions for us in groans that cannot be put into words (*Rm 8:26*).

At Pentecost 50 days after Easter, the Church exploded into life in the wind and fire of the Spirit. Some of the crowd accused Peter and the other apostles of being drunk, but what they were seeing was the transforming effect of the Holy Spirit.

Just before the ascension the apostles had asked, "Lord, has the time come for you to restore the kingdom to Israel?" (*Ac 1:6*). They got not the answer they wanted, but a fairly clear hint about the real nature of the kingdom of God:

> You will receive the power of the Holy Spirit which will come on you, and then you will be my witnesses not only in Jerusalem but throughout Judea and Samaria, and indeed to earth's remotest end (*Ac 1:8*).

During Christ's earthly life, people had generally come to him as individuals. He called James and John from their boat, and Matthew from his counting house. Andrew brought his

---

The Holy Spirit works through particular gifts to build the body of Christ's followers, the Church. These may be called "charisms," a Greek word meaning gifts.

Some are permanent and are called hierarchical: as for instance the sacrament of holy orders of bishop, priest and deacon.

Some are occasional, like prophecy and healing. Not everyone has these and the same person may not have a particular gift all the time.

At Pentecost the Church exploded into life in the wind and fire of the Spirit. The Spirit is often represented by a dove.

This same Holy Spirit is active in all aspects of the life of the Church. His gifts or charisms are varied. They include the grace and authority conferred on members of the hierarchy by the sacrament of ordination as well as the spiritual talents of great poets and preachers like St. Francis of Assisi, or those of the great apostles of mercy like St. Vincent de Paul or Dom Helder Camara. They include everyday gifts of faithful perseverance and love in family obligations and in unpublicized help for our neighbors.

As St. Paul pointed out, "There are many different gifts, but it is always the same Spirit" (1Co 12:4). The Spirit who transformed the crowd into a new community at Pentecost is the same Spirit who keeps the Church together in unity now.

brother Simon, and Philip fetched Nathaniel. But with the coming of the Spirit at Pentecost the call, and the effect, were now communal, showing us how

> God has willed to make human beings holy and save them not as individuals, without any bond or link between them, but as people (*Vatican II on the Church, no. 9*).

There seem to have been two stages to that incorporation into the Church. In his sermon on Pentecost Peter said:

> You must repent ... and every one of you must be baptized in the name of Jesus Christ for the forgiveness of your sins, and you will receive the gift of the Holy Spirit (*Ac 2:38*).

This double process, now crystalized for us in the two sacraments of baptism and confirmation, had a parallel in Christ's own life.

Just as the Spirit had brooded over the waters of chaos at creation, so he overshadowed Mary when Christ was conceived. Later, after John had baptized him in the River Jordan, Christ was led by the Spirit into the desert to begin his public life with a forty-day fast.

Just as the Spirit enlivened the human Christ, so too he is the life-principle of the Church. Indeed he has been called "the soul of the Church."

Christ promised his apostles that the Holy Spirit would bring back to their minds everything he himself had taught them. The same Holy Spirit inspires all authentic teaching in the Church, and all true development.

Everyone baptized into the Church is baptized in the name of the Father and of the Son and of the Holy Spirit. The Holy Spirit is the mutual love uniting the Father and the Son. The Church is itself the means by which we are actually inserted into the life and love of God. God's love, revealed to us as the doctrine of the Trinity, leads him to create us so that we may share in that life and love. The movement is circular. Caught up in that love we respond to it by the same power of the Holy Spirit dwelling within us. Sometimes we are consciously aware of his presence, and are stirred to strong and courageous faith and true joy. More often we are not. Yet we believe that through our baptism he is always with us.

Spreading the good news

No religion ever spread so rapidly. St. Peter's preaching converted 3,000 people on Pentecost day itself. The faith, called at first "The Way," spread like wildfire through the Jewish communities of Palestine, Samaria and Syria. Within 30 years of the death and resurrection of Christ it had spread right through the known world.

The key figure in the explosion of Christianity to the non-Jewish world was St. Paul. Born in Tarsus, in modern-day Turkey, he was a Pharisee who studied in Jerusalem. He was fanatical in his persecution of Christians. After his dramatic conversion on the road to Damascus he went from city to city preaching the Good News and founding Christian communities.

The Holy Spirit was given to the Church on the morning of the first Pentecost to be with her until the end of time and to accomplish in her a unique mission: to make present, for all generations and throughout the world, the redemption that Christ acquired once and for all. He comes as the one sent by the Son, as the one who prolongs and completes the task of the Father.

His mission, then, is not to add anything whatsoever to our Lord's revelation. Christ has merited everything for us by his passion which saved the world, but it is through the Spirit that the fruits of the redemption are "ripened." The Holy Spirit – this Spirit of life who gives life – comes to us to clarify from within the Master's words, to guide us "into all truth."

The new Catechism (CCC 688) links our knowledge of the Holy Spirit closely with the Church, where we encounter the Spirit:

In the Scriptures, which the Holy Spirit inspired

In Tradition, of which the Fathers of the Church are perpetual witnesses

In the Magisterium (teaching authority) of the Church, which the Spirit assists

In the sacramental liturgy, where the Holy Spirit puts us into communion with Christ

In prayer, in which the Spirit intercedes for us

In charisms and in ministries, where the Church is built up

In the signs of apostolic and missionary life

In the witness of the saints who show holiness and continue the work of salvation.

Prayer

Come Holy Spirit
Fill the hearts of your faithful
and enkindle in them
the fire of your love.
Send forth your Spirit
and they shall be created
And you will renew
the face of the earth.

Questions

1 In Ephesians 4:11, St. Paul gives a list of the different ways the Spirit works. "To some his gift was that they should be apostles; to some, prophets; to some, evangelists; to some, pastors and teachers ... to build up the body of Christ." What other gifts could be added to this list as we look at the parish today?

2 At the first Pentecost, described in chapter 2 of the Acts of the Apostles, people looked at the disciples who had just received the Spirit and thought they were drunk. How do we recognize the Spirit working in people? What fears do we have of the work of the Spirit?

The Holy Spirit was given to the Church to guarantee her fidelity to the mission confided to her. But it is also the work of the Spirit to introduce her progressively into the fullness of the truth. A distinction has to be made between what belongs to authentic Tradition and what arises from traditions that are purely human. Much confusion comes from the fact that customs and usages, perhaps a century or less old, are confused with true Tradition which goes back to the beginnings and which, in the course of time, has sometimes been obscured.

Often what seems revolutionary is simply a return to the sources.

The Lord did not wish to leave this process of discernment to the whim of individual interpretation or to the mercy of our prejudices. It is his Spirit who leads each phase of development. It is he who, as soon as new problems crop up, helps to bring the answer that is truly in keeping with Tradition.

14 The Church is one and holy

The word for Church in Greek is "ekklesia," which means "called out." Essentially this means the same as the Hebrew "qahal." The idea is that God is calling out his own people to address them; if you like, it is God's own roll call.

God's people become "Church," therefore, insofar as they respond positively to his call to celebrate his presence, to listen to his word, and to share in his life.

The "Catholic" or "Roman Catholic" Church presents a very distinctive claim to being linked with this original apostolic church founded by Jesus Christ. The leader of this Church, called "the Pope" ("Pope" means "Father," or "Papa"), the Bishop of Rome, claims to be the successor of Peter, the leader of the apostles, called "the Rock" by Jesus himself. In the Catholic faith, to be linked with the Pope in visible "communion" is an essential part of being fully Christian.

Outside the Church no salvation?

Contrary to what many people think, the Catholic Church does not teach that only its members get to heaven. It might have seemed like this, because we used the expression "outside the Church there is no salvation." But we are becoming more and more aware that people who are not Catholics are also members of the Church, because they can be united with Christ.

The Church teaches that anyone of good will may come to the vision of God in heaven.

The word "Catholic" (from the Greek *kath holos*, "according to the whole"), means "universal." At the time of the 4th and 5th century Councils, where important doctrines about Christ were defined, the word "Catholic" referred to those Christians who accepted the whole doctrine about Christ. They believed that he was both God and man, whereas "heretics" believed only parts of the "whole" doctrine.

"Roman" also refers to the rite (that is, the tradition and style of liturgical worship) of one section of the Catholic Church. Other sections follow other rites. See CCC 1200 – 1203.

After the Protestant Reformation, when Europe divided into different denominations, "Catholic" referred to those Christians who accepted the Bishop of Rome, the Pope, as the successor of the apostle Peter. Roman Catholics claim that to accept the "whole" (Catholic) doctrine of Christ implies visible communion with the Pope. This is a vital principle of universality. Only in the Roman Catholic Church is visible communion complete, because only there is that visible and historical link with the apostolic Church founded by Christ.

The Church does not only contend that anyone of good will may come to the vision of God in heaven. She also teaches that any Christian, who is a member of any church, in some sense belongs to the body of Christ, the Church, while lacking the fullness of visible communion which we believe is only in the Catholic Church.

The Catholic Church teaches that Christians who are members of any church belong to the body of Christ, the Church, even if they lack the fullness of visible communion in the Catholic Church.

Saint Paul

St. Paul described the Church as the Body of Christ. This was an obvious comparison with the human body in which the well-being or illness of any one member affects the health of the whole body. He was familiar with the Biblical idea of husband and wife becoming one body, one flesh. Above all he had a growing appreciation of the mysterious contact between the body of the Christian and the glorified body of Christ which takes place in the Eucharist (*1 Co 6, 10, 11*) and when Christians become one body with Christ (*1 Co 10:16, 17*). He was sure that one day all our bodies will be transformed into the likeness of Christ's glorified body (*Ph 3:21*). This led to his great song of praise of the resurrection when

this perishable nature has put on imperishable and this mortal nature has put on immortality (*1 Co 15:54*).

All these insights led St. Paul to see Christians as one body "in" Christ. He stressed this in the Letter to the Romans and his First Letter to the Corinthians. In the Letters to the Ephesians and Colossians he goes further and describes Christians simply as the body "of" Christ. In being the one body of Christ, Christians have Christ as their head – from which there is a movement of life into the rest of the members and he directs and coordinates their activities. Christ's headship is not merely over his Church. It is over the whole creation. He is the very source and destiny of everything that is created (*Col 1:15–17*).

The unity of both head and members is made possible by the work of the Holy Spirit, because there is but one body and one Spirit (*Ep 4:1–4*). The Spirit of God lives in each Christian as in a temple. He creates and conserves union between Christ and his members.

All this has daily implications for believers. They must live in close dependence on each other and on Jesus Christ. They must respect their bodies which are the dwelling place of the Spirit of Christ. The Christian is not just a body of flesh but a Spirit-filled body. Life in Christ demands a high standard of moral behavior. The Christian, for example, cannot at the same time share his body with a prostitute and with Christ (*1 Co 6:15*).

The bread that is broken when Christians share the Eucharist is a sharing, a communion, in the body of the Lord (*1 Co 10:16, 17*). Each Christian has his own role and his own gift, but all gifts must be used for the good of the whole body.

The new Catechism (*CCC 777–780*) tells us that the "Church," a word which means "assembly," signifies those who are called by God to form his People, and who, receiving their nourishment from Holy Communion, become the Body of Christ themselves. The Church, founded by the words and actions of Jesus himself, was created by his death and resurrection, and was finally revealed as the mystery of salvation by the effusion of the Holy Spirit. It will be consummated in the glory of heaven when all the faithful will be gathered into eternal happiness.

The mystical body

For centuries, the Church has been called the "Mystical Body of Christ." This tendency received a new impetus from an encyclical letter of Pope Pius XII in 1943. He stated that there was no more fitting title for the Church. The word "mystical" was originally applied not so much to the Church as to the body of Christ as received in the Eucharist. Whatever words we use, there is an obvious and intimate link between the body of Christ received in the Eucharist and the community of people we call the Church. Christ has only one body, his glorified body. In it all the mystery, all the secret plan of God reaches its fulfillment. Christ's glorified body is like a magnet drawing not merely all Christians but all of the human family and the whole of the universe into unity with itself.

The uniqueness of Jesus leads to the uniqueness of his Church. Catholics are used to describing the Catholic Church as the "one true Church." The bishops at the Second Vatican Council taught that the sole Church of Christ "subsists in" the Catholic Church which is governed by the successor of Peter and by the bishops in communion with him.

"Subsists" is a puzzling word. In practice, it means that the Catholic Church sees itself as possessing all the sacramental life and structures willed by Christ. But the bishops declared that many elements of sanctification and of truth are found outside the visible confines of the Catholic Church and are forces impelling towards Christian unity. This statement is one of the great foundation statements for the ecumenical movement. Much of its meaning has yet to be unpacked.

Each of us takes a particular starting point which colors our understanding of the Church.

Some see the Church primarily as institutional; some as a community; some as a herald of good news; some as a servant of God and humanity; some as a people on a journey. All these "models" should throw light on each other, and they come together when we see the Church simply as a community of disciples of the Lord.

Communion

Being in communion need not mean identical worship, or even belief.

> The Church ... is held, as a matter of faith, to be unfailingly holy. This is because Christ, the Son of God, who with the Father and the Spirit is hailed as "alone holy," loved the Church as his Bride, giving himself up for her so as to sanctify her (*Ep 5:25–26*); he joined her to himself as his body and endowed her with the gift of the Holy Spirit for the glory of God (*Vatican II on the Church, no. 39*).

> For it is through Christ's Catholic Church alone, which is the universal help towards salvation, that the fullness of the means of salvation can be obtained (*Vatican II on Ecumenism, no. 3*).

> The Church is holy by embracing sinners in her bosom, because she has no other life in her than that of grace; it is in living her life that her members make themselves holy; it is in straying from her life that they fall into sins and disorders which prevent the full manifestation of her sanctity. That is why she suffers and does penance for their faults, from which she possesses the power to cure her children by the blood of Christ and by the gift of the Holy Spirit (*Thérèse of the Child Jesus, Autobiography*).

Communion is primarily a gift of God. The Greek word *koinonia*, as it appears in the First Epistle of St. John, means a relationship between persons which comes about because they share mutually in one and the same reality. The reality with which we are concerned is the very life of God made available to us in his mystical body the Church. So the gift of communion is, first and foremost, the gift of salvation, the re-establishment of that relationship between God and people which was once ruptured by sin. But Christ has made it clear that the saving relationship between ourselves and God is re-established precisely in and through our mutual relations, our koinonia, as members of his body, the Church:

> He has willed to make people holy and save them not as individuals without any bond or link between them, but rather to make them into a people who might acknowledge him and serve him in holiness (*Vatican II on the Church, no. 9*).

We must share with, care about, accept responsibility for those others who are members with us of the communion of saints.

Note that holiness or sanctity is not just freedom from sin, or moral rectitude. In the Scriptures and in the teaching of the Church, sanctity is being God-like through the life of God in us. As the new Catechism says (*CCC 826*), charity is the soul of sanctity to which we are all called. To love as God loves (because God is love, as John says in Scripture) is to be holy.

Other faiths?

> The Catholic Church rejects nothing in other religions which is true and holy. With sincere respect she takes account of those ways of acting and living, those commandments and teachings which, though they differ in many respects from what she herself holds and teaches, nevertheless often reflect a ray of that Truth which enlightens all human beings (*Vatican II on Non-Christian Religions, no. 2*).

The mysterious secret of God's compassion and love for all his children is veiled. Every individual, everywhere, is linked to God's salvific will; it is Catholic teaching that no one is debarred from the offer of grace and salvation.

Developing the Church's understanding of redemption through Christ, theologians have acknowledged that the grace-encounter leading to salvation comes also to non-Christians, not independently of Christ, but through him. While for Christians the "ordinary means" of salvation are available, for non-Christians, "extraordinary means" are possible. In this view, non-Christian religions can be seen, at best, as a preparation for the Gospel.

Will Christian theology widen its horizons still further, and come to acknowledge that non-Christians who embrace God's will are saved not merely by exceptional means, in isolation from their own religious culture and devotion? Might these religions have, in God's providential design, a corporate function: to provide for their followers the place of encounter with divine grace and salvation, even if not without error?

Questions

1 "Perfection is an ideal the Church constantly holds out to us, but it does not exclude the great majority of us who muddle along in spite of failure and low-voltage faith." People outside the Church often think membership is only for those who can keep the rules. Is that what we believe?

2 How can lay Catholics help to promote and bring about necessary developments in the life of the Church?

15 The Church is catholic and apostolic

The Church claims that its message, life, and worship are not man-made, but come with the authority of God. They go beyond what human beings can work out for themselves; they are about our sharing in the life of God both on earth and in eternity.

This means that the message itself must have the guarantee of God's authority in order to be trustworthy.

God began by giving the message of salvation in the form of a "covenant": a deal with Abraham (*Gn 12*) promising land and a family, a "seed" greater than any other nation. God then made a covenant with Moses, giving him the law (the Ten Commandments), guidance for happiness on earth. When the people of God had settled in the promised land or Israel, God sent a prophet, Nathan, to tell King David, the Anointed (Messiah), that he had a covenant from God as well. He, David, was to have an eternal dynasty (*2 S 7*).

The people were unfaithful to the covenant, and suffered misfortune. But the prophets told of a new covenant, to be made with the "house" (the dynasty) of David. This covenant would change their hearts, and they would "know" God Yahweh (*Jr 31:31*).

Then came Jesus, sent from God his Father, a "son of David" (*Mt 1*). Jesus' miracles, his teaching, and the love he showed to outcasts and sinners, were proof that he was sent by God to found a new kingdom, and to make a new "covenant" or "testament" with the human race. Above all, his resurrection from the dead was proof that God was with him, in spite of his dreadful death on the cross, and was a seal of the new covenant.

Jesus sent out his apostles with his authority to preach and to found churches. They "laid hands on" (ordained) their successors the bishops or "overseers," to govern the Church in their place. Christ sent his Spirit to be with the whole Church until his final return.

Christ our Lord himself is the sole basis of the Church's authority.

Christianity claims to be based on a revelation. God is not impersonal. He is our Father and has revealed himself in history through the man Jesus Christ. The Bible tells us about him. But how do we know which interpretation of the events and stories in the Bible is the true one? We must look at the Christian churches. Is there one which claims to teach with the same infallible authority as the apostles and the fathers? The answer is what it always was: the Roman Catholic Church.

While on earth, Christ spoke with authority, and those who came to believe in him accepted his authority as infallible, from the Father. But what was to happen after his death? Were his disciples to be left without truly trustworthy guidance? This is where the infallibility of the Church comes in.

The Pope is the successor of Peter, Bishop of Rome.

Bishops and Pope

Paul in his Letter to the Ephesians says that the Church, or what he calls "God's household," is built upon the foundations of the apostles and prophets, Jesus Christ himself being the cornerstone (*Ep 2:20*).

This theme of building the Church on a secure foundation is more familiar from Matthew 16 where Jesus changes Simon's name to Peter (Rock). This change of name assigns him his vocation. Jesus says:

> You are Peter and on this rock I will build my community (*16:18*).

Though the emphasis is different, there is no contradiction between these two texts. Peter is himself one of the apostles. Apostles are people sent out as authorized delegates.

The Church is built on them. Building up "God's household" is always a divine activity in the Old Testament. Even if Peter is the foundational rock, Jesus himself remains the cornerstone.

Peter has a special place among the Twelve. His name occurs 124 times in the New Testament; John comes next with 38 mentions. Peter is given the specific task of "strengthening his brethren" (*Lk 22:32*) and feeding Christ's sheep (*Jn 21:15–17*).

A key passage of Vatican II reflects these New Testament themes: "Just as the role the Lord gave individually to Peter, the first among the apostles, is permanent and was meant to be transmitted to his successors, so also the apostles' office of ministry in the Church is permanent, and was meant to be exercised without interruption by the sacred order of bishops" (*Church in the Modern World, no. 20*).

But his leadership role does not cut him off from the rest of the apostles. Neither could exist without the other.

The Pope has a special place, as already indicated here: for he is the successor of an individual apostle, Peter, bishop of Rome, while the other bishops are successors of the apostles taken as a body.

The General Council

The best expression of the team-nature of the college of bishops is seen in a general or ecumenical council. At Vatican II, for example, it was impossible to drive a wedge between the successor of St. Peter and the successors of the apostles.

Pope John XXIII and then Pope Paul VI "presided over the whole assembly of charity" and therefore were members of the Council – not above it, still less against it. The whole college signed the Council documents, beginning with Pope Paul.

This is a somewhat ideal picture, and of course a Council cannot be in permanent session. In between Councils, that is most of the time, there have been famous historical quarrels about just where final authority lay.

There have been two extreme positions, both of which have been rejected by the Church.

Council versus Pope?

"Conciliarism" held that a General Council was superior to the Pope, could on occasions depose him, and was the only way to reform the Church "in head and members." In the thirteenth and fourteenth centuries, with popes and antipopes competing for an office that was often seen as one of domination rather than service, this was an attractive theory.

The opposite position isolates the Pope from the college of bishops, and makes them mere rubber stamps of his authority – branch managers as it were in the multinational corporation that is the Church.

The Second Vatican Council in the 1960s restored the balance between the Petrine ministry and the bishops.

For the first time residential bishops became members of the Roman Curia. A regular Synod of Bishops was set up to express "continuing collegiality" and make episcopal advice available to the Pope.

These moves were meant to stimulate consultation and communication – the life-blood of the Church. If they have not always succeeded, that can be attributed to human nature: the Church will not reach final perfection until the end of time.

Bishops of a region are now grouped together in an "episcopal conference." This is a revival of something very traditional. They do what patriarchates used to do in the ancient world.

Catholic unity does not mean being uniform: the Church is the home of "reconciled diversity."

At the same time diversity exists not for its own sake but for the more effective and adapted preaching of the Gospel. All the European bishops come together in the Council of European Bishops of which the Bishop of Rome, naturally, is a keen member.

But although bishops are the official "teachers and witnesses" of the faith of the Church, they do not in any sense "own the Church."

Thus the two infallible Marian definitions – the Immaculate Conception in 1854 and the Assumption in 1950 – were not novel doctrines propounded by the Pope after consultation with his bishops. They were pronounced infallible in order to validate long-held beliefs of the ordinary people in the Church.

The college of bishops with the Pope in its midst exists to serve the whole People of God and give it shape. Authority in the Church exists so that all may unite freely, and yet in order.

Magisterium

From the Latin *magister*, teacher. This usually refers to the official teaching body of the Church, in particular the bishops led by the Pope. But the word essentially refers to teaching authority of the whole Church, of which the bishops and the Pope are the official representatives, in apostolic succession from the apostles and Peter.

Infallible?

Since it is God's instrument for the achievement of his plan for the salvation of humanity, the Church, as Church, cannot be teaching fundamental error. Christians gradually realized that an ecumenical council, that is a council representing the whole Church as such and not just some region or section of it, will be protected from error when it commits itself positively to some specific interpretation of revealed truth. Thus after various conflicts in A.D. 343 a regional council at Sardica recognized the role of the Bishop of Rome as final arbiter in a dispute between other bishops. It was gradually perceived that the "official" solution to such disputes, given in the name of the Church and in the light of the teaching and experience of the Church as a whole, must also be infallible.

But the Bishop of Rome, successor of Peter though he be, is no more protected from greed, pride or ambition than the rest of Church members. Vatican I defined that Peter was appointed by Christ prince of the apostles and thereby endowed with a primacy of true and proper jurisdiction in which the Bishop of Rome is his successor. He thus has power over the universal Church, and possesses that infallibility with which Christ wished his Church to be endowed. These legal phrases have carefully limited the occasions on which the Pope can be seen to be enunciating the faith of the whole Church, and thus protected from error.

But infallibility, mere protection from error, does not guarantee the aptness, the clarity or the completeness of a statement. These will often come not from the magisterium of pope and bishops, but from the community which must respond to and assess the insights and teachings of ordained ministers.

The growth of the institutional Church has, at times, detracted

"The Magisterium exercises a function of its own which the Spirit has not entrusted to others. But this function demands that the Magisterium draw from the very life of the People of God the reality to be discerned and judged, promulgated or defined, for it must exercise all its activity upon the word as received and lived in the Church" (Jean Tillard, *Sensus Fidelium*).

from the role of lay people. Perhaps the most significant movement in the Church recently has been greater recognition of the common priesthood of all God's people, and the part all have to play in the building up of the body of Christ.

Sensus Fidelium (Understanding of the Faithful)

This refers to the Catholic belief that the whole people of God have an infallible understanding of the truth of Christ. Because the whole Church is entrusted with the message of Christ, and is given by the Spirit the competence to keep this message faithfully and preach the Gospel, the whole body of Christ cannot err in matters of faith.

The church is catholic

The new Catechism (*CCC 830*) explains that the word "Catholic" means "universal" in the sense of "according to the whole, totality." It is Catholic because Christ is present everywhere in the Church; because Christ is Head of the whole Church everywhere; and because it has the right and full profession of faith, sacramental life and ministry in apostolic succession. The Church is essentially Catholic, from its beginning at the day of Pentecost right through to the Second Coming of Christ.

The church is apostolic

The Church is apostolic (*CCC 857*) because it is founded on the apostles, in a threefold sense:

1. The Church is based upon the "foundation of the apostles" (*Ep 2:20; Rv 21:14*), who were chosen witnesses and sent by Christ himself.

2. The Church guards and transmits, with the help of the Spirit who dwells in the Church, the apostolic testimony, the deposit of faith, and the true words in that meaning understood by the apostles.

3. The Church continues to be directed and governed by the apostles until the return of Christ, thanks to those who succeed in their pastoral charge: the college of bishops, "assisted by priests, in union with the successor of Peter, the supreme pastor of the Church [that is the Pope]" (*Vatican II on Missionary Activity, no. 5*).

Question

One of the things which most people know about the Catholic Church is that the pope is infallible. Not so well known, but equally important, is the teaching which comes from the "sensus fidelium," by which we mean the widely held beliefs of ordinary people.

What implications does this have for our responsibility to reflect on our faith and to develop our "sensus fidelium"?

16 Mary and all the saints

All mainline Christian churches hold Mary in high esteem and accept that she was the Mother of God, that in Luther's words

> ... the same One whom God begot from eternity she herself brought forth in time.

They differ, however, on what kind of honor should be paid her.

The position of the Orthodox Churches is close to that of the Catholic Church. In the eyes of the Reformed Churches, however, certain Catholic Marian teachings and devotions lack Scriptural basis and involve "glorification" of Mary.

The Catholic Church made an important contribution to ecumenical dialogue in the eighth chapter of the Dogmatic Constitution on the Church (Vatican II).

The chapter opens with a reminder that the reason why Christians ought to "reverence the memory" of Mary is that it was through her that the Son of God "truly came into our history." Because (53) she is therefore

> Mother of God and of the Redeemer ... united to him by a close and indissoluble tie ... beloved daughter of the Father and temple of the Holy Spirit ... she far surpasses all creatures, both in heaven and on earth.

The chapter then recounts what the Scriptures and the Fathers tell us of the role of Mary in the plan of salvation. In the Old Testament she is

foreshadowed in the promise of the victory over the serpent,

> the virgin who shall conceive and bear a Son

and

> she stands out among the poor and humble of the Lord, who confidently hope for and receive salvation from him (55).

For the Fathers she is the second Eve, through whom life came, as death had come through the first Eve, and she is

> all holy and free from every stain of sin, as though fashioned by the Holy Spirit and formed as a new creature (56).

Her assent to the Incarnation was required and having said yes

> she devoted herself totally, as a handmaid of the Lord, to the person and work of her Son, under and with him, serving the mystery of redemption, by the grace of Almighty God (56).

Mary's role did not finish "when her earthly life was over":

> Taken up into heaven ... by her manifold intercession [she] continues to bring us the gifts of eternal salvation. By her maternal charity, she cares for the brothers and sisters of her Son, who still journey on earth surrounded by dangers and difficulties, until they are led into their blessed home ... This however, is so understood that it neither takes away anything from nor adds anything to the dignity and efficacy of Christ the one Mediator (62).

Mary is like the Church and the Church is like Mary.

Devotion to Mary has inspired great art in both Western and Eastern traditions.

The Church ... by receiving the word of God in faith becomes herself a mother. By preaching and baptism she brings forth sons and daughters who are conceived of the Holy Spirit and born of God, to a new and immortal life (64).

The Council urged "that the cult, especially the liturgical cult, of the Blessed Virgin, be generously fostered" (67).

But it insisted that all devotion to Mary must lead to Christ: "Let them rightly illustrate the duties and privileges of the Blessed Virgin which always refer to Christ, the source of all truth, sanctity and devotion." And it warned: "Let them carefully refrain from whatever might by word or deed lead the separated brethren or any others whatsoever into error about the true doctrine of the Church. Let the faithful remember moreover that true devotion ... proceeds from true faith, by which we are led to recognize the excellence of the Mother of God, and we are moved to a filial love towards our mother and to the imitation of her virtues" (67).

Mary and tradition

The Catholic Church maintains that doctrines about Mary have developed under the guidance of the Holy Spirit, within the tradition of the Church.

Not all these doctrines are contained explicitly in Scripture. This raises the whole question of the relationship between Scripture and Tradition in Catholic thought.

God's revelation is handed on according to Catholic faith, in Scripture and Tradition. The Church must teach nothing contrary to Scripture, because Scripture is the Word of God written. Also, the Church's teaching must be related to Scripture, because there is a unity in God's revelation. But,

the Church does not draw her certainty about all revealed truths from the holy Scriptures alone (*Vatican II on Divine Revelation, no. 9*).

Therefore the Church claims to teach nothing contrary to Scripture about Mary.

Mary mother of God

The Council of Ephesus (A.D. 431) defined that Mary was truly the "Mother of God" (Greek: *theotokos*). This title "theotokos" was disputed by the "Nestorians," who held that Mary was not the Mother of God, but simply the "Mother of Christ" (*christotokos*), of the man Jesus, to whom the person of the Word of God united himself. This made two "persons" in Jesus, the man of whom Mary was the mother, and God the Word, which to the Catholic bishops, led by St. Cyril of Alexandria, was heretical. Thus from early on, the Catholic doctrine of Mary has defended the true doctrine of Jesus as truly God the Son, the Word made flesh.

The perpetual virginity

The new Catechism includes teaching about Mary within the article of the Creed on the Communion of Saints. This is the most logical place, because

"She conceived in true reality without human seed from the Holy Spirit, God the Word himself, who before the ages was born of God the Father, and gave birth to him without corruption, her virginity remaining equally inviolate after the birth" (*Council of the Lateran, A.D. 649*).

Mary has her unique place in the Church within the communion of saints. As a member of the same Church as ourselves, and in communion with us in heaven, she helps us in a special way as a fellow Christian. This is the way in which the new Catechism explains the role of Mary in the Church and in our lives:

Mary is our mother

God has given Mary to us as our mother. This is shown to us from the beginning of her existence on earth, right through to her bodily assumption into heaven.

As the Catechism explains (CCC 968), she becomes our mother in the order of grace:

> Thus, in a wholly singular way she cooperated by her obedience, faith, hope and burning charity in the work of the Savior in restoring supernatural life to souls. For this reason she is a mother to us in the order of grace (Church, no. 61).

For this reason, the Catechism argues (CCC 971), public devotion to Mary is legitimate, quoting first Luke 1:48, when Mary exclaimed in her own prayer of thanks to God, called the Magnificat, "All generations will call me blessed":

> This cult, as it has always existed in the Church, for all its uniqueness, differs essentially from the cult of adoration, which is offered equally to the Incarnate Word and to the Father and the Holy Spirit, and it is most favorable to it. The various forms of piety towards the Mother of God, which the Church has approved within the limits of sound and orthodox doctrine, according to the dispositions and understanding of the faithful, ensure that while the mother is honored, the Son, through whom all things have their being (Col 1:15–16) and whom it has pleased the Father that all fullness should dwell (Col 1:19) is rightly known, loved and glorified and his commandments are observed (Church, no. 66).

Mary full of grace

Mary is different from us. We acknowledge the difference in the Hail Mary: she is "full of grace" and we are "sinners." But we must not think of her exalted state as setting up a barrier between her and us. It is precisely because she is the Mother of God that she is at the center of the mystery of Christ and the Church and is herself a preeminent member of the Church.

The unique privilege of the Immaculate Conception prepared Mary for her divine motherhood. It was in virtue of the redeeming power of Christ her Son that she was, from the first moment of her conception, preserved from original sin. How are we to understand this?

As G.K. Chesterton remarked, there are two ways of "getting home." One is to stay there. The other is to wander all over the world till, hopefully, one returns to the place from which one has set out. With the exception of Mary, mankind chose the second course. Through God's grace she always remained "at home" with him. She was most perfectly redeemed by not having been allowed to fall. She was without sin from the first moment of her existence. Our vocation also is to be "without sin": "glorious with no speck or wrinkle ... holy and faultless" (Ep 5:27). But whereas Mary through God's grace was sinless from the beginning, we with God's grace shall be sinless at the end.

Mary gave herself totally to God and became the virgin Mother of God through her free consent to his invitation. Her bodily virginity symbolizes the new creation in Christ and challenges us to live in undividedness of heart and affection to Christ.

Mary is most intimately related to the Church. As the link between the old and new dispensations, she receives the Word of God on behalf of Israel and all humanity. In conceiving and giving birth to Christ she realizes in her own person the vocation of God's people: to give to the world its Savior. At Cana Jesus gives his first great "sign" as the result of her request and changes water into wine. She stands at the foot of the cross as the Church is born symbolically from Christ's side in the water and blood, symbols of baptism and the Eucharist which constitute the Church. She is in prayer with the disciples at Pentecost when the Church launches out on its mission which will continue to the end of time.

Finally in her assumption, Mary anticipates the resurrection of the body. She is the perfect disciple faithfully following Christ, ready to take risks, and at the same time always learning more about him. In heaven she intercedes for us. But we must not think of her as coming between us and Christ in any way. Christ, our Redeemer, is immediately and personally present to each of us. Nobody comes between us and him. But though he himself is always interceding for us, it is his will that all his saints including Mary should be part of the work of intercession. However, her intercession under Christ is unique because she has given us the very source of all intercession, Christ himself.

Devotion to Mary has its basis in the New Testament:

All generations will call me blessed (Lk 1:48).

Questions

1 How would you organize parish devotions to our Lady? Explain your aims and what understanding of Mary you would want to develop.

2 Over the years there have been vast changes in the roles of women. Are these changes contrary to the Christian way of life, seeing that Mary lived out her life obscurely in a country village?

17 The resurrection of the body

What will heaven be like? The picture of harps, clouds and winged angels, which forms the basis of so many robust jokes, is imagery which can be misleading if taken literally.

One of the sets of imagery which St. Paul uses is that of the Roman triumphal procession. In his early First Letter to the Thessalonians he speaks of a final coming of the Lord, when, at a signal given by the trumpet of God, both living and dead will be taken up into the clouds "to meet the Lord in the air" (*1 Th 4:16–17*). This is a little more developed soon afterwards: the procession ends with the presentation of the kingdom by Christ to the Father, when he has abolished every ruling force and power and has made his enemies his footstool (*1 Co 15:23–26*).

The same sort of imagery is used in the synoptic Gospels to sketch Christ's liberation of the Church or of his chosen ones at the Day of the Lord. But what is meant by all this is not easy to say. Another perspective is given by Jesus' statement in John (*Jn 16:33*) "I have conquered the world," and Paul's .

> He has stripped the sovereignties and the ruling forces, and paraded them in public, behind him in his triumphal procession (*Col 2:15*).

A different model for the final state of things is given elsewhere in both John and Paul. For John,

> eternal life is this: to know you, the only true God, and Jesus Christ whom you have sent (*Jn 17:3*).

So eternal life would consist in knowledge, not of intellectual propositions, but of a person (or persons). God has the profoundest and most fascinating and lovable personality that could be imagined. It is the discovery of this personality which is the unparalleled and indescribable thrill of eternal life.

Paul puts it slightly differently but in the same mold: we are somehow absorbed into the sphere of the divine, taking on the attributes which properly belong only to the Godhead:

> What is sown is contemptible but what is raised is glorious; what is sown is weak, but what is raised is powerful; what is sown is a natural body, and what is raised is a spiritual body (*1 Co 15:43–44*).

The risen person takes on the imperishability, the glory and the power which are all primarily properties of God. And these three aspects of the transformation are summed up in the transfer from the natural plane to the

Jesus reveals the imprint of the nails of his crucifixion to doubting Thomas.

spiritual, that of the Spirit of God.

These are no more than hints and pointers, but Paul warns us against attempting to probe too far into this matter:

> Someone may ask: How are dead people raised, and what sort of body do they have when they come? How foolish! (*1 Cor 15:35-36*).

The golden thread which shows the way throughout is that Christ is the first fruits of all who have fallen asleep, so that just as in Adam all die, so in Christ all will be brought to life. Whatever the quality of his risen life, it is ours to share.

The resurrection of the body

Most civilizations believe in some kind of existence after death, the survival of what we call the "soul" or the "personality."

But Christian faith professes much more than this. We believe in the resurrection of the body, that is of the whole person. The discovery of the empty tomb, and the appearance of the risen Christ to his amazed disciples, is a sign that in Jesus the whole of nature, material and spiritual, will be redeemed.

Second, belief in the resurrection of the body is a statement that it is not just a question of our rising individually from the dead, but together as the whole human race, in what is called the "general resurrection." Our final salvation will be not only individual, but together in perfect unity with Christ and the whole of the human race united in him. St. Paul tells the Thessalonians to "encourage one another" with this faith (*1 Th 4:18*).

On this earth, we do not merely learn to be related to God on a one-to-one basis. We learn to relate to each other: because Christian faith tells us that we will be related to each other in eternity also.

There is a strange consequence of the doctrine of the general resurrection: that is, a period of what Paul calls "falling asleep" in the Lord before the final event of history, when we shall rise together body and soul. If we die before Christ returns, we wait for him to come. In that condition, we see God; but it still is a period of waiting before the final fulfillment of the resurrection.

The idea that God will in the end act like a judge, and condemn souls to hell fire, seems hardly to be the kind of God anyone of us would want to believe in.

But God does not fit easily into any image we create: not even the image of a decent fellow who will always let bygones be bygones in the end.

Heaven, hell and judgment

Heaven, hell and judgment remind us first of all that this existence gives us all desperately important choices. It matters whether we decide to follow Christ or not; and it matters eternally. God said to his people the Israelites, as they were about to enter the promised land,

> Today, I am offering you life or death, blessing or curse. Choose life, then ... (*Dt 30:19*).

The doctrine of heaven, hell and judgment reminds us that our choice for God is not once and for all. It is a daily decision. And it is not sufficient for us to say that we follow Christ. We must do his will.

Third, the doctrine of heaven, hell and judgment is a doctrine of hope. We know that no one will

In the parable of the sheep and the goats (*Mt 25:31–46*), the "goats" are condemned to hell because they did not feed the hungry, clothe the naked, and visit the prisoners. They are surprised; just as the "sheep" are surprised, because in feeding the hungry they did not realize that they were helping Christ. The King answers, "In so far as you did this to one of the least of these brothers of mine, you did it to me" (*Mt 25:40*).

The new Catechism (*CCC 1059*) issues us a solemn challenge: "The Most Holy Roman Church believes and confesses fervently that on the day of judgment all people must appear in their own bodies before the tribunal of Christ to render an account of their own acts."

Chinese legend

A Chinese legend tells of a man who dreamed of heaven and hell. In the first dream he found himself in a huge hall where many people were gathered around great tables laden with food. Their problem was that the chopsticks they had been given were so long that it was impossible to use them to lift food to their mouths. The people were becoming angry, pushing and fighting in their efforts to reach the food. This was hell.

In the second dream the man found himself in a hall exactly the same, with tables of steaming hot food. But in this dream each person was using the giant chopsticks to lift the food to the mouth of the person sitting opposite. In this way all were satisfied. This was heaven.

go to hell unless, in a sense, they have decided that that is what they want. A person who truly wants to love God and to be with God forever will be given the grace and help to fulfill that desire.

Heaven is difficult to imagine. Similarly with hell, the Scriptures give us graphic language. But the idea of the flames of hell is most likely an image rather than the reality. Hell is basically, and most frighteningly, love lost.

We do not know how many people, if any, will undergo that terrible fate. It is up to us to pray that none will. What we do know, from the Church's teaching, is that many millions right back to the good thief crucified beside Jesus have gone and will go to heaven, to rejoice in the eternal vision of God.

Purgatory

The idea of the holiness of God, however limited, requires that we should be purified before entering his presence.

This is the basis of the Church's doctrine of purgatory. It is found indirectly in Scripture and developed from the earliest centuries. Our Lord says that the sin against the Holy Spirit shall not be forgiven "either in this world or in the next" (*Mt 12:32*). St. Gregory the Great concludes from this that other sins can be remitted in the world to come. St. Paul speaks of the Christian teacher being judged by his fruits

> though he himself will be saved; he will be saved as someone might expect to be saved from a fire (*1 Co 3:15*).

There is a saying: "Lex orandi, lex credendi" (the belief of the Church is rooted in the way the Church prays). So the doctrine of purgatory was explained from the very early practice of praying for the dead, and believing that such prayers could help them. The doctrine became linked to the notion of the treasury of the Church, whose prayer and good deeds assisted the dead as well as the living – as well as with the recognition that even after forgiveness, sin left traces or scars upon the soul, and that there was need for satisfaction which might not be completed on earth.

Heaven in our midst

Christians pass over to the new reality by baptism. "You have died," Paul says, "and your life is hidden with Christ in God." We already are in eternal life. It is not merely a question of looking forward to it after death. The decisive transition has taken place. Physical death no longer has the finality it once had.

The Christian's true life is not extinguished by it. The continuity between now, when we live by faith and signs, and after death, where we hope to live by sight and in fullness, is real. We lack adequate means of representing to ourselves what eternal life is like. For this reason we find it vague and unreal. We simply know that it is a fulfillment and a crowning of all we have striven for and all we have longed for; that no effort of ours towards good is lost, nothing we have loved is forgotten.

We are speaking, in a way, of that "beyond in our midst" which the liturgy celebrates. In the Mass we pray that we may be kept free from sin and protected from all anxiety "as we wait in joyful hope for the coming of our Savior, Jesus Christ." It is those who "hunger and thirst for righteousness" who will be filled, those who long passionately for the day when peace and justice will spread throughout the earth.

The liturgy must foster our sense of the discrepancy between the way things are and the way God wants them to be. It must challenge us to live up to its wonderful vision of a life where all are truly brothers and sisters in Christ, sharing the same bread and cup and becoming one body.

But there is always hope. Liturgy, which means "public work," is the action of Christ and the Christian community. Its possibilities are limitless.

The bottom line

ANAKEPHALAIOSASTHAI is Greek for "to bring together as head."

This longest word in the New Testament is found in one text only, Ephesians 1:9–10.

> God has let us know the mystery of his purpose, according to his good pleasure which he determined beforehand in Christ, for him to act upon when the times had run their course: THAT HE WOULD BRING EVERYTHING TOGETHER UNDER CHRIST, AS HEAD, everything in the heavens and everything on earth.

Paul had to invent a new Greek word to say what he wanted to say.

His great vision was, at the end of time, to see everything "heading up" in Christ.

Prayer

Glory to him whose power, working in us, can do infinitely more than we can ask or imagine; glory be to him from generation to generation in the Church and in Christ Jesus for ever and ever. Amen (*Ep 3:20-21*).

Questions

1 "All the way to heaven is heaven and all the way to hell is hell." What do you understand by this comment of St. Catherine of Siena?

2 What guidelines would you propose for telling children and young people about heaven and hell?

3 "Some people are afraid to live and others are afraid to die." What has Christian faith to offer both these groups?

18 Liturgy and the sacraments – Introduction

Liturgy

The second section of the new Catechism is devoted to the most important actions of our lives as Catholics: the celebration of the liturgy, a Greek word meaning "service," the service we render to God of praise, adoration, confession of our sins and thanksgiving for all his gifts to us. Our English word "worship" conveys a similar idea, being a shortening of the old English word *worthship*, that is, giving to God what he is worth!

The Catholic liturgy is rich in meaning. "Going to a religious service" almost tends to cheapen the idea, because, in the modern world, we have lost the sense of wonder and mystery which is essential if our worship is to enrich our lives. Perhaps we need to go to an Eastern Christian liturgy, with icons and Greek chant, in order to recapture this sense of mysterious presence.

The new Catechism (*CCC 1077*) quotes from Vatican II's Constitution on the Sacred Liturgy, the first document which the Vatican Council produced, to try to convey something of this wonder and mystery:

> The liturgy, then, is rightly seen as an exercise of the priestly office of Jesus Christ. It involves the presentation of our sanctification under the guise of signs perceptible to the senses and its accomplishment in ways appropriate to each of these signs. In it full public worship is performed by the Mystical Body of Jesus Christ, that is, by the Head and his members (*Liturgy, no. 7*).

Within the general context of Christian worship, the new Catechism locates the seven sacraments as the most important worship we offer to God, because the sacraments are worship offered to God by the command of Christ, and also are acts of worship where Christ becomes specially present by the action of the Holy Spirit.

Sacraments

Sacraments are visible signs, instituted by Christ, by which we enter into the mystery of God's saving plan for us.

Christ himself is God's own sacrament. Everything he said and did on earth was a visible sign of God's love. When he went to heaven, he left the Church to be his body, the sign of his rule on earth, his sacrament.

The Council of Trent defined that Christ instituted seven sacraments.

Not all are of equal value. Supreme is the Eucharist, the source and the summit of the whole of the Church's life.

Central to every sacrament is the "sign," for example, water in baptism. Ordinary things of this earth are taken and, joined to a word, for example "I baptize you ..." become means of grace.

Essentially sacraments are prayers of the Church through Christ to the Father. But, as instituted by Christ, they have the authority of his Word. This effectiveness of the sacrament does not depend upon the worthiness of the minister involved, but achieves its effect "by the work worked" (*ex opere operato*): that is, by the power of God.

Each sacrament also must have a minister who represents the action of Christ. Generally, this minister is ordained, either priest, bishop, or deacon. Ordination, itself a sacrament, confers the authority of God upon the ordained person to represent Christ in the sacrament. But two sacraments, marriage and baptism, do not require an ordained minister. The sacrament of marriage is truly the "lay sacrament," because the ministers of the sacramental union are the man and woman themselves. Husband and wife together "make" the sacrament.

Baptism, in the normal way, is conferred solemnly in church by an ordained minister. But, in case of danger of death, any person can baptize, even one who is not a Christian, providing he or she intends to do what the Church does in the sacrament.

For the sacrament to be fully effective, there must be faith and commitment on the part of the person receiving it.

On the other hand, we are all human, and none of us is completely worthy to receive any sacrament. We say before receiving Holy Communion,

> Lord, I am not worthy to receive you, but only say the word and I shall be healed.

The Holy Spirit helps us to receive worthily.

Even a validly conferred sacrament can be fruitless, if the person receiving it is insincere. St. Paul reminds the Corinthian Christians "Anyone who eats the bread or drinks the cup of the Lord unworthily is answerable for the body and blood of the Lord" (*1 Co 11:27*).

19 Baptism and confirmation

Every society has conditions of entry; and some have initiation rituals. Such ceremonies indicate the seriousness of what is being undertaken, give a chance for the new members to demonstrate publicly their commitment, and give them a sense of being welcomed by the community which they have joined.

Since becoming a Christian is not something which we can do by ourselves, but needs the help (called the "grace") of God and of the Christians whose company we hope to join, it is most appropriate that God left his Church to perform solemn ceremonies of initiation for new members of Christ's body. The new Catechism says there are three Christian initiation ceremonies: the sacraments of baptism, confirmation, and the Holy Eucharist.

In the early Church, most converts to Christianity were adults, making a full, and often dangerous, commitment to Christ, with martyrdom a real possibility. The sacraments of baptism, confirmation, and Eucharist were performed in one ceremony, at the Easter Vigil, and were great and solemn occasions.

Churches in the 3rd century had "baptistries," where the candidates were plunged naked into the water, and came up "reborn to new life." A white garment was put on them, and then they were "anointed" with chrism (oil), before receiving the holy bread and wine of Communion, the Body and Blood of Christ.

As time went on, and the whole of Europe became at least nominally Christian, more and more infants were baptized, children of Christian parents. By the Middle Ages, infant baptism had become the norm, and adult baptism was becoming more rare.

The result was that baptism was no longer the sacrament of

Infants are baptized in the faith of the Church, with their parents promising to do all they can to bring the child up to make a personal commitment of faith.

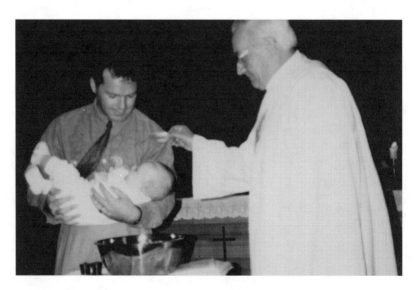

By the 20th century, the Western Catholic practice was fixed this way:

Baptism: infants of up to three months.

Eucharist: 7-8 years.

Confirmation: from 7 to 14 years.

We sometimes use the expression "before the flood" as an indication that something belongs to a past world now lost to us. At the time of Noah the rising waters of the flood destroyed a world bent upon its own destruction. The receding waters revealed - and stayed to irrigate – a world with hope restored.

It is in the nature of baptism that it should be celebrated once only for each Christian, just as it is in the nature of God that he does not go back on his word; and it was in the nature of Christ's sacrifice that it is valid for all time and in eternity. The bond is unbreakable. Failure on our part does not lead God to revoke it. Rejection only diminishes us, not his love.

the personal commitment of the individual Christian. The children's parents and the church community had to make the commitment for them.

Another result was that confirmation became separated from baptism and was given later in life, when the bishop visited. While a priest (or indeed a layperson in case of urgency) can baptize, the usual rule (now changed somewhat) is that only the bishop is allowed to administer confirmation, the ceremony of the laying-on of hands (signifying the gift of the Spirit) and anointing with oil. The sacrament of Communion also became separated from initiation; although, in the Eastern churches, infants are still given all three sacraments of baptism, confirmation, and Holy Communion.

Since the Second Vatican Council, there has been greater emphasis upon adult initiation. Whereas in the recent past, adult initiation was carried out as a private ceremony, we can now expect to see such initiation carried out quite publicly.

Baptism – new life

Baptism means new birth. It brings us into contact with the power of Christ's redeeming love. That does not mean that others are excluded from it, only that in this sacrament we know for sure that we are made one with Christ. Christ who is the firstborn of creation and the firstborn from the dead brings us into being as a people who now belong to the world of resurrection where he is Lord and Savior.

Christ died and rose again. Through baptism we are caught up in that mystery. There is a before and after which marks a real change in our condition. In baptism we leave behind the world that sin has marred with its alienations. We cannot entirely escape from it. But we join Christ and enter a new world that God is reconciling with his love, where Christ is the instrument of the Father's will.

Grace is new life through Christ and the gift of his Spirit.

Faith

Baptism is for those who have come to faith. Babies who are baptized must be brought to the ceremony by those who have faith, or must be linked in some way to a community of faith so that the gift in them may grow. Indiscriminate baptism which takes little consideration of the presence of faith or offers no prospect of an environment of faith is misplaced unless the danger of death makes the act itself, done in good faith, one which may stand alone.

"You will receive the power of the Holy Spirit ... and then you will be my witnesses" (*Ac 1:8*).

If God accomplishes so much in baptism, it is easy to see its importance. The Church has always acted with urgency, because

> no one can enter the kingdom of God without being born through water and the Spirit (*Jn 3:5*).

But the grace poured out is already at work. It is seen most clearly in those who are preparing for baptism and in the community providing a welcome.

In baptism God is at work, but there are many human participants. The minister says "I baptize" yet it is Christ who is baptizing through him. By his intention he brings his will in line with the intention of Christ. The baptized person is brought into the community of believers as into a family. Unique though each new member is, he or she is now a member of Christ's body, the Church. The Church is seen in relationship with Christ as actively participating in his work of bestowing new life.

Baptism is a bond between all Christians, ensuring that all are linked in some way as members of Christ's Church. Catholics believe that their Church contains all the means of holiness and full visible unity, and that baptism has been their gateway into that Church. They also recognize the elements of holiness and unity in other churches and pray that their common baptism may bear fruit in reconciliation.

Infant baptism

In the new Rite of Christian Initiation of Adults, the Catholic Church places a new emphasis upon adult baptism. Baptism and faith are inextricably united in the thought of the New Testament. No faith, no baptism. Thus the norm for baptism was adult commitment in faith.

But does this deny the validity or the advisability of the baptism of infants? Catholic teaching states that it does not.

There is no clear evidence of the baptism of infants in the New Testament, and little in the early Church. That is because the early converts were all adults. But from early on the children of believing parents were admitted into membership in the Church. For instance, in the Acts of the Apostles a new convert, the jailer at Philippi, was admitted for baptism, together with "all his household" (*Ac 16:31*). This may have included his children, even infants.

The sacrament of baptism is invalid without the response of faith. But where the infant is concerned, its faith is supplied by the parents, and above all by the church community. This faith, at the beginning given for the child, needs to grow into the full personal commitment of faith through education and formation, above all in the home.

Why are infants baptized? Ultimately, because Catholic faith is that baptism is "necessary for salvation,"

> is the sign and the means of God's prevenient love, which frees us from original sin and communicates a share in divine life. Considered in itself, the gift of these blessings to infants must not be delayed (*Instruction on Infant Baptism of the Sacred Congregation for the Doctrine of the Faith, 1980*).

What happens to children who die without baptism? This constitutes an enormous problem. One thing is clear: infants who die, clearly without having committed sin, will not go to hell, because no one goes there except through his or her own fault.

Confirmation

Because the sacrament of confirmation was originally part of the whole initiation ceremony, theologians have long debated what confirmation as a sacrament gives that baptism does not. If the Holy Spirit is given at confirmation, with the laying on of hands and the anointing with oil making us "other Christs," does not baptism give us that gift of the Spirit also?

There is one text in the Acts of the Apostles which tells of Christians, in Samaria, who had been baptized, but who still had to receive the Holy Spirit; for as yet the Spirit

> had not come down on any of them: they had only been baptized in the name of the Lord Jesus (8:16).

The apostles went, laid hands on them "and they received the Holy Spirit."

From the beginning, therefore, the Church understood that there was a special gift of the Holy Spirit in addition to baptism; we now call this "confirmation." But what is that gift?

Some scholars have seen the special contribution of the sacrament of confirmation as the gift of the Spirit to give us talents to become fruitful members of the Christian community

In Western countries, confirmation is usually of young people, and not of infants as with Eastern Christians.

The new Catechism links the sacrament of confirmation with that gift given to the apostles at the day of Pentecost, as a deepening of the grace given to us at our baptism.

CCC 1303 explains that confirmation grants five special gifts by the laying on of hands and the anointing with chrism:

Confirmation makes our sonship more complete, whereby we say Abba Father (Rm 8:15)

Confirmation makes us more deeply one with Christ

Confirmation makes grow in us the gifts of the Spirit

Confirmation links us more closely with the Church

Confirmation gives us strength (confirms us) to witness to Christ

The new Catechism then quotes the words of Ambrose, the great bishop of Milan:

Recall then the spiritual sign which you have received, the Spirit of wisdom and intelligence, the Spirit of counsel and might, the Spirit of knowledge and piety, the Spirit of holy fear, and keep what you have received. God the Father has marked you with his sign, Christ the Lord has confirmed you and he has sent into your heart the earnest of the Spirit (St. Ambrose, On the Mysteries, 7,42).

Gifts of the Spirit

THE SPIRIT OF WISDOM AND INSIGHT

THE SPIRIT OF COUNSEL AND POWER

THE SPIRIT OF KNOWLEDGE AND FEAR OF YAHWEH (Is 11:2)

Questions

1 What do you think about baptizing infants?

2 At what age do you think people should be confirmed?

3 Investigate the evidence for baptism in the New Testament.

(see 1 Co 12:4–11, the famous "'charismata"), whereas baptism is more oriented towards the person's becoming a member of the Church.

The Church teaches that confirmation is a strengthening and "confirmation" of the gifts already received at baptism. Where confirmation is delayed until teenage life, the sacrament becomes a way in which the young person can make the act of individual commitment to Christ which was made for him or her at infant baptism.

The gifts of the Spirit

In the early days, and sometimes today, the gift of the Holy Spirit is linked with "speaking in tongues," that is, an ecstatic state where the person utters strange speech which can only be interpreted by one who has the special "gift of interpretation." As with all types of mystical experience, this gift is not to be despised, but is to be treated with the same caution and common sense St. Paul shows when dealing with the charismatics in Corinth (see 1 Co 14).

Above all, following Paul's teaching, we are not to seek for these exceptional gifts, but rather for the greatest gift of all, "love" or "charity" (see 1 Co 13).

In addition, we pray for the "gifts of the Spirit" which the Church's tradition links with the sacrament of confirmation. These gifts are listed in Isaiah 11:2. Isaiah prophesied in the 8th century B.C. foreseeing an anointed Messiah to come in the line of David, who would have special gifts for ruling his people. With the coming of Christ the Messiah, these gifts are for us all, not just for specially chosen rulers.

20 The Eucharist

Baptism and confirmation can be given once only in our lives.

However, the third sacrament administered at the initiation of a Catholic, Holy Communion, the most important sacrament, is given to an adult for the FIRST time at initiation. The Church intends us to participate in this sacrament as often as we can, at public assembly in our parish church.

Catholics are obliged by Church law to go to Mass every Sunday. Why is the Mass so important?

The Lord's Supper

In the Passover feast, the Jews commemorate the night when the children of Israel, led by Moses, escaped from slavery in Egypt. (The full account of the Passover and the Feast of Unleavened Bread is in Ex 12.)

The Mass was first celebrated by Jesus himself, on the night he was arrested in the Garden of Gethsemane (*Lk 22:14–20*). It was the time of "Passover" (Hebrew *Pesach*, hence our word "Pasch" or "Paschal Mystery").

During the meal, Jesus broke bread, and introduced something quite new when he said

Take, eat, this is my body.

Then he took a cup of wine and said,

Drink of this. This is my blood, the blood of the new and everlasting covenant, for the forgiveness of sins. Do this in my memorial.

From the beginning, this service (called in the Acts of the Apostles "the breaking of bread," Ac 2:46) was celebrated on the "Lord's Day," that is Sunday, to commemorate Christ's resurrection. In a sense, every Sunday for a Christian is Easter Sunday, because on every Sunday we commemorate that first Sunday morning, when the women, coming to anoint Jesus' body, found that his tomb was empty. This was Jesus' Passover, his passing over from death to life; and the Mass is our "passing over" from a life of darkness to a life of light and virtue. Such a new life begins only imperfectly on this earth; but there is a promise of final fulfillment in heaven.

The priest is a special sign of Christ's presence. He presides over the congregation in Christ's name, and Christ working through him changes the bread and wine into his own Body and Blood.

The Introductory Rite

Mass begins with the sign of the cross,

In the name of the Father, and of the Son, and of the Holy Spirit. *Amen.*

The community confess their sinfulness and need of God. The confession is a reminder of the eternal mercy of God and of Christ's mission to call sinners back to the Father. This is answered with a hymn of praise "Glory to God."

The introductory rite ends with the special prayer of the day. Called the collect, it introduces the theme of the feast or season or the particular celebration: for example, a marriage, or a saint's day.

The Liturgy of the Word

The readings from Scripture follow when God himself speaks to his people and Christ proclaims the Gospel.

It is important that the readings at Mass are read clearly, with understanding, and that God's word is received with faith, allowing it to nourish our lives and make us better followers of Jesus.

The homily (or sermon) is an integral part of the Liturgy of the Word and should not be omitted on Sundays and holy days except for a serious reason. It explains the meaning of the Scriptures, especially the Gospel reading, and tries to show how we can put its message into practical effect in daily life.

Preparation of the Gifts

Representatives of the laity then bring the bread and wine for the sacrifice and also the congregation's gifts in the collection. This symbolizes the offering each member makes of themselves and all God's gifts.

Bread for our strength, wine for our joy

The Eucharist

This is the central part of the Mass. The priest prays that the Holy Spirit may come down on the gifts of bread and wine to make them holy so that they may become the Body and Blood of Christ. Then by the power of Christ's word, the bread and wine are changed into his Body and Blood. At the end of the prayer the congregation joins with the priest in offering Christ's Body and Blood to the Father.

> Through him, with him, in him, in the unity of the Holy Spirit, all glory and honor is yours, almighty Father, for ever and ever.

Our "*Amen*" is one of the most important acclamations at Mass. It is a statement of faith that Jesus is really present.

Christ is present

The Church believes that Jesus Christ is really present in many ways. He is really present in the community, for

> where two or three meet in my name, I am there among them (*Mt 18:20*).

He is really present in the Scriptures, and in all the sacraments. But the phrase "Real Presence" normally refers to his presence in the consecrated bread and wine at Mass.

The Church has explained this in various ways across the centuries. For the Jews, remembering makes the event present again, so Jews who became Christians understood our Lord to be present through the Church remembering him. Jesus instructed the Church to

> do this in memory of me.

So by this remembering we re-experience his presence and his saving work.

The new Catechism gathers together teaching from many sources on the Real Presence of Christ in the Eucharist.

First of all it says that the presence of Christ in the Eucharist is unique (*CCC 1374*). This is because, as the Council of Trent stated, in the most Holy Eucharist are "contained truly, really and substantially the Body and the Blood conjointly with the soul and the divinity of our Lord Jesus Christ, and, in consequence, the Christ whole and entire" (*Denzinger-Schönmetzer 1642*).

This is based upon taking Christ at his word when he said "This is my body" and "This is my blood" at the first Mass. This has always been referred to as a *conversion*, a supernatural and yet imperceptible change brought about solely by the word of Christ. This literal understanding of Christ's words is not new in the Church.

Real change

In the action of the Mass, the substance of bread and wine is changed into the Body and Blood of Christ, while the appearance of the bread and wine remain. This is called transubstantiation.

On October 11, 1551, the Council of Trent issued its famous teaching on the Eucharist, emphatically asserting

> Bread and wine are changed, converted into the Body and Blood of Christ.

The New Catechism (*CCC 1375*) quotes St. Ambrose, bishop of Milan, sixteen centuries ago:

Be well persuaded that this (the Eucharist) is not that which nature has formed, but that which the blessing has consecrated, and which the force of the blessing has carried over that of nature, because by blessing nature itself finds itself changed ... The word of Christ, which is able to make from nothing that which did not exist, is it then not able to change existing things into something which they were not up to then? Because to change things from their nature is not less than giving to those things their nature in the first place (*On the Mysteries, 9,50,52*).

The crisis of corruption in the Church and the ensuing Reformation led to controversies about many matters, including the sacraments. For instance, Martin Luther believed in the Real Presence, but he also thought it possible that the bread and wine might be the Body and Blood of Christ, and at the same time continue to be bread and wine.

In Catholic theology, the bread of the Eucharist is often called the Host (the Sacrificial Victim), to denote our faith that this bread has become the true body of Christ and is offered to God the Father for our salvation.

It then adds the phrase

> which conversion the Catholic Church most fittingly calls transubstantiation.

The essential Catholic doctrine is that a real but mysterious change, not visible to the senses, is effected by the Holy Spirit at the consecration. The bread and wine become the Body and Blood of Christ.

The saving sacrifice

The Holy Eucharist – the Lord's Supper, the Mass, the Blessed Sacrament – is a divine jewel. It is the Church's great act of liturgical worship. It is our meeting with God, and with one another, for prayer, praise and thanksgiving. It is our way of keeping holy the Lord's Day, and our weekly encounter with the Word of God.

At a deeper level, the Eucharistic mystery is the Real Presence of Jesus Christ under the appearances of bread and wine, sanctifying our churches and places of worship, testing our faith and calling us to adoration. It is the sacred fellowship-meal bringing into unity the members of Christ's body, the Church. It is Holy Communion with Christ, not only for the community but for each individual to whom it is a personal gift of grace and divine life. It is the sacrifice of the Mass, by which Christ perpetuates the work of our redemption.

The one sacrifice

> "As often as the sacrifice of the cross, in which Christ our paschal victim was immolated (*1 Co 5:7*), is celebrated at the altar, the work of our redemption is made operative" (*Vatican II on the Church, no. 3*). Those words of the Council repeat the constant belief and teaching of the Church through the ages.

> Dying you destroyed our death, rising you restored our life ...

These words at Mass proclaim the centerpoint of Christian faith. Jesus of Nazareth, the incarnate Son of God, became one of us in order to live with us, die for us, and raise us up to live eternally with God. Through his death upon the cross Jesus cleansed human nature from the deadly contagion of sin, and conquered the evil which separates us from God; through his victorious resurrection he revivifies those he has redeemed by imparting to them the power of his own divine life.

Central in Christ's saving sacrifice was his self-giving love, his merit and obedience to his Father's will, his example and moral influence for humankind. But central also is the divine power that works through the dying and rising of God made man. This power changes humankind and the created world; it inwardly transforms with a share of his divine life those whom he justifies by faith and love – even the infant at the baptismal font – and energizes them with the Spirit.

Through the mystery of Christ's death and resurrection the work of our redemption was accomplished once and for all. He entrusted to his priestly Church the power of making it available and operative in all times.

> Our Savior instituted the Eucharistic sacrifice of his body and blood, so that he might perpetuate the sacrifice of the cross through the centuries until his coming (*Vatican II on Liturgy, no. 47*).

That is the meaning of the Mass.

The Communion Rite

After saying or singing the Lord's Prayer together, and prayer by the priest, the members of the congregation offer each other the sign of peace, that peace of God, wholeness of heart and mind, which Christ came to give. The sign of peace is a final preparation for receiving the Body and Blood of Christ. Catholics are taught to receive Holy Communion with great devotion, because the bread and wine has become the very Body and Blood of Christ.

There are certain conditions we are supposed to fulfill before we can receive the sacrament of Holy Communion worthily. We must, for example, be in a state of grace, that is, free from grave sin.

The following is a translation of a beautiful old Latin chant, set to anthem by Mozart. It makes a good meditation after receiving Holy Communion.

O Sacrum Convivium

O Sacred Banquet,
In which Christ himself is received!
The memory of his Passion is recalled.

The mind is filled with grace,
And the promise of future glory
Is given to us. Alleluia!

The Mass is called

THE LORD'S SUPPER: referring to the night that Jesus celebrated the first Mass with his disciples.

HOLY COMMUNION: the act of receiving the Body and Blood of Christ.

THE EUCHARIST: the central part of the rite, the Prayer of Thanksgiving or Blessing, when the Words of Institution are recalled. The word "eucharist" means "thanksgiving."

THE MASS: a word meaning "dismissal," most likely coming from the Latin ending to the liturgy, "Ite, Missa est," which means literally, "Go, you are dismissed." Some scholars think that people started calling the whole service "the Mass" because in the early days people who were not fully in communion with the Church were "dismissed" after the homily.

Questions

1. Work out a way of explaining to young people who complain that Mass is boring why the Eucharist is so important within a Christian community. Why not find some young people and ask them what they think of your idea?

2. Are there any ways in which the Sunday Eucharist in your parish could become more truly a celebration for the community? What kind of things prevent it from being so? Could you offer any helpful suggestions to your priest or liturgy committee?

21 Penance and reconciliation

Every society has to have built-in ways of putting things right when they go wrong.

A Christian may have great euphoria and an intention never to do wrong when he or she is initiated into the Church in adult life, but he or she is only too aware of how easy it is to sin. And the Church has the proviso ready for this: the sacrament of penance, confession, or reconciliation.

If we call it "confession," this will underline the aspect of our willingness to bring this matter to the Church's representative, the priest. If we call it "the sacrament of penance," this will emphasize our willing attitude to be prepared to be "converted," and change from self to God's way. But nowadays it is more generally called the "sacrament of reconciliation," emphasizing that the effect of this confession and change of heart is to be one with God and with our neighbor again.

The earliest records of what later became called the "sacrament of penance," in the New Testament, show clearly that it was originally a form of excommunication for some serious and public sin.

St. Paul, for instance, tells the Corinthian Christians (c. A.D. 57) quite categorically to "turn out of the community" (1 Co 5:2) a man who committed incest.

> You must banish this evil-doer from among you (1 Co 5:13),

thunders Paul, quoting the Law of Moses (Dt 13:6).

Attitudes today appear to be softer. Perhaps we have gradually realized that we are all black sheep in some way. But the same basic elements remain: a consciousness that sin, especially serious sin, alienates us not only from God but also from his people; and the even stronger realization that by repentance, change of heart, the worst sinner can be forgiven and come back.

The apostles and their successors have power to "bind and loose" in the name of the Christian community. They can act on behalf of Christ and his Church, in imposing the conditions of return to the fold and of guidance for the reinstatement of the repentant sinner.

But how has the sacrament of penance with the modern confessional come to look so different from the time of Paul?

Penance yesterday

The apostles did not use the word confession. They simply called on people to repent and be baptized (Ac 2:38). It was not long before some kind of special service, or process of reconciliation, figured in the Church. But how the Christian confessed at that time, we do not know. We do know, however, that, as well as some form of confession of sins, there was a period of penance, followed by an act of reconciliation. Like baptism, this could happen only once in a person's lifetime.

By the fourth century, the Church was developing reconciliation. Confession of sin in some form was made to the bishop; the sinner was consigned to the

"You shall confess your sins in the Church, and neither shall you go to your prayer in a bad conscience" (*Didache* IV 14, second century A.D.).

94

ranks of the official penitents, which meant exclusion from Eucharist and community (a kind of portrayal of the real effect of sin) for a period of penance. Reconciliation took place by the imposition of hands on the head of the penitent by bishops and priests in the presence of the community. Eventually this took place during Lent with the service of reconciliation on Holy Thursday.

In Ireland and Britain there was a different system. More detailed confession of sins was made to a priest; absolution was immediate and only then followed by a penance. This could be repeated as often as the sinner needed Christ's forgiveness. Irish missionaries carried this practice to mainland Europe, where the practice of public reconciliation had declined. The "new" form of reconciliation, despite condemnations from local councils, caught on and, in time, developed into the present practice of "private confession."

Penance today

The sacrament of reconciliation today can be celebrated in many ways. The familiar "private confession" is still private, but frequently has a reading from the Bible to show how repentance is a response to God's call and how we should examine our hearts in the light of God's Word, not our own weakened will. The priest grants absolution – an act of reconciliation with God and the Church. The barriers of sin are broken down. The sinner comes away happy in the forgiveness of Christ.

A second form of the sacrament is the penitential service which is celebrated with the assembled community. The only private activity is the confession of sin and absolution. This form of celebration is a powerful sign that reconciliation comes through the Church, the community, which we have damaged by our sins. Together we listen to God's Word, examine our hearts, pray for our forgiveness and that of our brothers and sisters, and are reconciled with them and with God.

The third form of the sacrament has no individual, detailed confession of sin and has a general absolution. This is for any emergency, such as in time of war when there is not time for priests to hear individual confessions (CCC 1483). Because the Church teaches that the individual confession of all serious sins is required by divine law, a penitent conscious of such sins should confess those sins privately to a priest, even after receiving general absolution.

Sign and reality

Reconciliation is a sacrament, and therefore a sign: a sign that Jesus came into this world to reconcile us to God and our neighbor. Any celebration of reconciliation is a celebration of the mercy and love of God. It is also a sign that the repentant sinner is actually forgiven, reconciled. And it does not end there. The celebration of reconciliation, especially by a community together, builds up the whole Church into a living, effective sign to the world of the presence in its midst of the redeeming Christ.

Confessing sins makes us aware of our weaknesses and sharpens our sense of responsibility for our actions before God and the Church. Perhaps at times we have placed too much emphasis

Love your enemies. The Pope talking to Ali Agca, who tried to assassinate him.

Benefits

The act of going to confession makes us look more carefully at our life and examine our conscience.

We are able to discuss problems with the priest. Often, problems become worse when they are not discussed early.

The priest undergoes a long training in theology, psychology and counseling.

Confession is completely confidential. The priest will never reveal anything that is said, even to the police. He is bound by the strictest law of secrecy.

The priest gives encouragement which helps us to grow in the Christian life. He then gives a "penance" which is undertaken to show willingness to live a new life.

When the priest gives absolution we experience the forgiveness of Christ.

Often, people stop going to confession because they no longer feel that it is of benefit. Sometimes, this might be the fault of the priest, who might be unsympathetic. If so, we should try to find a better confessor.

The fault might also be that of insufficient preparation on the part of the penitent. Some basic guidelines for the fruitful use of the sacrament are:

Guidelines

Make a careful examination of conscience, using perhaps a good booklet such as *Making a Better Confession* by Con O'Connell, O.F.M. (Liguori). We should not make this just a "shopping list" of sins, but a request to the Holy Spirit to reveal ways we have failed to live up to the fullness of life in Christ.

We should not be frightened to be frank about sins, if something is on our conscience. The priest has probably heard it all before, and it is not nearly as bad as we thought.

The new rite recommends reading a passage of Scripture before going into the confessional.

We do not expect to "enjoy" going to confession, any more than going to the dentist, or to the doctor. But we may well feel liberated after receiving the forgiveness of Christ. Like all healing, the process may be painful, but the result is joyful.

Never be frightened of routine. We all have some faults which cling like leeches. The story goes of a man going into the confessional and saying to the priest, "Same old sins, Father"; to which the priest replied, "OK, then. Same old penance."

on the confessing and obscured the forgiving. Sacraments are, above all, celebrations of the actions of Christ. Joy, not fear, should be the hallmark of reconciliation. Jesus ate and drank with sinners. If we were to rediscover that sense of joy in the sacrament of reconciliation, we might be better signs of God's loving forgiveness and bring to the world that healing it needs.

Love and confessional

Perhaps we may have been told as children, "If you are naughty God won't love you." That was wrong. God always loves us. Our sins harm our love, not God's.

We want to love God. So we are sorry. There cannot be sorrow without love. It is always important to remember that we come to the sacrament for love. We feel guilty. This is natural because we have done wrong. But it is knowing that God's love is still there that really matters, not our guilt.

We know we should tell all serious sins in confession, but what about the things that are not so important? We twist the truth a little to keep ourselves out of trouble. We slip home from work early. We forget our prayers. Do we need to confess these things?

The answer is "No." Our friends do not expect an apology for every little thing that goes wrong.

But some of these smaller things do trouble us. They tell us that we are not loving enough. We should confess these. It also helps to say why we think they are happening. Not to make excuses, but to give simple reasons.

We are human and we need to know that we are forgiven. When Jesus was on earth he met that human need in people.

Why go to confession?

If a Christian has not committed a serious sin, there is no obligation to seek absolution in the sacrament of reconciliation. It is sufficient to confess sins privately to God or publicly at the beginning of the Mass for the forgiveness of venial sins or of imperfections.

But the Church offers the gift of the sacrament of reconciliation for our personal growth in Christ even when we are not in a state of mortal sin. To come to the sacrament once a month, or at major seasons, is a unique way of realizing the joy of Christ's forgiveness.

The new Catechism explains clearly the rules about the confession of sins.

First (*CCC 1457*) the Code of Canon Law makes the rule that a Catholic must confess, at least once per year, the grave sins on his or her conscience (*Canon 989*). What is "grave sin" will be more thoroughly discussed in the next section of this book.

Secondly, the new Catechism explains (*CCC 1458*) that the confession of "daily faults," or "venial sins," though not obligatory, is nevertheless highly recommended by the Church. The regular frequentation of the sacrament of penance or reconciliation, as the Catechism explains, enables us to grow in the life of the Spirit and to become merciful like the One who gives us mercy.

The new Catechism quotes St. Augustine, who speaks of confession of sin in his usual powerful way:

A man who confesses his sins acts already with God. God accuses you of your sins; if you accuse yourself, then you join yourself with God. A human being and a sinner are in a manner of speaking two distinct realities: when you speak of a human being, then it is God who has made that human being; when you speak of the sinner, then it is the human being oneself who has done it. Destroy that which you have done in order that God might save what he has made ... When you begin to detest that which you have done, it is then that your good works commence, because you accuse these bad deeds. The commencement of good deeds, that is the confession of bad deeds. You do the Truth and you come to the Light (*St. Augustine, Commentary on the Gospel of John, 12.13*).

He said,

> Your sins are forgiven

or

> Your faith has made you whole

or simply

> Go in peace.

He left the Church his power to forgive.

> Whose sins you shall forgive they are forgiven.

That is why we confess to God and to the Church through the person of a priest.

> As the minister of Jesus the priest says

> Through the ministry of the Church, may God give you pardon and peace

and then

> I absolve you from your sins, in the name of the Father and of the Son and of the Holy Spirit.

Indulgences

"Indulgence" simply means "forgiveness," where the intercessory life of the whole communion of saints is made available to us.

The first principle of "indulgences" is that the members of the Body of Christ can help each other. From the earliest days of the Church, Christians who were doing public penance for sins committed after baptism were helped by the prayers of the martyrs, and sometimes had their penance reduced by those prayers. We also can ask other members of the body of Christ, who have run the race of life and won, to help us in our daily struggle.

The second principle of "indulgences" is that a Christian, after being forgiven by the grace of Christ in baptism, needs daily to be "sanctified," the process by which that forgiveness is applied in daily growth.

We must be careful not to misunderstand indulgences. Pre-Vatican II, people used to speak of "500 days' indulgence," a language which dates back to public penance, where 500 days' public penance might have been given and then dispensed with by an indulgence. It is fruitless to try to "quantify" indulgence to this extent. Rather, indulgences are used to realize more fully our communion with the whole Body of Christ, living and dead.

Questions

1 When we say the "Our Father" we ask that God will forgive us our sins "as we forgive those who sin against us." If forgiving is the duty of every Christian, why the need for a special sacrament of forgiveness? Why the need to confess to a priest?

2 There are those who say that the frequent reception of the sacrament of reconciliation, confession, is no more than a "license to sin." Discuss.

22 The ministerial priesthood

The priest's work is varied, demanding, lonely and often very hard, with its own particular tensions. In fact, many priests at one stage or other during their ministry will be tempted to give up. What keeps them going, and still more, happy and fulfilled in their vocation? Basically, the priesthood is being in love with and loving the Church, God's people. Paul wrote to the Ephesians that

> Christ loved the Church and sacrificed himself for her...(Ep 5:25).

Just as Christ's love led him to die on the cross, so the priest gives his life to help people draw closer to God, and into communion with each other.

The priest's ordination consecrates him in a special way to the Church, as the leader and the representative of Christ in the Christian community.

It is in the Mass, the Eucharist, that the priest's role is most fully expressed. He represents the whole community in offering the one sacrifice of Christ to the Father. All Christians are "other Christs." But at the Eucharist the priest fulfills the role played by Jesus at the Last Supper, giving himself to his disciples.

And furthermore, the priest's role at the Mass symbolizes his role throughout his life. At Mass, he represents Christ offering the perfect worship to his Father. The priest then helps God's people in their daily lives to form a community of love, sharing and witness: lives which themselves are offerings pleasing to God.

The priest's life, like all professions, is often humdrum, and concerned with mundane affairs like raising money for the upkeep of the church. He is something of a general practitioner, expected to be counselor, friend, small business manager, spiritual director, preacher, parish politician, school administrator, school teacher, youth club leader, registrar, employment referee. No task, however secular or unusual, which builds up the Christian community, is foreign to the priestly ministry – provided that his prayer life, the heart of his vocation, is not neglected.

The priesthood in history

It has been said that the priesthood is "the second oldest profession."

This may not be very complimentary to priests, to put them second historically to the ladies of the night. But it makes a valid point: that nearly all ancient civilizations had a man, or woman, whose role it was in that community to offer worship to their god in their name.

Because sacrifice is central to most religions, the priest's job was to offer the sacrifices prescribed by that religion. His duties also included teaching and handing on traditions. The priest also exercised a role of leadership. When Christianity flourished, it developed its own priestly system.

In the 16th century, Europe suffered its greatest religious cleavage, the Protestant Reformation. One of the most important issues dividing Protestants and Catholics was that of the nature of the Christian priesthood. Should the Christian Church have priests, just like most other religions?

The Protestant Reformers answered with a definite "no." They believed that Jesus Christ was the only priest.

The Catholic reply, given in the 23rd Session of the Council of Trent (1563), was totally opposite.

For over four hundred years, this controversy has raged between Christians. The Catholic Church maintains that Christ did initiate in his Church (either while on earth, or after his resurrection, through the Spirit) a permanent order in the Church, which we now call the order of bishops, priests, and deacons. This permanent order took time to develop; but its main lines were established by the end of the first century, with Ignatius of Antioch.

Only those in holy orders, in fact bishops and priests, can offer the sacrifice of the Eucharist for and with the people of God, and represent Christ in the sacraments.

But, in an ecumenical age, we are beginning to realize that we have much to learn together with other Christians, without compromising our faith. The Second Vatican Council saw the need to realize much more profoundly the insight that all Christians, both priest and lay, have a vital role in the whole "priestly people of God." A priest is ordained

> to preach the Gospel, to shepherd the faithful and to celebrate the divine worship (*Church, no.28*).

A priest's role is complex and varied.

The common priesthood

St. Peter wrote to the early Christians:

> You are a chosen race, a kingdom of priests, a holy nation, a people to be a personal possession to sing the praises of God who called you out of the darkness into his wonderful light (*1 P 2:9*).

He borrowed the description of Israel, the People of God, from the Book of Exodus (*19:5f*), which sets them apart from the rest of

The priest's ordination consecrates him in a special way to the Church, as the leader and the representative of Christ in the Christian community.

the nations and gives them the role of priest among the earthly kingdoms. Because of her special relationship to God, Israel is allowed to "draw near" to him to do "service" for all the world (see *Is 61:5f*). Peter applies this description to the new People of God who are incorporated into Christ by their baptism, and in whose unique priesthood they have a share.

The New Testament idea of priesthood moves the emphasis away from the duty of priesthood in the individual sense to a sharing in the being and mission of Christ, the sole priest of the New Covenant. Each and every Christian, therefore, participates in the prophetic, priestly and pastoral identity and activity of Jesus Christ.

The ministerial priesthood was instituted by Christ, and is exercised in various orders (bishops, priests, deacons). They share Christ's office of mediator, shepherd and head.

> These members in the society of the faithful would be able by the sacred power of their order to offer sacrifice and to remit sins.

The ordained are living images of Christ's headship over the common priesthood. They are required to teach and to build up the Church at local, diocesan and international levels.

The priesthood of the laity

All Christians share in the mission to preach the Gospel.

> They also share in the priestly, prophetic and royal office of Christ and therefore have their role to play in the mission of the whole people of God in the Church and in the world (*Vatican II, Decree on the Apostolate of the Laity, no. 2*).

The Church has an involvement in the renewal of the temporal order of the world and in this the laity has a special role.

The difference in nature and function between the common priesthood and the ministerial priesthood exists only to ensure a more complete collaboration in one mission. Their common goal is the evangelization, sanctification and transformation of the world.

Celibacy

One of the most controversial aspects of Catholic life is that priests cannot marry and in the West generally cannot be married. Why is this?

Celibacy is not "required by the nature of the priesthood itself" (*Decree on the Priestly Ministry*

"By their very vocation the laity seek the kingdom of God by engaging in temporal affairs and by ordering them according to the plan of God" (*Laity, no. 31*).

This tradition of celibacy, as the Second Vatican Council states, "is in many ways particularly suited to the priesthood" (*Life of Priests, no. 16*). It is following the example of Christ, who "prized highly that perfect and perpetual continence which is undertaken for the sake of the kingdom of heaven." It is easier for priests to keep close to Christ with undivided love. They are more free, in him and through him, to devote themselves to the service of God and people.

The Ordination of Women

The Catholic Church, in common with Eastern Orthodox Christians, allows only men to be ordained, resisting the more recent tendency within some other Christian denominations to begin to ordain women also.

The tradition of ordaining only men to the ministerial priesthood goes right back to the time of Jesus himself, who chose only men to be his apostles. The priest, especially in the Eucharist, represents Christ, who is God become MAN, not God become WOMAN. This does not mean that women are not important in the Church. On the contrary, apart from Christ himself, we believe that the most important role of all in God's plan was given to a woman, Mary, who bore the Son of God in her womb: a role, indeed, which no man could have fulfilled.

The new Catechism insists that, according to tradition, only a male (Latin *vir*) can be validly ordained (*CCC 1577*). The new Catechism adds that no one has the right to receive orders, but one must be called by God and submit to the authority of the Church, which alone has the right to call to orders.

Questions

1 Numerous Protestant clergymen, most of them married, have been given permission to be ordained Catholic priests. What advantages would married priests bring to the ministry and what disadvantages? Would you like to see the practice of married priests being more widespread in the Church?

2 Refer back to the list of things which the priest does. Which of these could not be done by women priests? What would be the benefit to the Church if women could be ordained?

and Life of the Second Vatican Council, no. 16). In the New Testament, and in the early Church, many bishops and priests were married; and today in the Eastern discipline of the Catholic Church, in the Eastern Orthodox Churches, and in most Christian denominations, many clergy are married.

The law, then, could change for Catholic priests in the West. The law could even have changed at the Second Vatican Council should the bishops have decided it; as they decided to change the law that Mass should be celebrated in Latin. But they decided against change in the law of priestly celibacy.

Even in the Eastern Churches a priest can marry *only before* ordination. This tradition, that men in orders should not marry, but are "married to the Church," goes back to about the 11th century. And, where the Catholic Church in the West has occasionally allowed relaxation in the law of celibacy (as for instance when ministers of other churches have become Catholics and want to become ordained priests), it allowed men, whether bishop, priest or deacon, to marry after ordination. To do this they must receive a dispensation from the Pope and renounce active ministry.

Is a celibate life more difficult than a married life? All states of life, married, single, or consecrated celibacy or virginity, have joys and difficulties. Each of us has our gift; and we should pray for each other to be faithful to it.

Priests are conscious that celibacy could lead to a self-centered life, without the demands of a close family relationship; or even to running away from close friendship. This underlines the need for the priest's training to provide means of personal as well as academic growth.

23 Marriage

Marriage is a covenant between a man and a woman. It is a sacrament of love instituted by Christ.

God's attitude to marriage is fully stated on the first page of the Bible. The Lord said that it was not good for the man to be alone; he could not flourish and develop without a companion. And this companion was the woman with whom he becomes one "flesh." "One flesh" means more than a physical union; it embraces the whole being, so that man and wife are depicted as one physical and psychological unit, one living, thinking, planning whole. This teaching is reaffirmed by Jesus when he annuls the regulations of the Deuteronomic Law permitting divorce.

The second account of the creation, then, treats only the unity between husband and wife; the first account, concerned with the stability and perpetuation of every species, leads on directly from the sexuality of human beings to the command to be fruitful and multiply. The procreation of children remains a primary reason for marriage.

Perhaps the way which most clearly indicates how marriage is to be treasured, and how warm and vital it must be, is its use as a figure of God's love for his people. Almost all the prophets see that the deepest human married love is only a shadow of God's love for Israel. Although the prophets' intention is to illustrate the divine reality by the human relationship, the dignity of the human bond grows by the illustration itself. God's unbreakable fidelity, his boundless devotion, his refusal to let go of Israel, has perhaps its strongest image in the prophet Hosea's pursuit of his faithless wife (*Ho 2*).

In the New Testament similarly, devotion of husband to wife, and his lavish care for her, is used as the image of Christ's devotion and generous self-giving to the Church for which he sacrificed himself (*Ep 5:25-31*).

Such is the ideal of devotion and generosity of spouse to spouse, voiced of course, in that socially male-dominated world, in terms of devotion of husband for wife. Custom might dictate that the dominant part was played by the husband and that infidelity was more severely punished in wife than in husband. But, alone of the peoples of the Mediterranean or Near Eastern world, Israel knew that the basic equality of partnership could not be revoked after the creation narrative provided woman as a companion, one flesh with her husband. And they were instructed by God to take equal responsibility for the care of creation.

Marriage for life

The Church teaches that marriage is for life. Christ said

> What God has united, human beings must not divide (*Mk 10:9*).

This is no easy task; but it has been achieved, through God's help, by millions of couples. Marriage is hard work. But if you put a lot into it, you get even more out of it.

Tolerating each other's drawbacks is the beginning of a stronger and more meaningful love than simply being "in love." It is love with no strings attached. Each one loves the other for who they are.

The result is a relationship which is honest and open, strong and secure. Everything is shared. No other relationship has the freedom, and at the same time the security, of marriage. It is basking in the sunshine of warmth and acceptance.

As we grow older and change, we grow together through continual communication and no secrets. There is a unity of thought that does not always need words, an understanding in a look or turn of the head.

Partners bring to their relationship their own unique experience of life which will be different. They will have different experiences of family, different values, expectations, and styles of behavior. Many will have learned from inadequate models inappropriate, ineffective and sometimes destructive ways of both relating and communicating.

It is not always easy to share prayer in married life. Having common belief should make it simpler. This is one reason why the Church prefers and

Although external pressures have certainly contributed to the increase in divorce, it must also be recognized that many people are totally unprepared for the intimacy and reality of marriage. They may marry too young. They may marry for the wrong reasons. Perhaps they are lonely, on the rebound, anxious to leave home, pregnant, or it may be simply because all their friends are getting married. They may be inflexible, incapable of coping with change, unused to expressing how they feel, and unpracticed in the ability to communicate with each other. Their self-esteem may be damagingly low: "How can I tell him his friends make me feel small? I feel so stupid all the time. He'd only laugh. He never listens to what I say."

encourages marriages between Catholics rather than mixed marriages. But sharing belief does not guarantee sharing practice. People can lapse and give up praying while still believing. Some people can be deeply in love and have a very wide understanding and union, but nevertheless find prayer together embarrassing and even counterproductive.

The habit of prayer together and going to Mass together should begin before marriage and continue within marriage. This helps the couple to grow together.

Marriage is for life.

In past days, many families said the rosary together. It is possible to share music in a prayerful way or even simply be together closely and silently, after a brief turning to God – say by sharing an "Our Father."

It is important also for parents to pray with children. But this must be simple and loving. They should be allowed their own expression in words and ideas, even if they are a bit offbeat. Long tedious prayers are not really suitable for children. They should learn to pray in love and trust.

If one partner will not or cannot share prayer with the other, the praying partner must not give up his/her prayer.

What is marriage for?

A married couple learns to sustain each other in every aspect of life. In order for any human being to do this there is usually a long and sometimes painful process of learning, which first tests and then deepens the love each has for the other. Second, there is healing. After the "honeymoon period," faults can soon begin to be revealed. A priceless grace of married life is for each to accept the other as he or she is. This acceptance is itself a primary form of healing. Mutual confidence develops, and one can help the other to overcome fears and anxieties.

Third, there is growth. As the years pass, crises arise, and the couple can guide each other through them.

The catechism of the Council of Trent describes one purpose of marriage as: "That one being afflicted, by the help of the other might more easily bear the inconveniences of life, and the weakness of old age" (*The Catechism for the Curate p.319*).

Mixed marriages and disparity of cult

The new Catechism (*CCC 1633-1637*) is fully aware that in many countries (as indeed in the U.S.) many Catholics marry partners who are baptized but members of another Christian denomination – called a "mixed marriage" – or who marry partners who are not baptized Christians – called "disparity of cult."

The Catechism first speaks positively of these marriages, which do not present necessarily an "insurmountable obstacle" to a happy marriage, and to the Catholic partner being faithful to his or her faith. But the difficulty must also be faced: that of disunion of religion in the very family itself. A further temptation presents itself: that of religious indifference (*CCC 1634*).

First of all, therefore, the Catechism states, there must be the permission of the local bishop who has the pastoral responsibility in the local area. He must ensure that there is the right kind of guidance for the couple. The Church also tries to ensure that the children of that marriage will be brought up in the Catholic faith. It is also important, the Catechism states (*CCC 1636*), that the couple, especially of a mixed marriage, understand what is common to their respective Christian communions, and to respect each other where there are differences of faith and discipline.

There is a particular responsibility, the Catechism states (*CCC 1637*), regarding the Catholic partner of a marriage where there is "disparity of cult." Where one partner is not a Christian, the Catholic partner, as Paul says (*1 Co 7:14*), sanctifies the nonbelieving partner who follows another religion. What a joy it will be, says the Catechism, if the Catholic partner succeeds in leading the non-Christian partner to conversion and faith.

Annulments

The Church teaches clearly that persons who are divorced cannot remarry. Yet some Catholics and some non-Catholics are allowed to marry in Church after they have received a Church annulment or dissolution of their first marriage. What is the real differ-

ence between a civil divorce and a Church annulment?

Marriage is a special and solemn agreement between a man and a woman to enter a life-long partnership which of its very nature is faithful and permanent, is open to the possibility of children, and is for the mutual benefit and support of each other. When partners give a proper and considered consent to marriage they are promising to remain faithful to each other

for richer or poorer, in sickness and in health, till death us do part.

Having given that consent, it is essential that they stick to it, for their own good and for that of the children and society. That applies to any marriage properly entered into whether the partners are Christians or not.

But for Christians, this agreement is also strengthened by the grace of the sacrament. Once a marriage is solemnly and properly entered into, and has been consummated, it cannot be dissolved under any circumstances because it is a solemn covenant made before God and the Church. That is why the Church does not accept that a couple can remarry after a civil divorce, because by granting a divorce, the state is claiming to break the bond of an existing and valid marriage.

This is substantially different from a Church declaration of nullity. When the Church declares a marriage to be null and void, it is a formal declaration by the tribunal judges that matrimonial consent, on the part of at least one party, was not sufficient to create an indissoluble bond. Therefore, the persons concerned are not bound in marriage, and are in fact free to marry. The essential difference is that by a civil decree of divorce, the state claims to break the bond of an existing marriage, whereas by a declaration of nullity, the Church judges that there was no legally binding marriage.

A marriage comes into being when the couple mutually exchange their consent. But if there is some radical defect in that consent then the marriage is in reality nonexistent, despite the outward appearances. There are many reasons why such consent can be defective, even though the spouses enter into the marriage in good faith and with the intention of making it last. It is the job of the Church tribunals to determine if the consent was invalid.

The breakdown of a marriage involves great suffering on the part of the couple, their children, and their families and friends. The Church, with a mother's love for her children, has for centuries used the annulment process to heal and strengthen the broken without abandoning the values of the Gospel in regard to Christian marriage. The number of such declarations has risen sharply throughout the last twenty years, but this is simply the Church responding to an increasingly acute pastoral problem, namely, the rise of breakdown in marriage. But while the Church is deeply concerned for those involved, she also has the serious duty to protect and strengthen the institution of marriage and so witness to the world its inherent value.

Questions

1 What are the main influences against marriage and family life in the modern world? What does Christianity offer to help people face and overcome them?

2 The pastoral care of married couples is the responsibility of the whole parish. What do we do in our parish to help foster and strengthen our married couples? What else could be done?

24 Healing

The sacrament of the sick – formerly called extreme unction – is healing in a special sense.

All the sacraments heal. Marriage heals selfishness; confirmation heals fear of witnessing; the sacrament of reconciliation heals sinfulness.

The new Catechism lists the sacrament of the anointing of the sick as the second sacrament of healing, the first being the sacrament of reconciliation, healing our sick hearts and souls.

The sacraments are a means of bringing wholeness, even in incurable illness. We receive healing also from others through acceptance, care, friendship. Prayer and scripture too are healing.

Healing is not the same as curing. Few of the many millions who visit Lourdes may be cured but many are healed. Some suffering is incurable, like loss in bereavement. But the pain can be lessened. New peace and courage are found. From the distress of bereavement people can look outwards again. They are healed by God, by time, by others.

Much of the Bible is about healing. Fallen human nature is wounded, and many encounters of life keep that wound open: the pain of childbearing, the brambles and thistles of life, the sweat of toil. And yet even with this curse comes the promise of a remedy, when the offspring of the woman will bruise the serpent's head (*Gn 3:15*).

Healing is promised by Jesus: "I have come that they may have life and have it to the full" (*Jn 10:10*). There are many ways in which we can lack fullness of life. Bitterness, sickness, sin, guilt, weakness in many forms, can crush our spirits. We can become crippled in our relationship to God, to ourselves, to others.

Jesus did not promise to remove the cross from our lives. On the contrary. But the cross can heal, allowing life to the full.

Most people who go to Lourdes are not cured of physical sickness, but receive spiritual health and strength to face their problems.

Later on, this healing is associated with the messianic era. A sign of the coming of the glory of the Lord will be that the eyes of the blind will be opened and the ears of the deaf unsealed (*Is 35:5*) – signs which Jesus explicitly notes that he has fulfilled when he alludes to this passage for the messengers of John the Baptist (*Mt 11:5*). As the consciousness of sin grows deeper, especially in the writings during and after the exile, such as Baruch 1–2, 4–5, the longed-for healing is expressed more and more in terms of healing from sin.

In the ministry of Jesus, sometimes forgiveness of sins is followed by healing from physical sickness (*Mk 2:10*). But Jesus refuses to accept that sickness or suffering is necessarily a punishment of sin, as some of his Jewish contemporaries mistakenly did (*Jn 9:3*).

The apostles continue this healing mission, and again the healings by Peter and Paul are signs of their deeper mission. They are repeating and continuing the healings of their Master.

In the list of gifts of the Spirit healing takes its place with teaching, guidance and tongues as one of the key activities in the work of the organic body of Christ.

The service of healing

The anointing of the sick is a sacrament which looks to one basic New Testament text – James 5:14–15. James says:

> Any one of you who is ill should send for the elders of the church, and they must anoint the sick person with oil in the name of the Lord and pray over him. The prayer of faith will save the sick person and the Lord will raise him up again; and if he has committed any sins, he will be forgiven (*Jm 5:14-15*).

Behind this text lies the whole concern of Jesus for the afflicted and weak, and his minstry of healing and reconciliation among them.

Some points should be noted in James's text as guidelines for our celebration of anointing. First. Who are called? Not the members of the community, interestingly enough, who had the gift of healing, but rather the elders (the words we now translate as "priests") – in other words the people who represented the unity of the community and ensured its fidelity to Jesus. Their coming to be with the sick member is a sign of solidarity of the community with one unable to come to its gathering.

Second. What does this community delegation do? Primarily it prays. The salvation of the sick person is attributed by James to "the prayer of faith." This prayerful visit is a focus of the prayer of faith by the community for the sick brother or sister, and this prayer is very powerful (indeed this thought leads James to digress on the power of prayer in the last few verses of his letter).

Third. The anointing with oil is carried out in the context of this prayerful concern. It communicates by the sense of touch. Its soothing and refreshing quality expresses the reaching out of the community of faith to the individual.

Finally, the anointing is done "in the name of the Lord." This refers to the Lord Jesus, who under this title is the one who humbled himself even to accepting death, and was raised up by the Father (*Ph 2:5-11*). The Church claims the power ("name" involves the whole power of the person) of Jesus who suffered and was raised up, and applies it to the sick Christian;

One of the prayers after the anointing expresses the solidarity of the community of faith:

"Father in heaven, through this holy anointing grant N. comfort in his/her suffering. When he/she is afraid, give him/her courage, when afflicted, give him/her patience, when dejected, afford him/her hope, and when alone, assure him/her of the support of your holy people, through Christ our Lord. *Amen.*"

its promise is that the sharing of life and destiny which he or she has entered into in baptism will be present and evident also in sickness and failing health, and will ultimately result in the Christian's being "raised up" with Jesus, as James promises.

To think that the sacrament has "worked" if the sick person gets better and that it has somehow "failed" if this does not happen is a misunderstanding of the sacrament.

The sacrament celebrates faith in the power of the risen Christ, who will conform our mortal bodies to the image of his glorious body (*Ph 3:21*). Despite sickness and suffering, despite death itself – which none of us can escape – we rest safe in the confidence that our ultimate destiny is assured in Christ.

Use of the sacrament

The Christian community and its priests have two important duties concerned with this sacrament. They should encourage the sick to receive it and they must protect the sacrament from being trivialized.

The rite of anointing gives the key by using the word "danger." Danger does not mean a threat to life, but rather a threat to the person. Illness can weigh down the whole person: people can be at risk in relationship to God; their life is disrupted; they cannot look outward; they no longer find a meaning for their lives.

Through the anointing of the sick and by other gifts to his Church, Jesus offers fullness of life no matter what our situation may be.

People who are gravely ill, physically or psychologically, and those very weak in old age should be anointed. Less serious illness can be a danger to wholeness, so that people lack fullness of life. Examples might help. Physical illness: chronic arthritis, certain forms of diabetes, angina, debilitating migraine. Illness with psychological factors: severe depression, alcoholism, acute anxiety or fears that interfere with normal living. There are also difficulties that appear spiritual but have psychological roots, such as scrupulosity and severe sexual problems.

Patients yearn to be treated as human beings and not as another number. They sense, although many have lost their Christian tradition, that healing has to touch body, psyche and spirit since all of these are interrelated. They know that modern medicine does not do this, hence their frustration and continued sickness. So they turn to alternative medicine and prayer to achieve the "inner healing" which eludes them in present-day hospitals and clinics.

Sometimes it is forgotten that medicine owes its greatest debt not to Hippocrates, but to Jesus. It was the humble Galilean who more than any other figure in history bequeathed to the healing arts their essential meaning and spirit. Physicians would do well to remind themselves that without his spirit, medicine degenerates into a depersonalized methodology, and its ethical code becomes a mere legal system. Jesus brings to methods and codes the corrective of love without which true healing is rarely actually possible.

Caring for the dying

A time comes in an advanced progressive and incurable illness when further attempts to cure become inappropriate. The role of those caring for the patient then changes, and continuing care concentrates on ensuring that the remainder of the patient's life is free from unnecessary physical and mental distress.

The first duty of the doctor and nurses is to gain the patient's confidence and trust by providing appropriate treatment to alleviate physical suffering. This does not include extraordinary or excessive measures which are quite inappropriate for a patient who is dying. It does require medications, therapies and nursing procedures which when correctly applied will relieve physical suffering, while avoiding diminution of mental alertness.

Other causes of suffering must then be considered – social, emotional, spiritual. A dying patient is still a living person and we should help them to "live" until they die and to use the remaining precious weeks to good purpose.

It is easy for dying patients to become isolated and lonely. They are weak, dependent, vulnerable and in need of that security which can only be demonstrated by love and kindness.

The most valuable thing we can give is time. This provides them with the opportunity to express their fears and anxieties, and these may well be dispersed by unhurried and repeated conversation. They may have particular worries concerning their families, financial or legal difficulties, emotional or spiritual problems, and these may need the involvement of the appropriate expert, especially a hospital or hospice chaplain.

As the patient's life disintegrates there may be a parallel disintegration of the family. Even before death the anguish of grief will be evident and the total care of the dying includes care of the family with bereavement support. Grief is the price to be paid for loving someone, and there is no shortcut through it. It is, however, a particular aspect of suffering for which a firm religious faith will give great solace.

In facing terminal illness, prayer can be wonderfully helpful. This works both for the dying person and for the relatives and friends. It can bring great

strength. In knowledge of the situation, shared through prayer, the approach of death can be faced, recognized and even accepted. Instead of empty phrases about "How well you look today," there can be genuine truthful expression of the real feeling, the real state of affairs.

Sometimes the dying, when they know the prognosis, want to

In death, we share the experience of the One who said "It is fulfilled" (*Jn 19:30*).

111

reminisce, share sorrows or regrets, make their peace with everyone, settle outstanding debts.

Through weakness, the dying person may only be able, without speaking, to hold the rosary entwined in his fingers following an Our Father or Hail Mary.

Many hours may be spent at a bedside in a mixture of hope, fear, sorrow, despair. To be able to pray during this time is most supportive when it is not possible to help in any other way, except by sitting and waiting.

Before and after death, before and during the funeral, grief can and should be expressed in prayer, singly or with others. Mingled with this is the hope of resurrection and the need to comfort and be comforted. Finally, the bereavement which will come to everyone can be an empty, lonely and often guilt-ridden period. Prayer does not end but eases the pain. It calms, enlightens, deepens faith and trust, and leads to the bereaved person's own resurrection in a new life in the world.

> "It was through one man that sin came into the world, and through sin death, and thus death has spread through the whole human race because everyone has sinned." (*Rm 5:12*).

Death

Death is the one certainty in life and it is the horizon that colors every choice we make. It is a constant reminder to us that life is radically limited. All our choices have to be made within this perspective which threatens and undermines the lasting value of all achievements. Perhaps the most painful awareness of this ultimate limit is in our relationships. Every genuine love experience carries with it the dimension of the eternal. And yet even the most beautiful experience of loving another is constantly threatened by the knowledge that death will mean the loss of the beloved.

But death is also positive. It brings life, with all its choices, actions, and values, to a completion. Death in this sense is the fulfillment of human freedom.

This is the law of biological life. But such an idea hardly resolves the deepest questions about death that lie in the human heart: Why must I die? Why am I afraid to die?

Revelation

The Scriptures assert that the deepest response to these questions lies in the connection between sin and death. The Book of Genesis explains how death became the punishment for sin.

Paul takes up this theme in Romans. In explaining Paul's ideas, theologians have suggested that he is not thinking primarily of biological death. Even if man had not sinned, he would have died biologically, but this biological death would have been a natural transition to life with God in heaven. But because man sinned, death means being cut off from everything that can fulfill the person.

Sorrow and hope

Belonging to Christ, companionship with him even in death, is the good news for all who search for an answer to the apparent meaninglessness of death.

Fear of death is the fear of the loss of everything dear. It is ultimately the dread of the loss of God, who is the ultimate source of life and humanity's only true destiny.

The Christian, however, has another story to tell, of God's entrance into the human situation of sin and death. The Old Testament called life beyond the grave Sheol, a shadowy existence in which there was no vitality, no praise of God; the dead were mere dust. Sheol was often described as solitude, aloneness, the pit from which the dead never return to life. The extraordinary Good News of the New Testament is that God's only son entered into this experience of death and Sheol for us. In Gethsemane he knew the dread of death. On the cross he knew our sense of abandonment when he cried out: "My God, my God, why have you forsaken me?"

Scripture teaches us that human death as we know it came about because of disobedience, because we human beings wanted to make ourselves as God. Jesus reversed this disobedience even to the point of the cross. He was so open to the Father's love that he allowed himself to become a corpse until the Father breathed new life into him in the resurrection.

We Christians cannot avoid death but we do have a story to tell of how God came to us in our death and overcame it from within.

The Gospel tells us that because of Christ's death, we will never more be alone.

Prayer

Lord, he whom you love is sick.

Lord, that I may see.

Questions

1 Choose one example of healing from each of the four Gospels which you think gives a clear idea of Jesus' attitude to healing. Explain your choice and what each one adds to a complete picture of Jesus the Healer.

2 Vatican II reminded us that the sacrament of the anointing of the sick is not for those only who are at the point of death. What suggestions can you offer about how this can be taught and practiced in a parish?

3 Gilbert Harding, a famous British broadcaster of the 1950s, was asked whether he was afraid of death. "No, I am a Christian," he replied, "I am not frightened of death. But I am frightened of dying." Do you agree with him?

4 How would you try to comfort a friend you knew was dying?

25 Moral teaching – Introduction

Moral questions are perhaps the most controversial in the world today. There are serious questions about euthanasia, as to whether we have the right to terminate life in a case where life seems pointless; or whether we should use contraceptives to solve the world's population problems. At the close of the 20th century, it is in these moral issues that the Church finds its teaching most under attack.

Many people bemoan the fact that children in America seem to have little sense of moral values. Politicians see a need to inject some inspection of spiritual and moral values into our school system.

This emphasizes the first and most important point. It is not sufficient just to tell people what to do and what not to do. We must consider the reasons why we should act morally. Many children who are a problem today are such because they have only known abuse and lack of love. What a difference it makes when we realize that the Creator of the universe loves each one of us infinitely and personally. As the psalmist says:

> Though my father and mother forsake me, Yahweh will gather me up (Ps 27:10).

The new Catechism begins this section by outlining the basis of Christian morality, of life in Christ. It insists that we are made in the image and likeness of God (Gn 1:26) and that fact gives us great dignity (CCC 1701). It also reminds us that we are called to eternal happiness with God, and that happiness is nothing other than God himself who is infinite goodness. The new Catechism (CCC 1718) quotes Augustine:

> Certainly, all of us wish to live happily, and in the human race there is no one who would not give assent to this proposition even if he may not have fully articulated it. (St. Augustine, On the Morals of the Catholic Church and the Manicheans, 1,3,4).

> How then is it that I seek you, Lord? Because in seeking you, my God, I am seeking the happy life; help me to seek you in order that my soul might live, because my body lives from my soul and my soul lives from you (St. Augustine, Confessions, 10,29).

How are we to achieve this happiness? The new Catechism (CCC 1724) states that the Ten Commandments (Dt 5; Ex 20), the Sermon on the Mount (Mt 5-7) and apostolic teaching show us the way to our final happiness in the kingdom of heaven. Happiness on this earth is also involved. The saints, in spite of all their sufferings and privations, are the happiest people on this earth. Christ promised that those who followed him would receive a hundredfold on this earth followed by life everlasting.

Freedom

The new Catechism insists that our freedom is the basis of all morality. Because we are free we are responsible. Machines and inanimate objects or even animals cannot be morally responsible. I cannot hold the pot of paint responsible which empties its contents over my head. I must hold the man responsible who left it precariously placed on his window ledge.

Philosophers and scientists have attempted to argue that we are not free, but like machines, or at least like animals: that we act according to impulse or instinct. But if that argument were carried to its logical conclusion, those very scientists and philosophers would find their own researches invalid; because by the same principle, they as human beings were not acting freely, but only like a machine or according to instinct.

From the Christian viewpoint, our freedom is based upon the fact that we are body and soul. We are not just machines; we are spirit as well as matter, which enables us to make rational choices, and not just to act from compulsion or instinct.

> The new Catechism *(CCC 1730)* quotes Vatican II's document on the Church in the Modern World:
>
> But that which is truly freedom is an exceptional sign of the image of God in man. For God willed that man should "be left in the hand of his own counsel" *(Eccl 15:14)* so that he might of his own accord seek his creator and freely attain his full and blessed perfection by cleaving to him. Man's dignity therefore requires him to act out of conscious and free choice, as moved and drawn in a personal way from within, and not by blind impulses in himself or by mere external constraint *(no. 17)*.

We are not just machines; we are spirit as well as matter.

Passions

Although in general we recognize that we act freely, according to choice, we realize also that there are constraints or limitations on our freedom. Sometimes, we may be physically constrained, or have pressure put on us.

The new Catechism *(CCC 1762-1775)* mentions also the fact that our passions are a factor to be considered in the process of making moral choices. Note that "passions" in this case do not refer only to sexual passion, but also to feelings and desires of various kinds. As human beings, we are body and soul, physical and spiritual. Our emotions have complex ori-

John Henry Cardinal Newman
(1801 – 1890)

gins, sometimes more biological than psychological. Depression may arise, not from our will, but simply because we are tired, anxious or ill.

The new Catechism roots our passions in what Jesus himself called the "heart" (*Mt 7:21*); not the pump that circulates blood around our bodies, but rather the seat of all our emotions. The heart is the driving force of all our activity, stimulated first and foremost by whatever we desire deep down.

Christian teaching is that our passions have become disordered through original sin.

Growth in moral life, growth in our life in Christ, is allowing the Holy Spirit more and more to take over in our lives, thereby enabling us to make free and right choices. That means that our "heart" will be purified, cleansed from disordered passion. That does not make us purely spiritual beings, angels. Our bodies will always have a part to play. After all, we believe in the resurrection of the body. A saint will enjoy a good meal, or if he or she is married, making love. What growth in the Christian life means is that there is a true integration between the passions and the rational will. The new Catechism quotes a psalm in this respect:

> My heart and my body cry out for joy to the living God (*Ps 84:2*).

Conscience

The new Catechism quotes the words of Cardinal Newman:

A conscience is a law of our spirit, but which surpasses our spirit, which gives us injunctions, which signifies responsibilities and duties ... It is the messenger of him who, in the world of nature as in that of grace, talks us across the cavern, instructs us and governs us. Conscience is the first of all the Vicars of Christ (*Letter to the Duke of Norfolk, 5*).

All would agree that it is right to act according to our own conscience. Unfortunately, in the modern individualistic world, what is often meant by that is simply that we ought to be able to do what we like. Even St. Augustine said,

> Love God and do what you like;

but he was talking about a person who first truly loved God. We cannot always guarantee that what we like is truly in conformity with the love of God and his will for us.

We all have a powerful law rooted in our soul, a voice within which tells us whether we are doing right or wrong. That is what we call "conscience," a force within us which is strong as our instincts, what the new Catechism calls a "judgment of reason" (*CCC 1777*).

This does not mean, of course, that our conscience is infallible. The SS officers who killed thousands in the gas chambers might even have thought that they were acting rightly, simply by obeying orders. Our conscience, as the Catechism insists (*CCC 1783*), must be informed, if it is not to become stunted and habitually erroneous. Studying Christian morality helps our conscience become informed by the light of the Word of God (*CCC 1785*).

Virtue

In our modern thinking, the word "virtue" has become rather debased. A "virtuous" person is rather a bore with moral scruples, while a girl who has "not lost her virtue" is one who has refused up to now to join the sexual revolution. It is not exaggerating to say that the modern world does not think too much of virtue.

But "virtue" is a fundamental concept in human life. We may define it as "a power of doing good" which acts within us, and which we have developed within ourselves by good habits (*CCC 1803*).

As Christians, we are in training constantly to become more like Christ. The new Catechism (*CCC 1804*) quotes the early Church Father Gregory of Nyssa, who says that

> The aim of a virtuous life consists in becoming like God (*St. Gregory of Nyssa, On the Beatitudes, 1*).

Thus the agenda of the Christian life is set out by Paul as he is quoted in the Catechism giving his advice to the Philippian Christians.

> Finally, brothers, let your minds be filled with everything that is true, everything that is honorable, everything that is upright and pure, everything that we love and admire – with whatever is good and praiseworthy (*Ph 4:8*).

The new Catechism (*CCC 1789*) gives three rules of conscience to apply in every case:

1 It is never right to do evil in order that good may come of it, e.g. it is not right to support the evil regime of Hitler in order to destroy Communism.

2 The Golden Rule (*Mt 7:12*): Do as you would be done by. Never do to others what you would not want done to you.

3 Always consider the good of others in what you do (*Rm 14:21*). It would be very wrong to try to persuade an alcoholic who was trying to break the habit to drink a glass of whiskey even though drinking a glass of whiskey is not in itself wrong.

The Catechism follows the Christian tradition in dividing the virtues into two:

Human or moral virtues (*CCC 1804-1809*)
These are virtues which we can acquire by human reason (called cardinal virtues) even if naturally we are helped by divine grace:
Prudence is practical wisdom, even common sense
Justice is a sense of fair play towards God and neighbor
Power is strength in difficulties ("guts")
Temperance is moderation in pleasures (not necessarily abstinence, but temperate use of food, drink, etc.)

Divine or theological virtues (*CCC 1812–1821*)
These are virtues which have as their principle the Holy Spirit, their aim to enable us to share in the divine nature of Christ, and their final direction to the praise and honor of God the Father:
Faith enables us to believe in God and what he has revealed
Hope enables us to have confidence in God's promises
Love enables us to love God and our neighbors for God.

There are traditionally seven gifts of the Spirit, listed in Isaiah 11:1–2 as gifts of the messianic figure to come:

Wisdom, Understanding, Counsel, Might, Knowledge, Piety, Fear of the Lord.

The list might also be put another way, to express the varied fruits of the Spirit in our lives, as Paul puts it, contrasting his "good list" of virtues and his "bad list" of vices:

> sexual vice
> impurity
> sensuality
> worship of false gods
> sorcery
> antagonisms
> rivalry
> jealousy
> bad temper
> quarrels
> disagreements
> factions
> malice
> drunkenness
> orgies
>
> love
> joy
> peace
> patience
> kindness
> goodness
> trustfulness
> gentleness
> self-control

(Ga 5: 19-23)

Questions

1 How can we help each other to develop morally?

2 Do you think that a moral life is possible without Christian faith?

The gifts and the fruits of the Spirit

(CCC 1830–1832)

These are permanent dispositions given to us by God in our baptism which help us to become open to the impulses of grace in our life.

If the virtues are to grow in us we must first encounter and defeat the enemy within.

St. Paul's advice for spiritual warfare is given in Ephesians 6:11–17.

> Put on the full armor of God so as to be able to resist the devil's tactics. For it is not against human enemies that we have to struggle, but against the principalities and the ruling forces who are masters of the darkness in this world, the spirits of evil in the heavens. That is why you must take up all God's armor, or you will not be able to put up any resistance on the evil day, or stand your ground even though you exert yourselves to the full. So stand your ground, with truth a belt round your waist, and uprightness your breastplate, wearing for shoes on your feet the eagerness to spread the gospel of peace and always carrying the shield of faith so that you can use it to quench the burning arrows of the Evil One. And then you must take salvation as your helmet and the sword of the Spirit, that is, the word of God.

26 Love, law and sin

Love is the most abused word in the English language. It is used to mean anything from self-sacrificing devotion to selfish lust.

Many different kinds of love are genuine. They spring from the fact that human beings have a physical and a spiritual dimension. We are related to the animals below, and to the angels above. Act according to these genuine loves, and we are acting morally. "Love," said St. Augustine, "and do what you will."

But love can also go wrong, due to our disordered nature as fallen creatures. C. S. Lewis's four loves can be changed. Affection can become possessiveness. Friendship can be for what we can get out of the other person. Eros can simply be desire for pleasure, rather than desire for the other human being. And even charity can be perverted by using God to further our own ego.

The Christian life is a journey in which we purify our human loves, with God's help, to make them genuine; and learn day by day to relate affection, friendship, and eros to charity, the highest love.

C.S. Lewis, one of the greatest Christian communicators this century, speaks of four loves: Affection, Friendship, Eros and Charity.

Affection is the tender love of parent for child, or of an old age pensioner for his dog. Friendship is what Lewis calls companionship in common activities. Eros is a passionate love between the sexes. Charity is the love which is God himself, and which is poured into our hearts by the gift of the Holy Spirit.

True love brings happiness.

The statue of Eros, Piccadilly, London, which represents passionate love between the sexes.

Love has no limits upwards

Christian theology is clear that love is the greatest of the virtues.

> The greatest of them [all] is love

says St. Paul (*1 Co 13:13*).

Paul also says that without love, none of the other virtues has any value in the sight of God.

> And though I have all the faith necessary to move mountains – if I am without love, I am nothing (*1 Co 13:2*).

Love has no limits. We can never say, "I have kept all the rules, I am home and dry." Always, we hear that command "Love God with ALL your heart and your neighbor as yourself." And we never know what the next demand of love will be. The young man who told Jesus that he had obeyed all the commandments did not receive the skeptical response from Jesus which an irate spiritual director might have given: "You could not have kept all the commandments; only Mary is sinless!" On the contrary, Jesus accepted the young man's assertion that he had kept God's law.

But Jesus saw that this for the young man was still not enough. To the question

> I have kept all these [commandments]. What more do I need to do? (*Mt 19:20*),

Jesus replied:

> If you wish to be perfect, go and sell your possessions and give the money to the poor, and you will have treasure in heaven; then come, follow me (*Mt 19:21*).

We are told that the young man could not go the whole way and follow Jesus' advice, but went away unhappy "for he was a man of great wealth" (*Mt 19:22*).

Traditionally the Church has interpreted this as an example of the challenge of a religious life, that is to say, a life lived according to the vows of poverty, chastity and obedience. Nevertheless, this brief, tragic drama has something important to say to every Christian. By reason of our baptism, we are all called to holiness – and we cannot foretell where our response to that call will take us. If we find ourselves "going away sad" from an invitation to live life more generously, we must pay attention to the sadness, consider what we may be missing, and turn to the invitation again.

To be truly, fully alive requires that we be ever open to change, development, growth. If we let the virtue of love direct our decision-making, the challenges we accept will bring us surprising joy.

There is always something slightly crazy about genuine love. A young man may for the first time in his life brave danger just to impress his girlfriend. The Scriptures tell us that "God is love" (1 Jn 4:8), and God has shown himself more than slightly crazy with love for the human race he has created in his own image and likeness. He sent his own Son to live a human life and to die for us all, to win our love and to enable us to share in his divine nature.

However, if love is crazy, it also has to face the humdrum. Christian teaching is that love is not simply a feeling, but is rather a commitment of the whole person, reason as well as instinct, will as well as heart. Love is actually a human decision, not just an impulse. That is why we can be commanded to love God, not just when we feel like it, but all the time. That is why married couples, monks and nuns, friends, make commitments of love which are permanent. Married couples have to face each other tired at breakfast time. Monks have not only to pray, but to live with people they sometimes find irritable.

Love and law are not contrary ideas, but are truly complementary to each other, in order that the four loves outlined by C.S. Lewis and discussed above, affection, friendship, eros and charity, can truly work in harmony, and not undermine each other, for all of us as the Body of Christ to grow until it (the Body of Christ) has built itself up in love.

The most fundamental law of love is that, if we truly love someone, we will not wish anything but good for that person. We will therefore resist anything which is seen as evil for that person.

Loving yourself?

Jesus also commanded us equally to love ourselves.

This can be difficult, as we are often plagued with a low opinion of ourselves.

Such a state can make us self-centered and distracted and can stop us from giving and receiving love, and experiencing life fully.

We cannot love ourselves, if we are struggling with problems of worthlessness, unless we are loved by someone first. We need to have another person reflect to us that we are loving and lovable.

Loving in Christian terms means loving ourselves as Christ would love us, seeing ourselves as Christ would see us. Jesus loved us so much. He laid down his life in sacrifice for us. He sees us with eyes of infinite love and compassion. It is obvious that we are very special to him.

Following God's example, great Christian saints have shown themselves not a little mad, Ignatius of Antioch for instance telling his fellow Christians that he truly desired to be eaten by the lions, to be a sacrifice acceptable to Christ.

Loving oneself also involves a decision to surrender our poor self-image and to have faith in the image presented by the one who loves us. There may be hesitation and doubt about surrendering that poor self-image. Would self-appreciation and evaluating my goodness amount to conceit? How should we behave towards someone complimenting us? It might be easier to brush it off, more comfortable to cling to the poor self-image as we may, at least, have learned to cope with it.

However, there should be no room for vanity when we remember that all our goodness, our talents and faculties, are a gift from the Creator, and not of our own making. This reality faces us squarely with who we are – creatures belonging to God, and not gods in our own right. Loving ourselves can be tough, but unless we do we cannot love anyone else.

Practical loving

When we hear of people whose needs are desperate, we immediately wonder what governments or charities could do to help. Our thoughts turn to money which seems a cure-all. Do we think of our own responsibility to show love to those in difficulty?

Love and service

God does not call us in some rare mystical experience, or merely indirectly in the commands of conscience, but first and foremost in the needs of our neighbors. Indeed love of neighbor is not only an expression of my love for him, but a test of that love. St. John is quite explicit about this:

> Whoever does not love the brother whom he can see cannot love God whom he has not seen (*1 Jn 4:20*).

But the connection was already made by Jesus himself in his description of the final judgment. Listing the works of mercy done to the hungry, the thirsty, the naked, the sick, the stranger, the imprisoned, he said:

> In so far as you did this to one of the least of these brothers of mine, you did it to me (*Mt 25:40*).

Christian love of neighbor is not simply an act of obedience to God who commands it, but a recognition in action that those in need are brothers and sisters in Jesus. To be one with him and with his Father we must build up a community where we are all truly brothers and sisters.

What does it mean in practice? First, that love is not mere talk or sentiment, but service. In daily living, our neighbor is the person who turns up needing help. His or her need is God's call to each of us.

Ask yourself

Who are the "poor" of my area? Do "labels" prevent me from seeing a neighbor in need among "the lapsed, the divorced, addicts, gays, ex-cons, AIDS victims, dropouts, punks, vandals?"

Do I have a secret feeling that God is interested only in nice, intelligent, respectable, well-behaved people?

Who is the stranger in my neighborhood?

Does custom, prejudice, fear or even law build a barrier to my Christian love?

Does protesting help?

Have I failed to love enough?

Jesus gave no definition of "neighbor" that would enable us to pick and choose, to exclude any. Judaism in his time considered hatred of enemies permissible, but Jesus said:

> Love your enemies, do good to those who hate, bless those who curse you, pray for those who treat you badly (*Lk 6:27*).

Christian forgiveness does not mean pardoning the enemy only after he has apologized. Even the pagans do that. Our model is the prodigal father who rushes to welcome the erring son before he confesses, and pours out his love in a way that restores the son's confidence and self-respect.

Jesus is uncompromising in his demands as to how often we must forgive anyone. "Not just seven times, but seventy times seven," without counting the times or the cost, because that is how our heavenly Father forgives us.

The love of God poured into our hearts which invites and enables us to love our enemies should make us particularly sensitive to the plight of the poor, the weak, the sick, the neglected or shunned. We have only to look at the company Jesus kept to see that Christian love should break through all barriers that keep people apart.

Spiritual warfare

The church is unambiguous in its affirmation that spiritual conflict exists at the highest level, between God on the one side, and the devil and his angels on the other.

It is not a struggle between equals. Christian faith rejects this utterly. The devil is only a rebellious spirit created by God. There is no question of him winning the final conflict. The gates of the underworld can never hold out

I Corinthians 13:1–13

Though I command languages both human and angelic – if I speak without love, I am no more than a gong booming or a cymbal clashing. And though I have the power of prophecy, to penetrate all mysteries and knowledge, and though I have all the faith necessary to move mountains – if I am without love, I am nothing. Though I should give away to the poor all that I possess, and even give up my body to be burned – if I am without love, it will do me no good whatever.

Love is always patient and kind; love is never jealous; love is not boastful or conceited, it is never rude and never seeks its own advantage, it does not take offense or store up grievances. Love does not rejoice at wrongdoing, but finds its joy in the truth. It is always ready to make allowances, to trust, to hope and to endure whatever comes.

Love never comes to an end. But if there are prophecies, they will be done away with; if tongues, they will fall silent; and if knowledge, it will be done away with. For we know only imperfectly, and we prophesy imperfectly; but once perfection comes, all imperfect things will be done away with. When I was a child, I used to talk like a child, and see things as a child does, and think like a child; but now that I have become an adult, I have finished with all childish ways. Now we see only reflections in a mirror, mere riddles, but then we shall be seeing face to face. Now, I can know only imperfectly; but then I shall know just as fully as I am myself known.

As it is, these remain: faith, hope and love, the three of them; and the greatest of them is love.

against the kingdom of God (*Mt 16:18*).

Temptation

Temptation is when we are "tested" to choose evil rather than good. Why do we feel attracted to evil? Because it looks good at the time. Original sin weakens our resistance to temptation, but does not destroy our free will. Sin is still our decision; we cannot pass the responsibility for our evil choices over to anyone or anything else, even to the devil.

What is the devil's role in temptation? Scripture calls the devil the Tempter. He aggravates the situation by encouraging us to choose evil. Jesus calls him the father of lies (*Jn 8:44*). He distorts our ideas of what is good, true or right.

Jesus has, as the Epistle to the Hebrews tells us, "been put to the test in exactly the same way as ourselves, apart from sin" (*Heb 2:18*). And "the suffering he himself passed through while being put to the test enables him to help others when they are being put to the test" (*Heb 4:15*).

Jesus' temptations are described in Matthew's Gospel as three, usually interpreted as the temptations of the world, the flesh, and the devil.

The devil tempted Jesus to take over the world by evil means. He claimed that he owned "all the kingdoms of the world and their splendor," and said "I will give you all these, if you fall at my feet and do me homage" (*Mt 4:9*). Jesus rebuked him with "The Lord your God is the one to whom you must do homage, him alone you must serve" (*Mt 4:10; see Dt 6:13*).

The devil, of course, was telling a lie. The world belongs to God, not to him. However, he

was speaking a half-truth. As a consequence of original sin, and human decision against God, the devil is able to influence human society. We pray that as Christians we will reject what is false in the world.

The flesh

Christ was tempted to turn stones into bread, to satisfy his hunger. He replied,

> Human beings live not on bread alone but on every word that comes from the mouth of God (*Mt 4:4; see Dt 8:3*).

Within us, given by God, are powerful desires, good in themselves, desires to eat and drink in order to preserve our life, and desires for sexual intercourse in order to increase and multiply the human family, to share ourselves with the one we love. These instincts are good. What is wrong is to respond to them in such a way as to abuse our bodies or destroy others.

The Church has great experience in dealing with sins and sinners and realizes that the "sins of the flesh" are often the result of weakness and bad habit, rather than of deliberate malice. "The spirit is willing enough, but human nature is weak" (*Mt 26:41*). We pray for Christ to help us in our particular weakness never to be discouraged in our attempts, by prayer and self-denial, to "use your body for the glory of God" (*1 Co 6:20*).

The devil

The devil took Jesus to the highest point of the Temple.

> Throw yourself down; for the Scripture says:"He has given his angels orders about you" (*Mt 4:6; see Ps 91:10-12*).

To see more clearly the devil's role in temptation, read the story of the temptation of Jesus (*Mt 4:1-11*).

The "sins of the flesh," gluttony and sexual impurity, are not to be lightly treated as so often they are today.

The "little bit on the side" and "the night out with the boys" can so often lead to families split by divorce, and lives ruined by alcoholism.

Not only would it have "tested" God and proven Jesus' powers, but it would have made a spectacular beginning to his public ministry.

Jesus replied, "Do not put the Lord your God to the test" (*Mt 4:7; see Dt 6:16*). As the obedient Son he would live in faith, trusting the Father's will even to death on the cross.

The devil in fact was asking Jesus to commit suicide, to disobey the commandment "You shall not kill" (in this case himself), demanding God his Father to save him "on the way down."

Christian morality is based upon reason. We are responsible for our actions. We have no right to do what is in itself evil, as Jesus was tempted to do, expecting God to extract us from our folly.

The first criterion of action is "Is it right? Or is it clearly wrong?" God has given us the commandments: "You shall not kill," "You shall not steal," "You shall not bear false witness," "You shall not commit adultery."

Very often, people are tempted even in the name of God to act contrary to these commandments. Many wars have been justified on a religious basis. As Scripture says, even Satan can appear disguised as an angel of light (*2 Co 11:14*).

Jesus was tempted by the devil but did not sin.

Demon possession

The existence of "the devil and his angels" to use the Lord's phrase (*Mt 25:41*), is established by Scripture and the constant teaching of the Church. And it is possible for them today, as in New Testament times, to occupy or possess the body (not the soul) of a human being. But this is very rare. The Christian, born of God's love, redeemed by the Blood of Christ, consecrated by the waters of baptism and nourished with the Lord's Body, should not be worried by theories of demonic possession.

The external manifestations of demonic possession and psychological illness can be very similar. Sound medical guidance and skill in the discernment of spirits is necessary to help distinguish between the two. All natural explanations should be examined before concluding the devil is the cause of some distressing state.

Solemn exorcism, that is, directly commanding the devil in the name of the Church, is reserved for priests specially appointed by the local bishop and marked by piety, knowledge, prudence and integrity of life (*Canon 1172*). On the other hand, all of us can pray for deliverance from evil spirits:

"Deliver us from evil" is the Lord's own prayer.

Questions

1 Use both Old and New Testament sources to show that God is love. How effectively, in your own experience, is this message being preached in the Church today? Are there any improvements you would suggest?

2 How do you understand the natural law? In your view is it possible to come to a knowledge of the natural law without Christianity?

3 What evidence do you find of the seven deadly sins in society? What remedies can the Christian community offer?

4 Compare the accounts of temptations of Jesus in the Gospels of Saints Matthew, Mark and Luke. Why do you think St. John does not include this episode in his Gospel?

5 How do you understand sin?

27 Church rules

All religions have basic rules for all their members. But we must be careful before we define whether a person is "good" or not in terms of whether religious rules are kept. A person may keep all the rules, yet be a spiteful or hateful neighbor. Again, a person may be "lapsed" from the practice of his or her faith, yet that faith may influence their life in profound ways, making them truly loving and merciful.

Also, to define a religion simply in terms of keeping its minimum obligations would do a great disservice to that religion. Religion, especially Christianity, is the growth of a relationship, a kind of marriage, between ourselves and God our Father through Christ and in the Spirit. And, as with any marriage, just to make it a series of rules is to take the heart out of it.

On the other hand, again as with marriage, no way of life which is permanent can flourish without discipline, without rules. The Church's rules can help us to be faithful to the covenant between God and ourselves. When life is humdrum, even when we do not "feel" good about our religion, the rules are there to keep us plodding on.

And again, to treat the Church's rules with contempt can put our spiritual lives in danger. On this earth, life with God is not once and for all, but is a process. Like plants, without nourishment we can die. The rules are there to make sure that such daily nourishment is there for our spiritual lives.

Through the centuries, rules have been given for the daily life of Christians, in the Catholic Church, with the authority of the local bishop, or, for the wider Church, with the authority of the Pope. These rules vary according to times and circumstances and changing needs. The latest revision has been published by Rome to enshrine the insights of the Second Vatican Council. The book is called "The New Code Of Canon Law" (it is called "Canon Law" because each of the 1752 rules is called a "canon," Greek for "rule").

Like any code of law, only a small proportion of its rules apply to the life of any individual. Many of the rules in the New Code of Canon Law are not relevant to most of us, referring to the setting up of parishes, taking religious vows, or the organization of a diocese.

The following canons are relevant to all, or at least to a large number of, Catholic Christians, and arise from our baptism and commitment to live the Christian way in the life of the Church.

Canon law states that each church member has the duty of witnessing to our faith, together

ensuring that "the Gospel reaches the whole world."

Moral authority

The Church acts as teacher and mother. As teacher, she must set before us clearly the demands of the Gospel. She must equally show the individual the concern and compassion of Christ. This concern as mother involves an appreciation of the circumstances of each person's life.

To discover the true moral teaching, the Church first looks to the life and teaching of Jesus, and then reflects on the experience of twenty centuries of Christian living. We can also learn a great deal about God's plan for us, and the natural law, by looking at his world, and at ourselves. In this way, we can often discover values and moral principles that we share not only with our fellow Christians but also with many other people who are trying to do what is right.

There is great danger of seeing "the Church" as Church authorities, but we all have a contribution to make to the Church's understanding of the Christian life. For example, public statements by bishops are often the result of lengthy consultation. There is, however, a history and a tradition of accumulated wisdom which is not of purely human origin, but is a gift of the Spirit. Catholics believe that the bishops are successors of the apostles, forming a "college" in union with the Pope, the successor of Peter. These have the authority, given them by Christ, to represent the mind of the whole Church.

Jesus promised that he would be with his Church until the end of time, and that he would send the Holy Spirit to lead us into truth. Thus a Catholic will

Ten Church Rules

1 All Christ's faithful have the duty to preserve communion with, and promote the growth of, the Church, lead a holy life, and strive that the Gospel reaches the whole world (*Canons 209–211, 225*).

2 All Catholics are obliged to accept the infallibly declared teaching of the Church (*Canon 750*), and to follow in obedience the pastors of the Church when they declare this teaching and discipline (*Canon 212*).

3 They are obliged to receive Holy Communion at least once per year during the Easter season (*Canon 920*).

4 They must attend Mass on Sundays and holy days of obligation, abstaining from such work and business which would inhibit worship on those days (*Canon 1247*).

5 They are bound to confess all "grave" or "mortal" sins, and are recommended to confess "venial sins" (*Canon 988*). Grave sins must be confessed at least once per year (*Canon 989*).

6 Ash Wednesday and Good Friday are days of fasting and abstinence (*Canons 1249-50*). Other days of fasting and/or abstinence are regulated locally, as are Fridays, when the Church insists all Catholics must perform some act of penance.

7 In order to be married, a Catholic should have been confirmed (*Canon 1065*), and must be married before a priest and two witnesses (*Canon 1108*), unless a special dispensation has been obtained.

8 All have a duty to provide for the needs of the Church, for its worship and support of its ministers. All must promote social justice, helping the poor from their own resources (*Canon 222*).

9 All have a duty to grow in the knowledge of Christian teaching appropriate to their capacity (*Canon 229*); and to educate their children in accordance with the teaching of the Church (*Canon 226*). Parents are obliged to choose those ways which can best do this (*Canon 793*), especially by sending their children to schools which provide for Catholic education (*Canon 798*).

10 Parents are obliged to have their children baptized within the first few weeks of birth (*Canon 867*), and to ensure that their children who have reached the age of reason are prepared for confession and Communion (*Canon 914*).

Theologians disagree whether there are any infallible moral definitions in Church teaching. But there is a substantial amount of teaching which a Catholic must accept as part of the Church's magisterium.

One strand of clear moral teaching is the absolute sanctity of human life. In other words, it is always wrong deliberately to take the life of an innocent person such as in the case of abortion, murder or euthanasia.

This also means that a nuclear attack where millions of human beings are indiscriminately killed could never be justified, although this does not settle the question of the morality of nuclear weapons as a deterrent.

The new Catechism links the Eternal Law with the Divine Wisdom (CCC 1950) and quotes the words of the great Christian thinker Tertullian:

Alone among living creatures, the human being is honored to have been made worthy to receive from God a law; as an animal endowed with reason, capable of understanding and discerning, he regulates his conduct by disposing of his liberty and of his reason, by submitting to him who has given everything to us (Tertullian, *Against Marcion*, 2.4).

always start from wanting to know the mind of Christ as the Christian community has come to understand it. The teaching of the Church is not just an ideal, but a real demand of Christ. He is always understanding and compassionate in the face of human failure and weakness, but he is always calling us to perfection.

The Church's teaching authority clearly regards certain acts as being "intrinsically disordered" or "objectively wrong." This does not necessarily indicate the moral guilt of this or that individual involved. The Church has great experience of human nature, and knows too well that mortal sin, that is, breaking off our relationship with God, is possible. However, this does not happen easily; it involves a free and deliberate decision, with full knowledge, to turn away from God and his Commandments. This must be in a grave or serious matter. But Christian life is not merely a matter of avoiding mortal sin, but rather a conscious desire to live as Christ would have us live each day. We must also remember that no sin is so great that it cannot be forgiven.

The natural law

The Catholic Church has always taught that the basic principles of right and wrong are known to every human being even if those principles are partly obscured by our sinfulness.

This "natural law," in all human beings, is expressed in the Ten Commandments. But it is more basic even than the Ten Commandments, since they are an expression given in divine revelation of God's law written in our hearts; and that law is founded upon a further law, that of the Eternal Law which is God's plan by which the universe and all things are regulated.

The natural law is a principle of conduct within us, motivating us to do good and to avoid evil.

It is not natural in the same sense as the laws which govern our physical life. Those that govern the heart, for example, operate whether I will them or not. But the natural law challenges our free will constantly. We are free to accept or to reject our conscience.

The law is "natural" insofar as it springs from our very nature as human beings. To murder another human being is against the natural law because destroying human life made in God's image is against human nature.

The natural law as Christians understand it has no meaning without God. Because God is author of life, we have an ultimate value, and have the "right" to everything which furthers life – food, shelter, friendship, etc. The natural law is the law of God. It ensures that morality is not just a case of what we feel is right. There is truly an order, a law within us, which we ignore at our peril.

Mortal and venial sin

Many people find it difficult to understand why the Catholic Church insists that mortal or deadly sin is possible. But the idea is very simple. Love can die. We know that this tragedy can occur; there are millions of broken marriages to prove it. What the Church teaches is that our love of God can die, by our own decision. The First Epistle of John puts it starkly:

> If anyone is well off in worldly possessions and sees his brother in need but closes his heart to him, how can the love of God be remaining in him? (*1 Jn 3:17*).

John is speaking of one whose love of God has actually died, who, as Catholic theology would say, is in a "state of mortal sin." The rule in the Catholic Church is that, for one in a state of mortal sin, he or she must go to confession before again receiving Holy Communion; since Holy Communion is for those who, however imperfect, do have the love of God alive in them.

Now it is very important not to become scrupulous about mortal sin. The full decision of mind and heart must be involved, and in a serious matter. "Venial sin," which is less serious sin, in other words daily faults such as a harsh word, an impulse of impurity, missing daily prayers, the expletive when we drop a hammer on our foot, these do not destroy the love of God in us, but only weaken it. While the Church encourages us to confess venial sins, sacramental confession is not demanded. They can be confessed privately or in the penitential introduction at Mass.

For sin to be mortal it must be so in object, intention, and circumstances. The new Catechism (*CCC 1750*) explains:

Object. This is the object of the act itself. If a man decides to kill his enemy by shooting him, this is clearly a serious sin in itself.

Intention. A man may give someone with a liver condition a bottle of wine which he has been forbidden, with the intention that he will die. Of course, giving someone wine is not objectively a wrong action. Indeed it may turn out that the person does not die, but survives drinking the wine. But, in virtue of intention, the man who gave the wine has

St. Thomas Aquinas, called the "Angelic Teacher."

To make the distinction between mortal and venial sin clear, the Catechism quotes the great theologian St. Thomas Aquinas:

When the will acts with regard to something against charity, by which a person is ordered towards our final end (God), the sin by its object is mortal; whether it is against the love of God, such as blasphemy, perjury and so on; or against the love of neighbor, such as homicide, adultery, and so on. These are in themselves mortal sins. When however the will of the sinner relates to that which in itself contains some disorder, not however against the love of God and neighbor, such as a hateful word, ... etc., then such are objectively venial sins (*Summa Theologiae, I-II, q.88,a.2*).

129

Questions

1 Which laws of the Church have you found most helpful and supportive for your own Christian living? What advice would you offer someone who was finding particular laws irksome?

2 Why does the Church have rules? Are there too many rules? Should we have more rules?

committed murder. But if, by giving a glass of wine, he does not intend his death, but simply that he may have a little joy in his life, in spite of the risks to his liver, then his intention is not murder, and there is no case of serious sin.

Circumstances. If I ask my enemy to meet me at 6:00 p.m. by the clocktower, that is a harmless suggestion usually. But if I know that an armed gang is waiting for him, and will shoot him, then, in terms of the circumstances of the case, I am morally guilty of his murder.

These are in reality little more than common-sense principles; but there are often complications in terms of what is morally right and wrong, or in terms of what is seriously wrong, and what will jeopardize our relationship with God and our neighbor, and even destroy that love of God in us.

We now proceed to look at each of the Ten Commandments in the light of all these principles. But first, we remember that we are not on our own. We have the help of the risen Christ, who conquered temptation for each one of us, and helps us daily in our struggle against the world, the flesh, and the devil.

28 Life in the world

Religious people are sometimes criticized for being "so heavenly-minded that they are no earthly use." This attitude springs from two mistaken attitudes to religion, which run deep in Western society.

First, religion is seen as a private affair, between ourselves and God. Our duty is to save our souls and go to heaven. Other people are seen as either a hindrance to our salvation, or simply there to be "used" for our path to God.

Second, religion is treated as an escape from the world. The world is like a battlefield which we have to go through in order to get to heaven. The things of this world are seen either as helps or as hindrances in getting through this battlefield. Either way, they are essentially ugly.

There is a grain of truth in both positions. There is a secret area of life which is between ourselves and God, a "space" which not even the closest loved one can enter. Often in Scripture, the Christian life is referred to in military terms, as a "fight of faith" (*1 Tm 6:12*); and Paul exhorts all Christians to "put on the full armor of God" (*Ep 6:11*).

But, alone, these attitudes spell the death of religion as an optimistic way of life.

Christian faith is essentially a communion, a sharing of the life of God in the spiritual family of the Church. Religious life in the Christian vision mirrors human life as it really is:

> Man by his very nature stands completely in need of life in society (*Vatican II on the Church in the Modern World, no. 25*).

The world is created by God as a sign of his love for us. It is not inherently evil. Our task, as Christians, is to transform this world into the kingdom of God

By Church we mean the community of men, women and children in this world who profess Jesus Christ as Lord.

Signs of the kingdom

Healing: Jesus cured "all kinds of disease and illness" (*Mt 4:23*). All kinds of healing are a sign of God's rule of love and power.

Learning: "I have come into this world," said Jesus, "so that those without sight may see ..." (*Jn 9:39*). Jesus cured blindness, not only physical but also spiritual. Education is bringing about God's kingdom, in curing the blindness of ignorance.

Feeding: "I am the bread of life. No one who comes to me will ever hunger" (*Jn 6:35*). Christ also showed his concern with our material needs. When we feed the hungry, we are sharing in his ministry.

Worshiping: "The kingdom of God is among you" (*Lk 17:21*). The human race is called to "converse with God" (*Vatican II on the Church in the Modern World, no. 19*). Acknowledging God's rule, therefore, involves worshiping him.

Sharing: Jesus said to Zacchaeus, "Hurry, because I am to stay at your house today" (*Lk 19:5*). Communicating with each other is an essential part of being human. With modern technology and transport God's kingdom COULD be brought much further forward.

Where is the kingdom?

The individual: God is present in each of us. He makes his home in us when we say "yes" to him.

Family and friends: God's kingdom is in our relationships when we recognize him in each other.

Society: God rules in human institutions, national and international, when justice and human rights are respected.

The Church: God is present especially in the Church which is the sign of his kingdom on earth.

even though we know that this will not be complete until God finally brings it to perfection in his own way and in his own time.

The kingdom of God

The whole life of Jesus was taken up with proclaiming the kingdom of God in word and deed. This kingdom has always been difficult to understand. Even when Jesus spoke about it people had problems in grasping its richness.

For this reason, Jesus spoke in parables about it. He likened it to treasure found in a field that changes one's whole outlook, or to a net cast deep into the sea, or to a wedding feast.

The kingdom proclaimed by Jesus is a new spiritual and social reality embracing all people through the love and mercy and justice of God, drawing them into one family. This new reality comes as a gift in this life when good news is brought to the poor, release to captives, liberty to the oppressed, sight to the blind, hearing to the deaf, healing to the sick, and life to the dead (*Lk 4:18; 7:22*). It is experienced as future promise when we realize that these present gifts have their true fulfillment in God.

The role of the Church is to continue this preaching and practice of Jesus. The Church is the sign and sacrament, the instrument and agent of the kingdom of God in the world. This means that the Church, like Christ, is always signaling the power and presence of the reign of God: reaching out to the estranged, building bridges between the divided, healing broken lives, and gathering the scattered into the one new community of the kingdom of God.

By Church we mean the community of women, men and children who profess

Jesus Christ as Lord (*Ph 2:11*),

and actively commit themselves to his service.

Within this community there are different callings and gifts:

To some, his "gift" was that they should be apostles; to some prophets; to some, evangelists; to some, pastors and teachers; to knit God's holy people together for the work of service (*Ep 4:11-12*).

All Christians are responsible for bringing about the kingdom of God – not just bishops, priests and sisters.

One of the great rediscoveries of Vatican II was that the Church's mission in the world is both religious and temporal, both spiritual and social. There had been a tendency to see this mission as mainly spiritual, concentrating on the salvation of souls for the next life. In contrast, the insight of Vatican II spoke about the human development and liberation of the person in this life, referring to it as essential to the preaching of the Gospel of Christ (*Justice in the World*, 1971).

Paul VI pointed out that

> the Church has the duty to proclaim the liberation of millions of human beings ... the duty of assisting the birth of this liberation, of giving witness to it, of ensuring that it is complete (*Evangelization in the Modern World*, 1975, no. 30).

The Church, continuing the work of Christ on earth, must confront social problems. Thus, the Church is concerned to promote the dignity of individuals, to defend their rights, to fight discrimination, and to struggle for justice. More specifically, the Christian community must be involved in problems of poverty, unemployment, drug abuse, loneliness, divorce and homelessness.

Thus, the Church as people of God is summoned to be a leaven in the world, an agent of social change.

This means the individual Christian is faced with new responsibilities. Being a member of the Christian community carries with it an explicit commitment to change society in the name of the coming reign of God set in motion by Christ.

Growing together?

The Christian needs the community, especially the Church, to grow morally. All members can make a contribution to the shared understanding of Christian faith and morality. Each member has to develop his or her own understanding and

convictions within the community, using its resources and the wisdom and experience of other members, especially leaders.

The responsibility of leaders is to promote personal convictions based on the established truths of the community. This requires respect for the integrity of the person and fidelity to acknowledged truth.

Faith and action

Every Church member must have regard for the way people develop in their understanding of moral truth. What is accessible to an adult is not always accessible to a child. Many people remain childish in certain areas of moral behavior. They must be helped to grow in understanding.

Moral development depends as much on good behavior as it does on good instruction. The witness and example of a life of love remains the most forceful form of instruction in Christian living. Good practice also leads to fuller understanding.

What I decide to do concerns other people as well.

Moral truth develops

Sometimes, the Church sets out her moral and social teaching as clear principles. Other times, particularly with new problems, Church documents serve more as a stimulus to discussion and reflection, rather than as static and dogmatic.

A tension can exist between individual conscience and teaching authority, between respect for persons and commitment to truth. Jesus' disciples need to take seriously the way people grow, how truth is more fully understood, and the personal responsibility before God which no person can assume for another or pass to another.

Social justice

The new Catechism devotes a section to social justice (CCC 1928–1947). It founds the social teaching of the Church on the dignity of the human person, "another self" (CCC 1931). There are legitimate differences within society. We are not all the same, nor do we have the same gifts. Rather, we need enrichment from each other (CCC 1937). But there are also inequalities which are due to greed and injustice (CCC 1938). People need to remember our solidarity as human beings, divinely ordered.

As we look at the Ten Commandments, therefore, we will be looking at their social as well as individual implications. We are first and foremost given the responsibility for our own salvation, just as we are first and foremost given responsibility for our own individual health and strength. We may not "trade" the salvation of our soul for anything, even the salvation of someone else's soul. Among the temptations put forward to Thomas More, the English Chancellor who refused to accept King Henry VIII as head of the Church of England, and who was in prison awaiting execution as a result, was that in staying alive he could do much good. But what good would it do, he explained to his interrogator, if I went to hell for not following my conscience and you went to heaven for following yours? The command not to do evil first and foremost applies to refraining from doing anything which might prejudice our individual eternal destiny, which is the whole purpose of our existence. We may not do evil that good may come.

But the Church recently has emphasized our responsibility in society; and, as the world comes much closer through technology, our closeness as human beings becomes increasingly obvious. We can help or hinder each other in that common life.

The world

The use of the word "world" in the Bible carries two senses: one good, and the other bad.

In most texts, "the world" has a good meaning. It refers to the universe, made and loved by God.

The new Catechism quotes the Vatican II document on the Church in the modern world:

While there are rightful differences between people, their equal dignity as persons demands that we strive for fairer and more humane conditions. Excessive economic and social disparity between individuals and peoples of the one human race is a source of scandal and militates against social justice, equity, and human dignity, as well as social and international peace (29).

This is the world which Christ came to live in and to save (*Jn 3:17*). Into this world we are all sent to preach the Gospel (*Mt 26:13*).

In other texts, however, "the world" has a bad meaning. It refers to that dimension of the universe ruled over by the devil, or Satan. Thus the devil, in one of the temptations, shows our Lord all the kingdoms of the world, and offers them to him if he will do him homage (*Mt 4:9*). And, in the same sense, Jesus refers to the devil as "the prince of this world" (*Jn 14:30*).

Even in these texts, the omnipotent rule of God in his own world is not denied. It is only because the human race has given in to Satan that he has any rule, and only then because God allows it as a consequence of his creating us with free will.

Summary – the Christian in the world

The world is good, created by God ...

But evil also exists in the world.

Our vocation as human beings is to build up the world ...

But we look beyond this world to a new heaven and a new earth.

Created things have their own laws ...

But not independently from God their creator.

Evil in the world comes from our own free will ...

But there is also a personal spirit of evil active in the world.

Christ came to save the world ...

But he condemned the prince of this world, Satan.

The human race constitutes one family under God ...

But there is now a new family, the Church, being formed by Christ.

The whole world is destined for God ...

But this can only happen through Christ and his Church.

Questions

1 "Some Christians are so heavenly-minded that they are no earthly use." What, in your opinion, are some of the practical contributions Christianity has made to the world?

2 We cannot fail to be aware of the power of sin in the world. Try to recall those occasions when you were convinced of the power of God, of his goodness, and of the certainty that good will win in the end.

Keep thoughts on things above; but watch below as well.

29 The Ten Commandments

There are two opposite views regarding the Ten Commandments, and both are wrong. One is to see the whole of the Christian life as merely a set of rules and regulations, as did a group of Pharisees in our Lord's time, and as some Christians do at times. This takes away the beauty of God's gift to us in Christ, the grace of the Holy Spirit. It would be rather like a mother giving that bicycle (Introduction) with a frown on her face, instead of her lovely smile. Instead of giving it as a present, she would say, "I paid $100 for this bicycle, half my week's profits. Make sure you don't kill yourself on it!" Those with good parents can thank God not to have a mother like that. And we do not have a God like that. God gives us his gift of divine life with a welcoming smile and a party, just as he did with the returning prodigal son.

The other mistaken view is to deny that rules and regulations have any place in the Christian life. All down the centuries, there have been groups of Christians who have misinterpreted St. Paul's statement that we are not under law, but under grace. But Paul himself saw the need for us

On the mountain, from the heart of the fire, Yahweh spoke to Moses face to face.

136

to obey the commandments (*Rm 13:9*). God's gift is free to us. That is what Paul meant when he said

It is by grace that you have been saved, through faith; not by anything of your own, but by a gift from God ... *(Ep 2:8).*

But in order for us to hold on to God's gift, and to progress towards the promised land of heaven, we must obey God's "dos and don'ts," expressed in the Ten Commandments and as interpreted by the teaching of the Church. Not to do so would be irresponsible towards ourselves. The Commandments are there to help us have a full and happy life. They are the Maker's instructions.

Paul, in writing to the Christians in Corinth, a town famous throughout the empire for its corruption and sexual impurity, used the image of the Jews coming out of Egypt and going through the desert of this life to the promised land of heaven (*1 Co 10:1–13*). Some fell on the way, because they did not obey the Commandments: they worshipped idols, fell into sexual impurity, complained against God. But God, Paul states, will give the Corinthians the strength to withstand their trials.

God's grace is a wonderful gift; but he has not provided us with an easy option, rather with a dangerous route to the promised land. We can have great confidence in our ultimate success in salvation with God our Father's help; but only if we follow his Commandments.

The devil will work his hardest to prevent us making that promised land. The Bible calls him a roaring lion seeking someone to devour. Two opposite temptations may present themselves.

Complacency and despair

The first is complacency. When things are going well, it is easy to imagine that nothing will shake us on our path to God. The biggest danger in this secular age is for us just to consider that, with everything going well, it does not matter if we continue to go to church or to say our prayers. We are OK. We have done nothing which deserves God's judgment, we might say. In that case, we may be neglecting the most important commandment of all, to worship God alone, and thereby neglect our own salvation. We can lose our souls, our spiritual relationship with God, simply by neglect of our spiritual duties, most important of which is weekly Mass and our daily relationship with God in prayer.

The opposite temptation is despair. We try our hardest, and we do not make spiritual progress. That will tempt us to give up the struggle. In response to this temptation, God will strengthen in us the virtue of hope to help keep us on the road. God will provide a way of enabling us to put up with temptation. This "way out" is, above all, the sacrament of reconciliation or confession. This is Christ's own gift to encourage us on our journey, when we have failed to keep his commands but wish to try again to live as he wishes. That is always there, no matter how many times we have fallen.

Justice and rights

The Ten Commandments look like a series of "don'ts" but they are the basis of civilized society. Behind each of the negative state-

You can trust that God will not let you be put to the test beyond your strength, but with any trial will also provide a way out by enabling you to put up with it (*1 Co 10:13*).

Paul warns us: Everyone, no matter how firmly he thinks he is standing, must be careful he does not fall.

From the Pastoral Constitution on the Church in the Modern World, expressed at Vatican II. Note how these rights compare with and reflect the Commandments themselves.

- Food, clothing and shelter
- To choose a state of life freely
- To found a family
- To education
- To employment
- To a good reputation
- To respect
- To appropriate information
- To activity in accord with one's own informed conscience
- To protection of privacy
- To rightful freedom in matters religious.

Questions

1 Do you think that the Ten Commandments are out of date?

2 Do you think that the Ten Commandments lead to a negative attitude toward Christian morality?

ments, there is a positive principle. For instance, behind the commandment "You shall not steal" lies a judgment of value: "Respect your neighbor's property."

Tradition has it that the Ten Commandments were given by God to Moses on Mount Sinai. But rather than being a sudden revelation they in fact developed in Israelite society, which remembered the escape from Egypt (*Exodus*) and the "forty years" wandering through the desert trying to find a land to settle. They were the "bill of rights," the foundation of Israelite life. Through them they were led to recognize their responsibilities to God and to each other. They also learned to value their dignity and rights as children of God. They had to survive in a rough world. But these ten rules – which could be remembered by counting on their fingers – ensured that violence was checked, the society was kept together and true religion fostered.

Catholic theologians have always insisted that the Ten Commandments also spring from our own conscience. They are written in our hearts as well as in Scripture.

For the full text of the Ten Commandments, see Exodus chapter 20 and Deuteronomy chapter 5. Those texts differ slightly. The Ten Commandments are not actually numbered. The Catholic Church has followed St. Augustine's numbering, as follows:

1 You must have no other gods than me, no graven image
2 You must not misuse God's name
3 Keep the Sabbath day holy
4 Honor your father and your mother
5 You must not kill
6 You must not commit adultery
7 You must not steal
8 You must not give false evidence
9 You must not lust after your neighbor's wife
10 You must not lust after your neighbor's property

30 The first commandment: worshiping the true God

Then God spoke all these words. He said, "I am Yahweh your God who brought you out of Egypt, where you lived as slaves. You shall have no other gods to rival me. You shall not make yourself a carved image or any likeness of anything in heaven above or on earth beneath or in the waters under the earth. You shall not bow down to them or serve them. For I, Yahweh your God, am a jealous God and I punish a parent's fault in the children, the grandchildren, and the great-grandchildren among those who hate me; but I act with faithful love towards thousands of those who love me and keep my commandments" (*Ex 20:1-6*).

It took the People of God in the Old Testament centuries to grasp what "the Lord is God" meant. The prophets taught them that they actually owed God their love and service. He had brought them out of slavery in the land of Egypt, with great miracles, ending with the miraculous parting of the sea. They were "chosen ... to be his own people" (*Dt 14:2*).

In some ancient civilizations, if you save a person's life, that person is obliged to you for the rest of their life, and has to do what you ask.

With God there is no democratic vote; it is simply a case of "Your will be done," which Jesus himself said to his Father on the night of his passion.

Worship God alone

Once the Israelites had settled in the promised land, it still took them a long time to understand that Yahweh was their only God. There was plenty of competition in the Middle East. A whole pantheon of gods was worshiped in the area called the Fertile Crescent where the Israelites settled.

At first they kept their household gods. Rachel the wife of Jacob hid hers from her pursuing brother Laban (*Gn 31:34*) to bring her luck. It may be that even the serpent in the wilderness which eventually became a symbol of Christ's redemption in St. John's Gospel was originally a god. Scholars believe that, for many years, the Jews thought of God as their national god, for them alone, but not necessarily everyone else's God.

But, in time, God taught them clearly that he alone had created

The new Catechism (*CCC 2086*) quotes from the old Roman Catechism concerning the virtues of faith, hope and charity, which relate to God our Lord alone:

The first of the precepts embraces faith, hope and charity. Who speaks of God, in effect, speaks of a being who is constant, immutable, always the same, faithful, perfectly just. Whence it follows that we must of necessity accept his words, and have in him a faith and a complete confidence. He is all-powerful, merciful, infinitely inclined to do good. Who would not place in him all his or her hopes? And who would not be able to love him in contemplating the treasures of goodness and tenderness which he has showered upon us? Whence this formula which God uses in sacred Scripture whether at the beginning or at the end of his commandments: "I am the Lord" (*Roman Catechism 3,2,4*).

them, had called them to be his people, and that all other gods were just no-gods:

> To whom can you compare me, or who is my equal? says the holy one (*Is 40:25*).

Yahweh, their special name for God (*Ex 3*) was the only God who was alive and could help them. They learned about the one God by developing a relationship with him. We in our day can develop a relationship with God; the new Catechism explains how (*CCC 2096–2103*). We use adoration, prayer, sacrifice, promises and vows. These are acts directly oriented toward God. This is called traditionally the virtue of religion, whereby we develop in ourselves a reverence and love for the transcendent God. This virtue was acknowledged not only by Christians, but also by people of all civilizations, up to the present time.

Today, many people think that there is something weird about a person who is "religious." Vatican II on the Church in the Modern World reflects on this:

> In the past it was the exception to repudiate God and religion to the point of abandoning them, and then only individual cases; but nowadays it seems a matter of course to reject them as incompatible with scientific progress and a new kind of humanism (*no. 9*).

It is a fundamental law of our being to worship God, to develop this virtue of religion; and it is not only an insult to our God to ignore him, and so perhaps the supreme sin, but also the stunting of the growth of an essential part of our nature, the religious and spiritual dimension.

The new Catechism also emphasizes that this command-ment protects the right to religious liberty (*CCC 2104*). This is because the act of religion must be free, and therefore every human being must have the freedom either to make or not to make that act toward God.

You shall have no other gods before me

This commandment originally attacked the worship of local gods like Baal (the word means "Lord"), a fertility god of the spring whose consort was Anat, goddess of war, of whom archaeology has found vivid pictures and mythical texts three thousand years old.

Nowadays, the main attack on true religion is not Baal or Anat; although the new Catechism makes it clear that superstition, divination and magic are sins against this commandment (*CCC 2115*), and are by no means unknown in this day and age. Recent years have also seen the proliferation of religious sects which are so extreme that they must be considered to be forms of divination and superstition.

Atheism and agnosticism

The new Catechism sees that new attacks contrary to this commandment take today the forms of atheism and agnosticism. The atheist denies that there is a God; the agnostic says that he or she does not know. Often this is a sincerely held opinion, and as such, far from being a sin on that person's part, may be their way to God. It is up to Christians to try to persuade people of the truth of God's existence. Sometimes also, the behavior of religious people, whether in religious wars or terrorism, or in a simple lack of love, is a cause of a person's becoming atheist or agnostic.

But we must not exaggerate the proliferation of atheism and agnosticism. What is lacking is any commitment to a religious faith, to worship or a life of prayer. This is what the Second Vatican Council's document on the Church in the Modern World calls "practical atheism": living one's life as if God did not exist. With modern technology and science, and the influence of work and the media, there is that temptation for all of us simply to ignore God.

To ignore God is a sin, and if we are aware of it, a serious, even a mortal sin. It is the sin of injustice, failing to give God the just glory due to his name. It could become a mortal sin if a person deliberately abandoned the practice of religion through neglect. The love of God can die in us simply by never being activated. A husband does not need to be unfaithful to his wife to destroy their marriage. All he needs to do is to ignore her constantly. Many marriages have foundered simply through lack of communication. Our relationship with God can be destroyed if we take no steps to express our love for him in prayer, adoration, public worship, and confession of our sins.

Of course, not every person who abandons the practice of religion commits a mortal sin. Sometimes, such abandonment is caused by great pressure and distress, temptations against faith, or even by being badly treated by a fellow Christian, even by a priest. In such a case, those who cause such an abandonment are more responsible than the person themselves. Sometimes, also, we realize, young people abandon the practice of their religion just as a stage in their lives.

The one thing that this commandment teaches us clearly is that such abandonment and denial to our Creator of the honor and glory due to his name is very serious.

No graven image

The Israelites were forbidden to make any image of Yahweh their God.

Today people are not tempted so much to worship graven images of God. Rather, they substitute many kinds of false gods – money, power, sex, even another person – and worship these icons.

One note has to be made here concerning the Catholic and Orthodox use of pictures of Jesus Christ and of the saints, to which we give devotion.

In surveys in our secularist West, the majority of people still believe in a transcendent God. The latest world-wide survey on this subject showed that in almost every country the majority of people believe God exists. Top was the United States with 90% of the population believing in God.

Monica, the mother of Augustine, was distressed that her son had abandoned his religion. She went to the bishop Ambrose, who said to her, "Monica, the son of those tears will never be lost."

Hence, be very careful what you do. Since you saw no shape that day at Horeb when Yahweh spoke to you from the heart of the fire, see that you do not corrupt yourselves by making an image in the shape of anything whatever: be it statue of man or of woman, or of any animal on the earth, or of any bird that flies in the heavens ... (Dt 4:15–17).

The Israelites were forbidden to make any image of Yahweh their God.

Questions

1 What do I believe about God's relationship toward me?

2 What am I hoping for?

3 Do I believe God loves me unconditionally?

4 How do I express love for God?

5 Do I find it difficult to adore God? What helps me when I am distracted?

6 How do I express my adoration?

The new Catechism (*CCC 2131*) defends the use of these images by referring to the Second Ecumenical Council of Nicea, which in 787 (against the Iconoclasts, the Image Destroyers) defined that it was legitimate to reproduce the human form of the Word Incarnate Jesus Christ. Before the Incarnation, God had not revealed himself in any shape; but, with the coming of Jesus, who, as St. Paul says, was in the "form" of God (*Ph 2:6*), God was revealed in human shape. Thus, in praying before a statue of Jesus, Mary, or the saints, we as Catholics are not venerating the statue, but the person depicted by the statue (*CCC 2132*).

Catholics alone worship God. We do not worship any human being, even human beings so holy as Mary and the saints in heaven. Theologians make a distinction between *latria*, worship due to God alone, and *dulia*, devotion to a human being, to parents, and to venerated human beings such as the saints. The expression *hyperdulia*, "hyper-veneration" if you like, refers to Mary, because of her pre-eminent position in the body of Christ as the Mother of God and our mother. But even in her case, *latria*, to worship her as God, would be *idolatria*, false worship. Rather, devotion to her is simply devotion to another human being, even though she is considered perfect.

31 The second commandment: keeping God's name holy

You shall not misuse the name of Yahweh your God, for Yahweh will not leave unpunished anyone who misuses his name (*Ex 2:7*).

Again, you have heard how it was said to our ancestors, *You must not break your oath, but must fulfil your oaths to the Lord*. But I say this to you, do not swear at all ... (*Mt 5:33, 34*).

This second commandment emphasizes the respect due to the holy name of God. Most people would immediately think of "swearing," cursing the name of God or Jesus Christ when we drop a hammer on our foot. Such language is not to be encouraged, and is against the spirit of this commandment. But to use the name of God lightly or carelessly in this way is not a mortal sin. It is a venial sin, because the intention is not to insult the name of God. In fact, sometimes, when a person says, "Jesus, Mary, Joseph!" as an exclamation, it is possible that this is a prayer rather than a piece of careless talk.

But all disrespectful language about God is against the virtue of religion as the new Catechism explains (*CCC 2142*).

However, the second commandment means in its essence something deeper. Each one of the Ten Commandments has a mortal sin at its root.

The second commandment refers to a much deeper offense against God which we would usually call "blasphemy." It would be difficult to imagine the usual "swearer" intending contempt for God. Real blasphemy is much more serious.

Those who wrote the Psalms often "tell God off," complaining that God is not listening to them. This is not blasphemy, or even careless talk, but a person expressing deep feelings to God; just as a child will cry and complain to its parents, using strong language, but this is based on trust and confidence, not disrespect.

Intrinsically evil

The sin of blasphemy is generally considered by traditional moral theology to be the best example of a human act which is intrinsically evil, that is evil of itself and always so.

Recently, blasphemy, contempt for God, has come to public attention. The novelist Salman Rushdie wrote a book called *The Satanic Verses*, in which he expands the story to assert that the prophet Mohammed, in receiving revelations to write the Holy Koran, was on occasion the recipient of messages from the devil rather than from Allah. The Muslim community was deeply offended, but the author could not be charged with blasphemy under British law, because blasphemy, in Britain, technically can only be brought against one who has insulted the Christian God. Iranian Shiite Muslim authorities declared that Rushdie should be put to death and declared holy any Muslim who carried out his execution.

This shows how deep feelings can run concerning blasphemous language which insults a person's religion. Incidentally, Muslims are exemplary in their respect for God and the prophet. A good Muslim will, after mentioning the prophet Mohammed, say, "Peace be upon him."

Some people might argue that by letting off steam with blasphemy they are able to be nicer to others. But we would never admit that we could harm someone else in order to feel better; so why should we be able as it were to harm God by blasphemy in order to be less objectionable? Moral theologians have always seen blasphemy, and certain other human acts, as intrinsically evil.

The Christian name

The new Catechism (*CCC 2156–2159*) notes that we are baptized

> in the name of the Father and of the Son and of the Holy Spirit (*Mt 28:19*).

Each time we "bless ourselves" (make the sign of the cross) we are invoking the blessing of the holy name of God. We too, as human beings in Christ, become sacred, with the holy name of God. Thus the text quoted earlier (*Mt 5:33–34*) recalls Jesus insisting that his followers not only keep their oaths to God, but also to creation as a manifestation of God.

Questions:

1 Do you think that blasphemy should be a crime according to the law of the state?

2 Do you follow and agree with the concept, traditional in theology, of an "intrinsically evil" act?

32 The third commandment: remember the Sabbath

> Remember the Sabbath day and keep it holy. For six days you shall labor and do all your work, but the seventh day is a Sabbath for Yahweh your God. You shall do no work that day ... (*Ex 20:8–10*).

> And Jesus said to them, "The Sabbath was made for man, not man for the Sabbath; so the Son of man is master even of the Sabbath" (*Mk 2:27-28*).

A housewife used to say, as she put the clothes on the washing line on Sunday, "Six days shalt thou labor; and on the seventh do all the odd jobs."

It was fine for those who worked a five-day week, and could relax on Saturday and Sunday, to keep the Sabbath. For a busy shopkeeper like herself, the only time for housework was Sunday afternoon.

So much for the third commandment. For increasing numbers of people, with both partners working full stretch to pay the mortgage, a day of rest is becoming a dead letter.

More's the pity. In the Law of Moses, five thousand years ago, the Sabbath was introduced to protect the slave and poor worker from being exploited. God commanded that, at least on one day a week, everyone, rich or poor, must rest, even the donkey; because God himself rested on the Sabbath day.

Christians changed the Sabbath (Saturday) to Sunday, the "Lord's Day," because on that day Jesus rose from the dead. On the "eighth day," a Sunday, God began the new work of our redemption. But the idea remained the same. Peasants were exempt from work (servile work) on Sunday; their landlord could not exploit them for all seven days.

Conditions have changed. For many people who work in an office or school all week, hard physical work is good exercise, and a hobby. It is not "servile work." For them, to sit at the desk and negotiate on the telephone would be the equivalent of servile work. It could even be that putting the washing out on the line might, for some, be relaxation.

That is why the new Code of Canon Law does not use the expression "servile work" (see *ch. 24*).

But it does make clear that there are two obligations involved. The first is to keep Sunday holy by worshiping God, celebrating the supreme act of worship, the Eucharist. The second is to keep Sunday holy by "due relaxation of mind and body."

There are two heresies about work. The first is to imagine that our value as human beings is to be assessed in terms of our productivity. We admire "workaholics," people who constantly produce.

The second heresy is to imagine that work is related almost exclusively to economics: its value is to be assessed in terms of financial profit, to ourselves or to others.

For the Christian, work (paid or unpaid) is sharing in the creative activity of God, building his kingdom. In this sense, an

145

The disciples of Jesus were fishermen.

The Bible

The Bible presents both God and Jesus as workers. God is described as resting on the seventh day after completing his work (*Gn 2:2*). Jesus worked as a carpenter (*Mk 6:1–6*) and in his public ministry so that he could say toward the end of his earthly life

> I have glorified you on earth by finishing the work that you gave me to do (*Jn 17:4*).

Jesus chose working men for his twelve disciples, mostly fishermen. Many of his parables about salvation and the kingdom were built around the common working experience of his hearers.

At the Last Supper (*Jn 13:4–15*), Jesus gave a powerful example of the way his followers should regard their work. He washed the disciples' feet. This was a necessary but menial task, and usually reserved for the lowliest servant, yet Jesus chose it.

That incident can teach us that no task is below our dignity if we see it in terms of Christian service, and that the value of work does not depend on what is done and on what is paid for it, but on the person who does it.

Jesus' example points to another feature of our work – that it is necessarily a social activity, with or for others. To work is to cooperate with others, to depend upon them and they upon us.

In his encyclical on human work, Pope John Paul II drew attention to the fact that work is the foundation of family life; the family is both a community made possible by work and a "domestic school" in which we learn how to work (*Laborem Exercens, no. 43*).

unemployed person will also be working.

That is why stopping work is also important. Not only do we build up our resources physically and mentally for another round. God gave us the "Sabbath," time for re-creation, to admire our handiwork, and to thank him for giving us the courage, perseverance, and creative talent to see the job through.

Work: curse or blessing?

Work can be a pain: Getting up early, the rush-hour journey, the monotony, and the tension of working with people who are unpleasant or uncooperative or both.

While that view of work fits some human experience, it is not always so. Many people derive pleasure from their work, the companionship that often goes with it, and the knowledge that what they do is of benefit to others. Such people experience the blessings of work which God originally intended (*Gn 1:28*).

What is the Christian to make of these contrasts?

The Pope also stresses that human work is creative. We cooperate with God in the continuing act of creation, which is both the past event described in Genesis and a present process in which we are God's agents.

Vatican II in its document "The Church in the Modern World" and Pope John Paul have linked the pains associated with work with our redemption. John Paul suggests that through the way we accept the unpleasant aspects of our work we can find a small part of the cross of Christ.

The Pope is not saying we can earn redemption. That is a free gift from God. He is not suggesting that we should simply put up with bad working conditions or unjust treatment. Wherever possible we should strive to remove the cause of the problem, especially where it arises from greed, selfishness or mismanagement.

> It is hardly surprising that centuries ago theologians concluded that work was God's way of punishing mankind for original sin. They used Scriptural support for their view. Genesis tells us that after the man and the woman in the garden had disobeyed him, God told the man that only with suffering would he get food from the soil (*Gn 3:16-19*).

What is the point?

Christian tradition has seen work as a duty for all those capable of it for three reasons: to support ourselves and those who depend upon us; to be in a position to help others less fortunate; and to develop the talents God has given us.

St. Paul made the point forcibly in his second letter to the church at Thessalonika:

> We urged you ... not to let anyone eat if he refused to work (*2 Th 3:10*).

His criticism was directed not against those who could not work but those who refused work of which they were capable.

> In the parable of the talents, Jesus described how the fearful servant, the one who simply buried the talents he received, making no effort to increase them, was banished by his master (*Mt 25:14–30*).

Work and employment

But we should be clear that work and employment are not necessarily the same thing. Much real and valuable work is done in the home or in a voluntary capacity with no question of payment.

It is dangerous to equate the right to work with a right to *employment*. Only an all-powerful state could guarantee such a right, and that would mean giving over to the state the right to direct our labor wherever the authorities thought fit, without references to our wishes or abilities. That might be acceptable in a national emergency but not otherwise in a free society.

For some their right to work must mean a right to paid work. People who have no other means of supporting themselves have a right to earn a living. In times of high and persistent unemployment throughout the industrialized world, such people should have first claim to paid work. To demand or even to accept paid work, without any real need for an income, could well be to deprive others of the means of livelihood and support for their families and dependents.

In present circumstances, with no real prospect of return to full employment, the distinction between employment and work becomes highly important. One way of expressing Christian love is to help the unemployed preserve or recover the dignity they may feel they have lost.

Sunday trading?

Thomas Aquinas argued that one of the reasons why God instituted the Sabbath day was to cure the sin of avarice. If people work seven days a week, they tend to become greedy, think only of making money, and in consequence fail to care for the poor. Avarice also leads to dishonesty, because the greedy person thinks only of making money, not of justice. The prophet Amos, eighth century B.C., was quite prepared to attack the wealthy establishment of his day (*Am 8:4–6*).

Jesus was merciful to sinners. For example he said to the woman taken in adultery

From this moment sin no more (*Jn 8:11*).

But he reserved condemnation for two sins especially: religious hypocrisy and avarice. Jesus refused to arbitrate between two men who were squabbling over an inheritance, saying

Who appointed me your judge, or the arbitrator of your claims? (*Lk 12:13*).

Then he told the story of a man who, being successful in business, decided to build more and more barns. But he never enjoyed his hard-earned wealth. He died that night.

Sunday Mass

The second reason given by Thomas Aquinas as to why God instituted the Sabbath was that the Jews should remember creation. We need one day to remember that God created the universe and ourselves, and that he is our Lord and God.

From the beginning, Christian leaders saw the need for members of the Church to assemble for worship, and warned against slackness. The writer of the Letter to the Hebrews, only forty years or so after the death and resurrection of Christ, already

Many corner shops and chain stores now open seven days a week. What effect does this have on society?

has to warn his Jewish Christian readers:

> Do not absent yourself from your own assemblies, as some do, but encourage each other ... (*Heb 10:25*).

Why, then, should we go to Mass? Even more, why should we have to go to Mass? In most Western countries, if 25% of Catholics regularly attend Mass on Sundays, this is considered quite reasonable, particularly in urban areas. What about the other 75%?

Those who go to church must bear some responsibility for discouraging those who do not. Priests may preach boring sermons. The music at Mass may be poorly accompanied and sung. Churchgoers may even give a poor example by their lives.

With this in mind, some Catholics, after the Second Vatican Council in the sixties, proposed that Sunday Mass should no longer be an obligation, but optional. In their opinion, priests and people, those who do attend church, would be compelled to brighten up their ideas to fill more seats on Sunday.

The new Catechism (*CCC 2181*) has reaffirmed the ancient doctrine that deliberately to miss Mass on Sundays and holy days of obligation, without an adequate reason (e.g. sickness) is a "grave sin," requiring absolution in the sacrament of reconciliation before the person committing that sin may receive Holy Communion. The new Catechism takes a tough stand on this.

Of course, some priests should preach better sermons, music should be better, congregations should be more welcoming. But the new Catechism points out that the Mass is not part of the entertainment industry. It is not a matter of someone else's responsibility to make Mass more interesting. It is a matter of our responsibility before God as baptized Catholics to be present and actively participating in the assembly of God's people, the Body of Christ, of which each of us is a member.

Perhaps one reason why so many Catholics do miss Mass is precisely because they do not realize the seriousness of the obligation. But why should missing Mass on Sunday without a serious reason be a grave sin?

Disobeying a divine command

Sin, as the new Catechism explains, is an act of disobedience, a revolt against God (*CCC 1850*). Christ gave his Church the authority to bind and to loose, that is, to command Christians to certain courses of action which the Church decides are for their good and for the good of the whole body of Christ. Such commands, of course, have to be reasonable; but no one could seriously argue that the Church is making an unreasonable demand when it insists that faithful Christians be present at Mass once a week. This is a legitimate command of the Church; and Christ has promised that the Church's commands will be ratified by God:

> Whatever you bind on earth will be bound in heaven (*Mt 16:19*).

Some people may ask why Mass? Why does the Church not allow me to worship God in my own way? The answer is clear; the Church is following the command of Christ himself in requiring his followers to do this in remembrance of me

when he instituted the Eucharist (*1 Co 11:24*). This is why the Church puts the Mass at the top of her worship agenda, and requires all practicing Catholics to be present weekly.

The second reason relates to the first commandment, "You shall worship the Lord your God, and him only shall you serve." Many people believe it is not necessary to go to church to worship God. But beneath this assumption lies a common misconception about the nature of worship of God, namely that we can worship God as we please. But surely, we must worship God not as we please, but as he pleases? Otherwise, how can it be true worship, giving God what is his due? How can we give him his due, if what he requires through his Church, namely our presence at Sunday Mass, we refuse to give him?

Each Sunday, we receive a personal invitation from our Lord himself; and, from one of such divine authority, such an invitation is also a command.

Putting our spiritual lives in serious danger

To miss Sunday Mass regularly is to neglect our souls, our spiritual growth, which can die through neglect. If those who neglected to hear and obey the prophets were punished, asks the writer of the Letter to the Hebrews, then how shall we escape if we neglect so great a salvation? (*Heb 2:3*) If Catholics neglect to eat the flesh of the Son of Man in Holy Communion, or at least attend the Eucharist and be spiritually one with Christ in the assembly even if they are unable to receive Communion for any reason, then how can their spiritual lives not be weakened, and even die? The greatest gift of all, the Body and Blood of Christ the Son of God, is being refused regularly. How can this not be seriously harmful?

Failing to witness to Christ and his Church

The new Catechism points out (*CCC 2182*) that Christ and his Church are united inextricably as Bridegroom and Bride (*Ep 6:21–33*). For a Catholic, there is no such reality as being a Christian without being a member of the Body of Christ, the Church. Thus, when the Church assembles, and it lacks even one member, then the Church is to that extent weakened.

Not going to Mass not only harms our souls, it harms the souls of others, and indeed the whole body of Christ.

Christ said, "If you do not eat the flesh of the Son of man and drink his blood, you have no life in you" (*Jn 6:53*).

Questions

1 Why do you think people do not go to church?

2 How do you make Sunday a special day?

33 The fourth commandment: honor your parents

Honor your father and your mother so that you may live long in the land that Yahweh your God is giving you (*Ex 20:12*).

He [Jesus] lived under their authority [his parents] (*Lk 2:51*).

Children, be obedient to your parents in the Lord – that is what uprightness demands. The first commandment that has a promise attached to it is: *Honor your father and your mother*, and the promise is: *so that you may have long life and prosper in the land*. And parents, never drive your children to resentment but bring them up with correction and advice inspired by the Lord (*Ep 6:1–4*).

God and neighbor

This fourth commandment, as the new Catechism says (*CCC 2197–2257*), opens the second table of the Ten Commandments. The first table, the first three commandments, outlines our duties directly to God. The second table, the last seven commandments, outlines our duties to our neighbor ("love your neighbor as yourself"), made in God's image and likeness.

The principle of human relationships is that they are also divine. God works in and through them. God expects us to treat each other as we treat him. The famous story Jesus told about the end of the world, and the criterion by which he judged people, is both terrifying and instructive. To those who helped the needy, Jesus said, "in so far as you did this to one of the least of these brothers of mine, you did it to me" (*Mt 25:40*), welcoming them into heaven. To the goats on his left hand, he had the chilling message,

in so far as you neglected to do this to one of the least of these, you neglected to do it to me (*Mt 25:45*).

The first people we come to know on this earth are our parents, and our brothers and sisters. It is very apt, therefore, that this commandment deals with our relationships with what the new Catechism (*CCC 2204*) calls a "domestic church," in which we learn what it is to be a Christian community, as Jesus did himself with Mary and Joseph in the Holy Family.

Parents

The new Catechism first looks at the family as an institution and as the most essential element of our society (*CCC 2201–2213*). If the family is a "mini-church," it is also a "mini-society," called by the new Catechism an original cell of social life (*CCC 2207*) bound by nature and by blood.

The family today is under threat. Many of its problems, we shall argue when speaking of the sixth and ninth commandments, are related to the question of sexuality. When society does not value chastity, but promotes sexual promiscuity with all its vigor, then it is hardly surprising that families break up.

Parents therefore have a prime obligation to stay together in order that their family may itself

Light from the Council

One of the sixteen documents of Vatican II is the Declaration on Christian Education and it has the following to say (no. 3) on the role of parents in education:

"As it is the parents who have given life to their children, on them lies the gravest obligation of educating their family. They must therefore be recognized as being primarily and principally responsible for their education. The role of parents in education is of such importance that it is almost impossible to provide an adequate substitute. It is therefore the duty of parents to create a family atmosphere inspired by love and devotion to God and their fellow men and women which will promote an integrated, personal and social education of their children.

The family is therefore the principal school of the social virtues which are necessary to every society. It is therefore above all in the Christian family, inspired by grace and the responsibility of the sacrament of matrimony, that children should be taught to know and worship God and to love their neighbor, in accordance with the faith which they have received in earliest infancy in the sacrament of baptism.

In it, also, they will have their first experience of a well-balanced human society and of the Church. Finally, it is through the family that they are gradually initiated into association with their fellow men and women in civil life and as members of the people of God. Parents should, therefore, appreciate how important a role the truly Christian family plays in the life and progress of the whole people of God."

Children

Duty of Obedience and Filial Piety.

This recognizes those who have given us the gift of life. "With all your heart honor your father, never forget the birthpangs of your mother.

Remember that you owe your birth to them;

how can you repay them for what they have done for you?" (Si 7:27–28)

This means that children have the duty of obeying their parents. This is our first repayment, imitating Jesus who was subject to his parents.

be a stable school of love for their children. Their fidelity will be a sign of the fidelity of God himself who is their Father, who sent his Son to love them and die for them. In today's world, education in sexuality and personal relationships becomes especially important, precisely in order for their family to grow together, and for their children to have a similarly stable and fruitful marriage.

Obedience

Strangely enough, there is very little in the Old Testament about children obeying their parents, perhaps because, in their society, children had no option. But if it did not constitute a problem then, certainly in our present-day society we have our difficulties about "obedience."

It is clear to everyone that there are times when we must be prepared to disobey either our parents or our superior. After all, the apostles told the bosses in the priestly Sanhedrin (whose authority they recognized) that they must disobey their order to be silent and not preach the Gospel:

> you must judge whether in God's eyes it is right to listen to you and not to God (Ac 4:19).

There are times in all of our lives when we must nail our colors to the mast, and say "no" to an order from on high. This is because parents, and indeed all others in authority, constitute an imperfect image of God the Father.

However, although authority of any kind is an imperfect image, it still is an image of the Father's will. Christ himself became subject to his parents in Nazareth. This means we must try to see God's will manifested in those put in authority over us, even though sometimes this requires a gigantic act of faith. There is a

Family life is the basis of society, and should be safeguarded.

corresponding obligation, of course, incumbent upon those in authority not to abuse that authority; thus Paul says:

> Children, be obedient to your parents in the Lord ... (*Ep 6:1*),

but says almost immediately afterwards,

> and parents, never drive your children to resentment but bring them up with correction and advice inspired by the Lord (*Ep 6:1*).

Both sides of the authority coin need to make examinations of conscience occasionally.

Christianity brings about a whole new set of family relationships based

> not from human stock or human desire or human will but from God himself (*Jn 1:13*).

This is surely what the "Church" means. Whoever does the will of the Father in heaven is Christ's brother, sister, and mother, and so ours. This is also what Christ said to his mother from the cross, "Woman, this is your son," and then to the disciple, "This is your mother" (*Jn 19:26-27*). What a crime it is to see the Church simply as an institution, and not truly as a family. Paul invited Timothy to view the Church as a family back in the first century A.D.

Old Testament society

Old Testament society depended for its life upon a stable family. In the days before old age pension and social security, when families lived together in tribes, there was an absolute need for care to be taken of widows, orphans, and the old, who could no longer look after themselves; otherwise, they would die of hunger, starvation, and the cold nights of the Middle East.

> Never speak sharply to a man older than yourself, but appeal to him as you would to your own father; treat younger men as brothers, older women as mothers and young women as sisters with all propriety (*1 Tm 5:1-2*).

> One very humane law in the code of Deuteronomy (*Dt 24:13*), protected the pawnbroker by decreeing that, if a man had given his cloak in a pledge, that cloak had to be returned to him at night to keep him warm: "You must return it to him at sunset so that he can sleep in his cloak and bless you; and it will be an upright action on your part in God's view."

153

The book of Proverbs, a set of wise sayings in the form of advice from an old man to his son, sums up the Old Testament attitude on the need to care for our parents: "He who ill-treats his father and drives out his mother is a child both worthless and depraved" (Pr 19:26). Of course, one cannot conclude that a young couple acts against this advice if they persuade their aged mother or father to go to a "home" or to the hospital. Sometimes, the old couple genuinely wants to live elsewhere, either because they need more nursing care than could be provided at their children's home, or even because they find it as difficult to live with their offspring as their offspring find it difficult to live with them. This is not a matter of rigid rules, but rather the application of a simple test: is my action really and truly abandoning my mother and father who have given me life and love? Or am I really caring for them and loving them, wherever they might live, and whoever might be looking after them?

It is clear then that, even at this lowest level of interpretation, the commandment "Honor your father and your mother" calls for an examination of conscience. The number of old people is increasing in proportion to the rest of society, due to falling birth rate on the one hand and increased expectation of life on the other. Medical science is increasingly able to keep older people alive; but are we making their life worth living?

We must never think that this commandment is simply a command only to care for one's parents. The word used is "honor" (Hebrew *cabed*, which is the same word used for the "glory of Yahweh"). In other words, this commandment is saying that the respect we give to our mother and father must be something like the honor we give to God himself. That is surely the reason why, if a man cursed his father or his mother (note that in this law, and in a male-dominated society, women have equal rights with men), the law (Ex 21:17 and Lv 20:9) says that that man must be put to death – the same fierce punishment given to a man who cursed God.

Civil society

The new Catechism sees this as an order set up by God, who made us as human beings to live in society. This civil authority should be exercised as a service:

Everyone is to obey the governing authorities, because there is no authority except from God and so whatever authorities exist have been appointed by God (Rm 13:1).

The new Catechism, in putting this section on civil society within the commandment concerning obedience to parents, shows clearly that this authority from God does not give civil powers unlimited rights. The new Catechism reminds us that the moral measure of the rule of a civil government is whether its exercise conforms to the dignity of persons and the natural law. Indeed, many societies today do not recognize a natural law, but act more pragmatically, on the basis of what the majority in society agree should be done at any given time.

Christians have in particular the duty of praying for civil government.

The new Catechism also reminds citizens of a most unpleasant duty, of paying their taxes (CCC 2238); on the other hand, civil powers have the duty of protecting refugees from other countries who cannot find adequate resources in their own country (*CCC 2241*). The citizen also has the duty of refusing obedience when the civil authority commands something contrary to right conscience (*CCC 2242*).

Finally, the Catechism insists on the right of the Church to speak on civil affairs within her competence, and reminds states of their obligation to listen to the Church:

> If there is no ultimate truth to guide and direct political activity, then ideas and convictions can easily be manipulated for reasons of power. As history demonstrates, a democracy without values easily turns into open or thinly disguised totalitarianism (*Pope John Paul II, encyclical Centesimus Annus, no. 46*).

I urge then, first of all that petitions, prayers, intercessions and thanksgiving should be offered for everyone, for kings and others in authority, so that we may be able to live peaceful and quiet lives with all devotion and propriety (*1 Tm 2:1–2*).

Questions:

1 What do you think is the greatest problem facing the family today?

2 In what ways should Catholics become more involved in society?

34 The fifth commandment: respect for human life

The Law provided "cities of refuge" in the event of accidental killing (*Dt 19:6*).

You shall not kill (*Ex 20:13*).

You have heard how it was said to our ancestors, *You shall not kill*; and if anyone does kill he must answer for it before the court. But I say this to you, anyone who is angry with a brother will answer for it before the court ... (*Mt 5:21–22*).

We discussed earlier the whole question of what is intrinsically evil, and argued that blasphemy is such a case. Similarly, killing is and always will be wrong. But the act of killing itself must be clearly defined, and the new Catechism (*CCC 2258*), quoting the Vatican Sacred Congregation for the Doctrine of the Faith, does so:

> Human life is sacred because from its origin it implies the creative action of God and remains always in a special relationship with the Creator, its one and only purpose. God alone is the master of life and death from its commencement to its end: no one in any circumstance can arrogate to himself the right to destroy directly an innocent human being (*Instruction Donum Vitae, no. 5*).

This is a carefully worded statement. It does not say that all killing of a human being is necessarily wrong. What it says is gravely wrong is the direct killing of an innocent human being. This excludes:

- The indirect killing of a human being. An example would be the removal from a pregnant woman of a cancerous womb which is threatening her life. Even if a living fetus is in her womb, and removing that fetus causes its death, it is permitted as indirect killing.

- The killing, even direct, of a guilty human being, either in self-defense, or in war, or as a punishment for a crime committed. Traditional moral theology argues that the state has authority to authorize the punishment of criminals, and the defense of the realm, even to putting to death aggressors or those who threaten the state (*Rm 13:4*).

Note that neither of these exceptions, the indirect killing of an innocent human being, or the direct killing of a guilty human being, is always justified. It is only justified under certain circumstances, which we will discuss in a moment. First, however, we must look at the Scriptural basis of this command YOU SHALL NOT KILL, and see that its meaning was already established in Old Testament times, long before the birth of Christ our Lord.

Lo Tirsah

At first sight, the Old Testament seems inconsistent, if not hypocritical, in giving the commandment "You shall not kill." Even on a most cursory reading, the authors seem to approve of many types of "killing." War, for instance, is not only allowed but even encouraged. Israelites were expected by Joshua to kill men, women and children when they conquered a city, and to do so in the name of Yahweh (*Jos 6:17*).

Again, this commandment does not apply to animals, presumably because they are not made in the image of Yahweh. The sacrificial system of the Old Testament demanded thousands of animals to be slaughtered in the name of religion, not to mention animals killed for food. Also capital punishment seems to be most frequent. Any proven violation of the Ten Commandments was punishable by death. "You shall not kill," therefore, seems to have been a command with many qualifications.

This is where the knowledge of the Hebrew verb used is most important. The whole sentence "You shall not kill" is in Hebrew the briefest of sentences, *lo tirsah* "(do) not kill," the verb *rasah* being a special one, and not the most frequently used for "to kill" in the Old Testament. This is why there is some justification to support the older translations of the Ten Commandments which translated *lo tirsah* as "thou shalt do no murder."

> Scholars have researched this word *rasah* in great detail, and it appears that it is never used for God killing someone, it is never used for killing in battle, it is never used for the killing of animals, it is never used for judicial killing (capital punishment), and above all, it is never used to describe the killing of an innocent person, except by accident.

War and self-defense

Jesus Christ said that there would always be

> wars and rumors of wars (*Mt 24:6*).

In the two thousand years from his day to ours, this prediction has been amply fulfilled. In the twentieth century, war has become even more horrific. We now have instruments of death which could destroy our planet.

People who declare war will always justify their conduct. They claim they are exercising their rights. For instance, they will claim that, if they do not fight, they will be occupied by an enemy and lose their freedom. They would rather die free than live oppressed.

The following principles on self-defense seem to be implicit in the teaching of the New Testament and the great Christian writers:

a if nothing else but individual interests are at stake and the Christian has done nothing wrong, there may well be times when all must be ready to follow Christ as St. Peter wrote: "Christ ... left an example ... he has done nothing wrong" (1 P 2:21-22). And he was rewarded with crucifixion.

b I may be required to defend my own life because God has given it to me as a gift. It might also happen that my good name is tied up with the reputation of Christianity itself. I would then have the responsibility of defending myself. St. Thomas More, for example, used his razor-sharp mind on English law to defend himself and the Church against the overbearing King Henry VIII.

c When the innocent and helpless are involved, the strong Christian has a duty to defend them. Physical force may be needed but it must never be excessive.

d Civil authority must be able to use enough force to restrain those who disrupt society. This right is recognized by Saints Peter and Paul (1 P 2:13–17).

This problem is not new to Christianity, even if the problem is now so much greater. The question as to whether I should defend myself comes to all of us, in various situations: physical assault, verbal abuse, home, work, school. Should I take it, or hit back?

In St. John's account of Christ's ordeal before the high priest at his trial, our Lord is questioned about his teaching. One of the guards slapped his face because he thought that Jesus was being insolent. Jesus says immediately,

> If there is some offense in what I said, point it out; but if not, why do you strike me? (Jn 18:23).

He was acting in self-defense by pointing to the wrong that was being done to him. Yet, elsewhere in the same story, he chooses to remain silent. This is evidence that self-defense is complicated.

The Sermon on the Mount, especially

> Blessed are you when people abuse you ... But I say this to you: offer no resistance to the wicked (Mt 5:11, 39),

could give the impression that Christians should just let the strong have their way. But this could be no more than cowardice. The whole question is subtle.

Is self-defense justified for a nation?

As long as Christians were a persecuted minority, the question of national self-defense did not arise. Once the Roman Empire became Christian, the Church had to face a new situation. Many historians claim that Christians were pacifist until they were in power. Whether or not this is true, it was later in Christianity that the principles of the just war emerged.

- There must be a just cause
- War may be declared only by competent authority
- There must be a right intention, and not merely a desire to triumph
- War must be a last resort
- There must be a probability of success
- No war should be begun for trivial reasons.

Once war has begun there must be non-combatant immunity. There must not be use of terror by indiscriminate killing of civilians, for instance during bombing.

The prohibition on indiscriminate killing makes it clear that any weapon which can destroy a city cannot be morally used. However, there are smaller, more sophisticated weapons now available which some claim are legitimate because they can be aimed solely at military targets and have a limited effect. But others maintain this is illusory because the most serious effect is radioactive fallout which cannot be contained.

Some moralists maintain that the threat to use nuclear weapons is itself immoral. There are others who argue that nuclear deterrence had given peace to Europe for decades. And the arguments continue. In June 1982 Pope John Paul II told the United Nations:

> In current conditions "deterrence" based on balance, certainly not as an end in itself, but as a stage on the way towards a progressive disarmament, can still be judged morally acceptable.

The only final answer to those complex and worrying questions must be the growth of trust between the nations who recognize everyone as God's children.

The death penalty

When the new Catechism was published in Italy, a great stir was caused by the claim that it had legitimized the use of capital punishment. In fact, the media had inflated the matter beyond all proportion. This is a summary of what the new Catechism (*CCC 2266*) actually said: that to preserve the common good, public authority must deter crime, by proportionate punishment, and that where there is a case of extreme seriousness the penalty of death is not necessarily excluded. Similarly, the civil authorities can commission their army to repulse an unjust aggressor.

This therefore only concedes to the state the right to inflict capital punishment. It does not spell out under which circumstances capital punishment may be used, or even if it should ever be used. In these terms, therefore, the new Catechism says no more

Turn the other cheek?

One of the most challenging sayings of Christ is recorded in Matthew 5:38, 39. "You have heard how it was said: Eye for eye and tooth for tooth. But I say this to you: offer no resistance to the wicked. On the contrary, if anyone hits you on the right cheek, offer him the other as well ..." Is Jesus saying that it is forbidden to defend our rights? Clearly, he did not mean literally that we should "turn the other cheek," since he himself at his trial, being struck by one of the high priest's guards, answered him back, "Why do you strike me?" (*Jn 18:23*).

"Turn the other cheek" is an exhortation rather than a hard-and-fast law. The old law "an eye for an eye and a tooth for a tooth" was intended as a limit on seeking revenge. Jesus goes further than equal vengeance. The Christian should work for reconciliation, even at the cost of her own pride.

Capital punishment may or may not be the best procedure in order to deter crime.

than any state in the world, since every state would seem to grant itself the right to inflict capital punishment. The debate is always not as to whether the state has the right, but rather as to whether it is the best procedure in order to deter crime to use that right. The bishops of the United States have spoken out strongly and consistently against capital punishment. So has Pope John Paul II, in his 1995 encyclical *The Gospel of Life*.

Principles

It is because human beings are made "in the image of God" that the Church teaches the existence of the absolute right to life. Traditionally animals have not been seen as having the same rights, because they are not human. In recent years human beings have been more exercised about "animal rights." At least the principle of the love of God's creatures should make cruelty to animals repugnant.

The Church, and medical authorities until recently, have taught that life begins at conception with the fertilization of the ovum by the sperm. This is now being seriously questioned to meet the demands of experimental scientists. Advocates of test-tube baby techniques agree with the traditional teaching when they say "the conceptus even in the pre-implantation stage is a microscopic human being – one in its very earliest stages of development" (*A Mother of Life, 1981*).

For this reason, the Church teaches that the abortion of an unborn fetus is always wrong.

Abortion

The new Catechism (*CCC 2271*) points out that from the very first Christian century onwards, the killing of the unborn and the newborn child was forbidden. The document called the Teaching of the Twelve Apostles (*Didache*), one of the earliest Christian documents after the New Testament, makes this explicit:

> You shall not kill the embryo by abortion, and you shall not kill the newborn (*Didache 2,2*).

In the United States there have been around 32 million abortions since 1973 when Supreme Court decisions struck down most laws prohibiting abortion. There is no doubt that, in future centuries, people will look back in horror at this appalling statistic of mass destruction of life in the womb, and at how insensitive the consciences of "decent" Americans seemed to be to this crime.

Respect for life is now so eroded in our society that abortion can happen when the sex of the child is not what the parents wanted.

We must support any woman with a problem pregnancy, both during the pregnancy and afterwards. We must concern ourselves with helping persons with disabilities to lead as independent a life as possible. We should have compassion for those who have recourse to abortion – they are victims of our selfish society and need help. We must be well informed and speak out when we can.

We are not obliged to use extraordinary methods of preserving the life of infants with severe medical problems. However, we are obliged to use ordinary methods of treatment. A newborn child has a right to all normal care, to feeding, warmth and love. It is not acceptable to starve a child, or to sedate a child so that he or she is unable to feed.

Modern treatment methods may produce their own problems. Life support machines are used regularly in the case of the new-born. Very occasionally it becomes apparent that there is no hope of a cure and that a child is dependent on the ventilator. At this stage a decision has to be made about the wisdom of continuing with this treatment. Such decisions need to be taken by the parents with the appropriate professional advice.

Neonatal care is changing fast; the problems involved are changing as well. The staff of neonatal units need to be prepared to deal with ethical problems. They need the support of their chaplains in helping babies and parents during a vital time in a family's life.

Persons with disabilities

We are one Mystical Body in Christ. Able-bodied people often have a problematic attitude towards those with an obvious disability. They may ignore or overprotect the disabled.

Although social attitudes have improved, there is still a great feeling of not wanting to be bothered with persons with disabilities, possibly with the excuse that there is no time or that one does not know what to do. The disabled long to be treated as normal members of the community in the parish, at home and at work, no more and no less.

It is the job of persons with and without disabilities to work together to change attitudes so that all are looked on as children of God, with something to give and something to receive.

There is a need for humility, but we should also have a rightful pride in what we have achieved. Those who appear to have been given more of God's spiritual, mental or material gifts have a duty to share them with others, especially those who are disadvantaged.

Suicide

If direct killing of the innocent is always gravely wrong, then it follows that to kill oneself is wrong. The commandment "Love your neighbor as yourself" implies what is often forgotten, namely that we must love ourselves as well as our neighbor. To take our own life is the ultimate act of hating ourselves, of saying no both to our existence and to the unique talents that God our loving heavenly Father has given us.

Of course, we all realize that a person who commits suicide is very often in a state of unbearable depression and despair. Over the centuries, the Church has modified her discipline regarding the burial of those who have taken their own life. In the Middle Ages, Christian burial was forbidden for suicides; but in the Catholic Church today, this is never refused, on the principle that the poor person was not fully responsible for his or her terrible act.

Although we have every sympathy for those who are driven to commit suicide, it is wrong to imagine that nothing can be done to help a person who is tempted to this terrible act. Worldwide organizations of volunteers such as the Samaritans, who answer calls from those in despair, testify to the possibility of instilling hope in those who have come to imagine that their life is no longer of any worth.

But in the midst of despair, when life seems meaningless, a Christian can see his or her life as of infinite worth:

> You are worth more than many sparrows (*Mt 10:31*).

A story is told about the famous priest St. John Vianney, the Curé of Ars, who was hearing a confession from a mother who was distraught about her son who had just committed suicide by throwing himself from a bridge into a river. "Do not worry, my dear," said the holy man, "your son repented between the bridge and the river."

Christ loved each one of us so much that he died in agony for us saying,

Father, into your hands I commit my spirit (Lk 23:46).

Those who believe this, and thus believe that God has a plan for each and every one of us, can never think finally that life is worthless. When tempted to despair, will go to confession to find help from the Church, they will go to the doctor to find specialized help in the medical and psychological field, or will find befrienders such as the Samaritans.

But why should we not take the apparently easy way out of our troubles? After all, do not Christians believe that the next life will be much better than this present life, which is described in the "Hail Holy Queen," a prayer to Mary, as a "valley of tears"? This is where Christian doctrine of the Lordship of God over our lives is important. God is the author of life, and God determines when life is taken away. This thought is relevant when we consider what is called "euthanasia."

Euthanasia

Euthanasia (Greek for "easy death") is closely related to the problem of suicide, because it is argued that a person who wishes to die, because of age, or great suffering, or disability, should be allowed to have that wish fulfilled by being painlessly killed. In such a case, therefore, a person would be committing suicide by means of a medical agent such as a doctor.

The same moral argument applies as with suicide, whether indeed such "mercy killing" is with the full consent of the patient, or (as no doubt would often be the case in practice) by means of a little "helpful" persuasion from relatives or professional consultants. The Christian view is clear: that God is the author of life, and that God therefore determines when and under what circumstances our life on this earth is to be ended.

The question again arises as to the value of life. It is often argued that a terminally ill patient, or one who is old and incontinent, has no longer any reason for living. The growth in the lobby for euthanasia arises not only from the technology explosion, with methods of death being so much more efficient. It arises also from a false belief that life can somehow be judged in terms of its quality; and, if that quality is not apparent, then we human beings have the right to terminate it.

The Christian answer is that life cannot be quantified, or be subject to quality control, for we are made in God's image. As human beings, by virtue of our creation, we have a share in the infinite God, whether we are rich or poor, successful or failures, healthy or beset with illness. A terminally ill patient in these terms has just as much right – and indeed duty – to live as long as God wills, as does the doctor treating the patient, or the relatives.

St. Paul told the Galatians:

> Let us never slacken in doing good; for if we do not give up, we shall have our harvest in due time (*Ga 6:9*).

This applies again to everyone, to the apparently useless and rejected in our society too. The "harvest" of our lives is not how much money we make, or how much impact we make on society, but rather the harvest of good deeds. Those nursing the terminally ill testify to how they themselves are helped by the very people they are nursing. Parents of children with disabilities often testify that they draw closer to God through sharing in the life of one who needs them utterly.

Again, the Church rejects "mercy killing" for what it is, a crime against humanity. But this does not mean that doctors must strive to preserve life at all costs. To allow a person to die with dignity is not only allowed morally, but may sometimes be the only moral decision. "Extraordinary means" of preserving life (e.g., life-support systems; complicated and painful operations which do not have any real hope of restoring to health) may, and sometimes should, be dispensed with.

One of the greatest challenges to our society at the end of the twentieth century is this whole question of "playing God." And one important part of a Christian vocation is to testify to the value of human life in these agonizing situations.

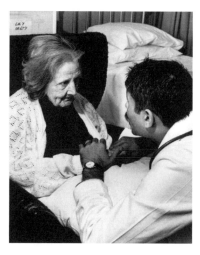

Growing old can be a painful experience in many ways.

Test-tube babies?

In current medical practice the aim is to try to obtain as many eggs as possible, to fertilize and then to select and implant three into the womb. What happens to surplus embryos or abnormal embryos? They are either frozen, experimented upon, or flushed down the sink. Frozen embryos may, or may not, be used at a later date. The whole process is not acceptable.

None of us has the right to have a child, for children are not material possessions, but gifts from God. Infertility causes deep distress, and we should be concerned to alleviate this, but not at any cost.

IVF (in-vitro fertilization) is a relatively new technique whose full moral and physical implications are the subject of much medical, ethical and theological debate. But the church condemns the deliberate "waste" of human fetuses.

Question

Think about one or more of the issues outlined in this chapter. How would you face such a problem yourself?

35 The sixth commandment: the virtue of chastity

You shall not commit adultery (*Ex 20:14; see Dt 5:17*).

You have heard how it was said, *You shall not commit adultery.* But I say this to you, if a man looks at a woman lustfully, he has already committed adultery with her in his heart (*Mt 5:27–28*).

The sixth commandment as stated refers to a specific example of sexual unchastity, namely sexual intercourse between a married spouse and a person to whom he or she is not married. This specificity is important, because, as with other commandments in the Decalogue, there were legal penalties for those caught in adultery, namely death (*Jn 8:1–11*, the account of the woman taken in adultery).

As the new Catechism explains, however (*CCC 2336*), within the tradition of the Church, this commandment has been understood as including the whole range of sexual acts. This is a moral question, operating independently of the question of whether an individual state attaches legal penalties to some forms of sexual immorality, for instance homosexuality, adultery or under-age sex. We are considering here the moral and not the legal question of what is right or wrong sexually.

The Church has always taught that every form of sexual intercourse is wrong except that exercised between married couples and open to new life. This rules out as objectively wrong adultery, fornication, acts of homosexual intercourse (not denying that some may have an orienta-tion towards members of the same sex), masturbation, and all other forms of sexual deviation. The new Catechism reiterates this teaching with authority and firmness, fully aware of the objections to it.

Such teaching will no doubt to many sound archaic, prudish, impossible to practice and legalistic. The widely-held opinion today is that any form of sexual practice is legitimate provided that no one is harmed (however "harm" is defined), and provided that an unwanted child is not produced. The one sexual absolute seems to be "Thou shalt wear a condom."

It is worth remembering, however, that less than fifty years ago the traditional Catholic teaching was held by most people in society, and certainly by all the major Christian denominations. That included the Church's teaching on the wrongness of using artificial means to prevent birth. Until the Lambeth Conference after the First World War, for instance, the Church of England held that contraceptive intercourse was always wrong. Muslims have always held the same sexual morality as the Catholic Church, apart from the divorce laws, as has orthodox Judaism.

Sexual immorality has always occurred. Leviticus 18, written well over 2,000 years ago and reflecting a still earlier civilization, mentions incest, adultery, homosexuality, and bestiality. The Church has always recognized how strong temptation can be, and the weakness of human nature, especially after the fall. Bad habits of unchastity, for instance masturbation, can be very hard to shake off. To rephrase the new Catechism (*CCC 2342*), the mastery of oneself is a "long haul"! That is why the sacrament of confession has been provided, to encourage and help those who are on this difficult journey.

The Church, and until recently society in general, has recognized that people fall into sexual temptation of various kinds according to their particular inclination. What is new in the present age is that many people do not recognize that there is anything wrong with sexual intercourse of any kind for pleasure (although sexual intercourse with children would seem to be excluded). In many people's opinion, the greatest sin is to acquire AIDS; and that, we are told, can be avoided by wearing a condom.

Why, then, is it wrong to have sex simply for pleasure? Why cannot various forms of sexual intercourse be a genuine expression of love? Why cannot I enjoy a form of sex which I like, whatever type, just as I enjoy a good film or a good meal, expressing my affection for someone? This takes us to the heart of what sexuality is according to Scripture and the Church's tradition.

The wedding ring is a sign to the couple and to the world that two have become one flesh.

One flesh

The Church teaches that the sexual act is only right when it conforms to the law of the two, man and woman, becoming one flesh in a union of love and life. This is the design, the law of the Creator God, when he created the human being male and female. As the Book of Genesis says, in describing the creation of the woman from the man,

> a man leaves his father and mother and becomes attached to his wife, and they become one flesh (*Gn 2:24*).

In Hebrew, "one flesh" means "one body," even "one personality." This is achieved through the sexual act, the procreative act, whereby the two become one flesh; but it is also achieved only through the lifelong partnership between the two, husband and wife, of which the sexual intercourse is the sign, even a kind of sacrament. Thus the sexual act of union is related essentially to the lifelong commitment of the couple.

This teaching is clearly stated by St. Paul in writing to the Corinthians (about A.D. 57), who lived in a sexually promiscuous city. The early Christians at Corinth were tolerating a case of incest, which Paul said would not have been accepted even among the pagans (*1 Co 5:1*). Paul wants the man

We can apply the two-become-one-flesh principle to the whole field of sexual morality:

Adultery

This is wrong because the one to whom the partner has become one flesh has now broken that union. The new union is false because the sexual act is not a sign of permanent union, but is only a transitory union, and breaks the bond which has been made lifelong between the couple who are married (CCC 2380).

Homosexual Intercourse

This is wrong because it is male and female who partake of the one-flesh union, ordered and decreed by God himself, not male and male or female and female (CCC 2357).

Masturbation

This is wrong because it is not a union of one flesh at all, but a solitary act, outside of any male-female relationship (CCC 2352).

Fornication

This, an act of intercourse between male and female outside of the married relationship, is wrong because "two becoming one flesh" is not just a physical union between the couple, but a lifelong commitment. Their physical union is a sign of permanent relationship in true married intercourse, which it is not in fornication (CCC 2353).

Contraception

This prevents within marriage the full giving of love and life, as the papal document *Familiaris Consortio* states (CCC 2370):

To a language which expresses naturally the reciprocal and total giving of the spouses, contraception opposes a language objectively contradictory according to which there is no act of giving oneself totally one to the other. It issues not only in the positive refusal to the overture to life, but also in a falsification of the internal truth of conjugal love, called to be a gift of the complete and entire person. This anthropological and moral difference between contraception and recourse to periodic rhythms implies two conceptions of the person and of human sexuality irreducible one to the other (*FC, no. 32*).

Contraceptives are readily available.

excommunicated, to bring him to repentance and to his senses (*1 Co 5:5*). Paul gives us his reasons (*1 Co 6:15–20*).

The Church's teaching can seem stark and unfeeling. It certainly is demanding; but it is not impossible. Millions of people have followed the Catholic Church's teaching over the centuries, and in spite of failure after failure perhaps, have never given up, have always sought help in the sacrament of confession, and have often won famous victories over temptation of all kinds in their own lives. Thus their marriage remained secure because they would not indulge in the habit at work of casual sex. They refused to meet at the local place where homosexuals meet. They refused to see the film that they knew could lead to acts of solitary impurity.

The real battleground of the spiritual life takes place in our daily lives. One example of success is St. Augustine. He who lived with a mistress for many years heard the voice of St. Paul in Scripture, "Let your armor be the Lord Jesus Christ, and stop worrying about how your disordered natural inclinations may be fulfilled" (*Rm 13:14*), and changed his whole way of life.

It is not always easy to make one decision and change everything. As Jesus himself said to his disciples when they were asleep on the night when he was arrested,

The spirit is willing enough, but human nature is weak (*Mt 26:41*).

This is often true in many areas of our moral life; especially in sexual behavior, the force of habit can be like a leech, holding us down to the past from which we want to free ourselves. How can we live from day to day according to the Church's moral teaching, especially within a world which rejects those moral principles as nonsense? The following are simple rules which have stood the test of centuries, some of which have been restated in the new Catechism:

A. Remember that sexual sins are not always committed with full deliberation and consent.

The church teaches that to misuse our sexuality in deliberate acts of fornication, masturbation, homosexuality, etc., as described above, is seriously sinful. Such acts require us to go to confession before receiving Holy Communion again. However, as we all realize, sexual passion being so strong that it can reduce our free will, the act itself may well be less than seriously sinful, because of diminished responsibility. (The most extreme example of this is a nocturnal emission of semen, which could be during sleep, and where there is no moral responsibility whatever on the part of the man concerned.)

In other instances, particularly where a married couple are leading a normal sex life, they may find the Church's teaching on contraceptive intercourse extremely difficult to follow. They may well wish to discuss their problem with a marriage guidance counsellor, who will talk about alternative possibilities, for instance the use of the infertile period, which could be the solution in many cases. But, with the best will in the world, couples could submit to the pressure of temptation, or perhaps one partner is determined to follow the moral teaching of the Church, and the other not. Here there is surely a case of diminished responsibility.

The golden rule is, always discuss these matters with your confessor, whom you will find sympathetic, knowledgeable, and used to dealing with these issues.

B. Remember that self-mastery often takes time.

The new Catechism was written with two thousand years of experience on the part of the Church in dealing with sinners. The Catechism argues that, in order for us to grow in unity and integrity as persons, we need to be guided not by instinct, but by free and rational choice (*CCC* 2338). This "self-mastery" is what is called "chastity" by Christian tradition, a much maligned word today. It means the ability to channel our passions into fruitful relationships. It is no more "unnatural" than redirecting a river which is about to overflow its banks and cause untold damage.

The new Catechism quotes Vatican II's Constitution on the Church in the Modern World regarding this self-mastery (*CCC* 2339). Such personal integration is a lifetime's work. As the new Catechism explains, we can never assume that we have mastered ourselves once and for all (*CCC* 2342).

Perhaps sometimes God allows us to remain with a habit unresolved, in order to prevent worse sins. It keeps us humble! The fiercest condemnations of our Lord were not against those who failed in chastity. He thundered most of all against those who were full of religious pride, and who loved money. At least sexual sin often makes us realize our human weakness, and may teach us something about love, even if imperfect love; whereas pride and avarice can make us feel happy and complacent with ourselves

God will also help us in the ups and downs that will inevitably follow: the falls and rises, the encouragements and discouragements. The new Catechism quotes St. Paul again (*CCC 2345*):

... the fruit of the Spirit is love, joy, peace, patience, kindness, goodness, trustfulness, gentleness and self-control; no law can touch such things as these. All who belong to Christ Jesus have crucified self with all its passions and its desires. Since we are living by the Spirit, let our behavior be guided by the Spirit ... (*Ga 5:22–25*).

Questions

1 Do you think that the Church will have to change its teaching on sexual ethics?

2 Is celibacy a real option for people today?

when our lives are not directed toward the good but toward our own self-satisfaction.

This is not to diminish the evil which sexual sin causes, through broken homes, self-loathing, misuse of people. But it is to encourage those who have started on the right road, and, particularly at first, may find it difficult, with perhaps many failures on that road, many stops and restarts.

C. Remember that we always have the help of God's grace.

In every age, people have transgressed the moral law, in sexual relationships as in every other sphere. What is different about our own day and age is that sexual self-control is seen not to matter. What the modern world has taken away, tragically, is the encouragement of the will to chastity.

Once, however, we realize the law of God in this area, as applied to our own lives, then the first act is to choose the good: to say, "I will not follow the path of wrong anymore," just as the alcoholic will make a determined decision never to drink again. Then, we have the most important gift of all: the help of God's grace. In fact, of course, it is God's grace which is working in us to make that radical decision for God and against the desires of the flesh.

36 The seventh commandment: respect for others' property

You shall not steal (*Ex 20:15; see Dt 5:19*).

You shall not steal (*Mt 19:18*).

The Church's teaching on sex is well known (*CCC 2401–2463*), even if often it is not correctly understood. But the Church's social teaching is much less well known. Some have called it "the Church's best kept secret."

During the twentieth century, the world has been in the grip of two rival and evil philosophies. One seems to be dead, except perhaps in China, the other still very much alive. They both relate in particular to material goods, and our acquisition and use of them individually and in society.

Communist totalitarianism

The first is the evil philosophy of Communism. This denied the right to private property for the individual, and made the individual virtually the slave of the state. The worker was a cog in the state machine, which arrogated to itself all human rights through the acquisition of the means of production. This system has now collapsed, mainly it seems through its own innate inefficiency. If you deny rights to an individual, in the end you lose the greatest resource you have in society: the people in it, who lose motivation to work and to produce the goods. The seventh commandment said, you shall not steal; and that includes the state, which has no right to steal unjustly the goods of its citizens and this includes denying them the right to own property.

Unbridled capitalism

The West rejoiced at the collapse of Communism. Religious people, who had suffered persecution from its atheism, thanked God for the end of the repression. But what have we in its place in Europe and in North America? What are we offering to the rest of the world, which is attempting to rival us in our prosperity?

The principle of investing money in a project to receive a share of interest or profit, the principle of capitalism, is not itself morally reprehensible. But, as the new Catechism states, any system which makes social relationships dependent entirely for their purpose on the profit motive is clearly immoral (*CCC 2424*) – just as immoral as Communism. It states that any system which turns people into forms of merchandise is likewise immoral (*CCC 2455*). But how much of our economic life in the

---

The new Catechism calls the paying of unjust salaries "stealing" (*CCC 2409*), that is, paying less than a living wage for work done, even if the worker accepts such an unjust wage because he or she has no choice. It also calls rigging the market "stealing," taking advantage to the detriment of one's neighbor because of privileged information about financial levels, or misappropriating funds, such as pension funds, perhaps by causing an automatic collapse of the market (*CCC 2409*). Respectable businessmen therefore can be guilty of stealing, just as much as a repeat offender sent to prison yet again for breaking and entering.

The desire for material goods is fueled by bargains and sales.

West is governed in precisely this way? How many people year after year are cast on the economic scrapheap, no longer useful to the market?

It is important to realize that what the Church calls stealing is not necessarily illegal in a particular country. It is a question of what is right or wrong morally, according to the natural law, the law of reason, conforming ultimately to the eternal law of God.

Communism and unbridled capitalism are both wrong because they take no account of the fact that the human person was made in God's image and likeness, and that all economic relationships in life must be directed toward the good of persons rather than toward profit or totalitarian power.

What are material goods for?

The Christian philosophy of material goods is based upon the fact that the human person, made in the image and likeness of God, was given dominion over the earth by God. If we are to rule the earth (*Gn 1:28*), we must acquire material goods for our needs: a place to live, food and drink, medicine and more recently machines to do our work, to build up the kind of world God wishes.

Catholic theologians have always argued that private property is necessary, in order to affirm our identity as individuals, and for the peaceful distribution of worldly goods. Otherwise, we would be continually fighting over the same loaf of bread. Finally, we are more careful to look after our own property, thus making a better world where its goods are cared for well.

However, this right to private property is not absolute, and must be balanced by other considerations (*Vatican II on the Church in the Modern World, no. 69*). The new Catechism argues, in line with the whole of Christian tradition, that the whole of the earth and its resources has been given to the whole of the human race. Because "the earth is the Lord's," he has given the whole of the earth to all of us (*CCC 2403*).

The Church teaches the right to private property, but only in the sense that a person may take what is needed for his or her needs from the common resources of the world provided by God (*CCC 2402*). This therefore requires first of all the virtue of temperance (*CCC 2407*).

This virtue teaches us to moderate our desire to possess earthly goods, remembering the needs of other human beings on this planet, and that unchecked avarice will destroy us as persons.

Respect for others' property

If we do not respect another's property, then we do not respect that person as a person.

The Church teaches that stealing something substantial, such as a large sum of money or a piece of property which was essential to a person's livelihood, could be mortally sinful, precisely because it hurts one made in God's image and likeness, a neighbor.

Stealing is often linked with violence to a person, precisely because wrenching from people what is valuable to them, and which they have justly acquired, is itself a form of violence and so is easily linked to further violence. A society which is greedy and acquisitive almost certainly will be also a violent society – as is ours at present.

Few of us perhaps may think that we could commit mortal sins of stealing. But there are many ways in which we can break this commandment.

Respect for creation

God has made human beings the lords of creation; but that lordship involves responsibility. Since all on earth belongs to God, we must respect creation as stewards of it. The new Catechism (*CCC 2415*) urges us to respect the integrity of creation, which involves essentially caring for our earth. The new Catechism also urges us to love animals, giving St. Francis of Assisi as a prime example of a saint who loved and was loved by animals (*CCC 2416*). However, the Catechism defends the right of humans to use animals for food (*CCC 2417*), and for experiments which will further scientific knowledge, excluding unnecessary cruelty; since we can use all the earth for our needs, provided we use the earth's resources temperately (*CCC 2418*). It is worth perhaps remembering that the risen Jesus ate fish with his disciples (*Jn 21:14*), taking living creatures of the sea for his sustenance. But the Catechism warns against giving animals priority over humans (*CCC 2418*), since humans are made in God's image. Many animals in the West are much better fed than humans in the Third World. The new Catechism sees that as an injustice, as a reversal of true priorities.

Social doctrine of the church

Many people say that the Church should not intervene in social and political matters, but stick to religion. The new Catechism rejects this view entirely. We understand the nature of the human

An example of stealing from the Old Testament was the story of King Ahab who stole Naboth's vineyard to extend his own royal garden, under the instigation of his wicked queen Jezebel.

When Naboth refused to sell his vineyard, because it was his family property, Jezebel and Ahab had Naboth falsely accused and put to death. The prophet Elijah met Ahab, and promised him God's punishment for murder and stealing (*1 K 21:18*).

The new Catechism lists varying ways in which we can act contrary to this commandment. It mentions work badly done (*CCC 2409*); appropriation of goods designated for common use; charging too high a price for goods; broken promises and contracts; not paying debts when we are able to do so; not paying just taxes for services rendered to us by the state; taking advantage of another's ignorance or distress to raise a price or make a person accept a deal which otherwise they would not enter into (*CCC 2410*).

The new Catechism argues (*CCC 2419*), quoting from Vatican II on the Church in the Modern World, "Christian revelation ... promotes deeper understanding of the laws of social living with which the creator has endowed man's spiritual and moral nature" (*no. 23*).

person in society better when we look at that subject in the light of God's revelation.

We have already seen how an understanding of the human person as made in God's image leads necessarily to respect for the other person's property. Looking now beyond the individual to the society in which that individual lives, we have also seen how both Communism and unbridled capitalism do not recognize human rights, but use property to enslave, either by giving the work force over entirely to market forces, or by sacrificing the individual to the collective will of the state (*CCC 2424*).

But, if we start with a Christian view of the human person, then, the new Catechism argues, we obtain enlightenment on social issues, understanding the fundamental basis of economic activity and social justice.

Economic activity and social justice

The right to work is seen by the new Catechism as a duty, stemming from God's command to us as humans to govern the earth (*CCC 2427*). By work, a person develops capacities in nature, and also can be a means of sanctification of earthly realities. St. Paul said,

> We urged you ... not to let anyone eat if he refused to work (*2 Th 3:10*)

but of course, he was referring to people who refused to work, not to those who cannot find employment.

The right to enterprise. The new Catechism underlines the right of each person to use talents and abilities to contribute to the benefit of all, and to receive the legitimate fruits of their efforts (*CCC 2429*).

Conflicts of interest. These arise from different parties promoting their own interests, in particular business interests, labor interests (unions), and public authorities. All have their part to play, says the Catechism (*CCC 2430*).

The responsibility of the state. The state has the responsibility of making sure that the market is not allowed to lead society to the situation of the unbridled capitalism referred to above; but to ensure that human rights are safeguarded (*CCC 2431*).

Business enterprises. These have the responsibility of looking not only to their own profit, but to the good of persons, even if profits are doubtless necessary to ensure investment for the future. They should afford secure employment to their employees (*CCC 2432*).

Access to work should be without discrimination of sex, disability, etc.

A just salary. This should be governed, not only by market forces, but also by the need of each person, that there should be a living wage for a week's work. The new Catechism explicitly states that the agreement of both parties is not sufficient to establish a just salary, since there may be pressures on the weaker party to accept a lower wage than is just. The just salary is established by what that individual employee needs to sustain a reasonable life for himself or herself, and for those dependent on him or her (*CCC 2434*).

A strike. This is legitimate when it is the only means whereby justice may be obtained, granted that there is a proportionate good to be obtained. In other words, it must be seen as worthwhile (*CCC 2435*). But it may not use violence to obtain its ends.

Social Security taxes. It is unjust not to pay these, if established by legitimate authority (*CCC 2436*).

The evil of unemployment. The new Catechism nearly always sees the deprivation of employment as an insult to the dignity of the one who is unemployed, and a menace to a stable life; unemployment also affects the home (*CCC 2436*).

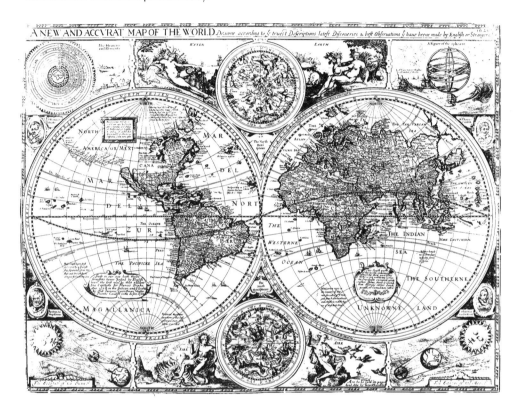

Justice and solidarity between nations

The new Catechism draws attention to the great gulf between rich and poor countries. It lists factors which keep poor countries poor: perverse structures which prevent advancement; lending debts which strangle a weak economy; commercial relationships which harm a country, particularly as related to armaments sales (*CCC 2438*).

The new Catechism insists that rich nations have an obligation to provide resources, by direct aid (*CCC 2440*) and even more by reforming international institutions to enable them to help poor countries, especially with agriculture, since the very poor are mostly peasants.

The new Catechism calls for a revival of the sense of God, which it describes as the basis of the

Can the idea of a global family ever become a reality?

complete development of human society. This will most of all ensure that material goods are put at the service of human beings, diminish exploitation, and make people open to the transcendent.

The main responsibility within the Church for working on these issues of justice lies not with the clergy, but rather with the lay people of the Church (*CCC 2442*), working in different ways according to their individual gifts. It is their responsibility

> to animate temporal realities with a Christian zeal and to conduct themselves in it as artisans of peace and of justice (*Pope John Paul II, encyclical Sollicitudo Rei Socialis, no. 47*).

Love for the poor

The Gospels are full of exhortations to help those in need. Christ himself said,

> Give to anyone who asks you, and if anyone wants to borrow, do not turn away (*Mt 5:42*);

and, to his disciples,

> You received without charge, give without charge (*Mt 10:8*).

Christ announced the Good News to the poor (*Mt 11:5; CCC 2443*).

The poor, in terms of Scripture, are those who need help. In the prophets, and later in the New Testament in the Letter of James, the rich are condemned for their hard-heartedness and love of wealth which deprives the poor of what they need (*Jm 5:1–6*).

The early Fathers of the Church insisted that, if we give the poor what is necessary to their life, we are giving them what is already theirs. This follows from the new Catechism's teaching that the world belongs to all human beings, and not to a privileged few.

That is why almsgiving is an essential Christian activity. It includes helping anyone in need with money, clothes, and personal comfort. As James again says in his Letter, it is not enough to give words of blessing to those in need: we must help them in practical ways (*Jm 2:15–16*).

Pope Gregory the Great, the pope who sent Augustine of Canterbury, then a monk in Italy, to convert the English, said:

When we give to the poor what is of necessity for them, we do not do them a personal favor, but we give them what is really theirs. We put into effect much more an act of justice than an act of charity (*Gregory the Great, Pastoral Rules 3, 21; CCC 2446*).

Questions

1 How can we practically help those who are poor and in need, first in our own country, then in the Third World?

2 What, if anything, surprises you about the social teaching of the Church as outlined above from the new Catechism of the Catholic Church?

37 The eighth commandment: telling the truth in love

You shall not give false evidence against your neighbor (*Ex 20:16*). Again, you have heard how it was said to our ancestors, *You must not break your oath, but must fulfill your oaths to the Lord.* But I say this to you, do not swear at all ... (*Mt 5:33–34*; see *CCC 2464–2513*).

This commandment forbids misrepresentation of the truth in human relationships. In the Old Testament, it was particularly aimed at false witness in court, where a person's life might be lost because of a lie told under oath. A dramatic example of false witness is the story of Susanna, chapter 13 of Daniel (found only in the Apocrypha or Deutero-Canonical Books). Susanna, a good wife who was young and beautiful, is falsely accused of adultery, for which the penalty was death; but the men accusing her, who had in fact tried to seduce her, are found out by the hero Daniel to be false witnesses, and so they suffer the death penalty themselves for perjury.

Clearly, where a falsehood could cause death or serious harm, it is a mortal sin. We cannot have the love of God in us, which includes love of neighbor, if we are prepared to destroy that person by false witness. It is not only in a court of law where a person could be destroyed by false testimony. A person can lose employment or reputation by a whispered lie or half-truth to the boss. So often, tragically, this is part of the workaday rat race. A Christian's conscience needs to be informed about the seriousness of a sin of this kind, which could be a real temptation for an ambitious career man or woman. It is just as bad, if not worse, than sins against chastity, or stealing property. To rob a person of a good name is at least as bad as stealing their virtue or their valuables; and indeed, may well lead even to destitution and being rejected by society.

If a person is guilty of false witness, then that person should go to confession and the priest

False accusation and slander are serious sins.

will ask him or her as part of the penance to undo the wrong committed and correct the falsehood by telling the truth, insofar as is possible.

Throughout our lives, it is easy to act against the truth in small ways: through gossip, judging another person, thinking the worst of their motives (*CCC 2477*); and, in this, the new Catechism gives clear guidance on how to live in the truth (*CCC 2465*) because God himself is the Truth, and his Word is faithful from age to age (*Ps 119:90*). In this way, we are helped, as the old saying goes, to "tell the truth and shame the devil," who is, as Jesus said, the "father of lies" (*Jn 8:44*).

Witnessing to the truth

Paul tells Timothy that

> you are never to be ashamed of witnessing to our Lord (*2 Tm 1:8*).

It is possible to work with a fellow Christian for years without knowing he or she is a practicing Christian, especially today when religion is sometimes a taboo subject. More important than what we say is our example in the practice of our Christian lives. However, this cannot give us an excuse not to speak about our faith when opportunity presents itself, as it often does, particularly when we are wide awake for such an opportunity. There is no doubt that Christianity, and indeed the Catholic Church, is losing by default, because so often people who believe in it are not speaking up for it.

We should examine our conscience, to see whether we are taking the opportunities presenting themselves to speak up for Christ. This might well include better informing ourselves about our faith in order to be better prepared for such testimony. The new Catechism refers to the martyrs, witnesses for Christ, who were happy to die rather than not confess Christ and his Church.

Telling the truth in love

Acting according to the truth will sometimes lead us to react differently depending on the circumstances. At one time someone might reveal certain facts about a person, though at other times they might withhold such information because to do so will harm that person. Here, it is a question of the demands of truth, and the even higher demands of charity.

A group of people will sometimes join together in running a person down, particularly in his or her absence. It is easy in such a situation to join in, and to gain quick popularity by revealing faults which

The Catechism quotes the great bishop and martyr Ignatius of Antioch (*A.D. 35–c.107*), who was thrown to the lions at the public games. Ignatius said this to his fellow Christians, who were trying to persuade him to tone down his message and so save his life:

I count as nothing the charms of the world, nor the kingdoms of this age. It is better for me to die in Christ Jesus, than to rule over the ends of the earth. It is him whom I seek, who has died for us; him whom I desire, who has risen for us. My birth approaches ... (*Ignatius, Epistle to the Romans, 4,1. CCC 2474*).

Ignatius saw his approaching violent death in the Roman circus as a new birth in Christ, because he lived for, and was prepared to die for, the truth.

are so far unknown to the group. The new Catechism says that this is wrong, since there is no reason why that person should be harmed. It is better for a person's faults not to be known, if there is no sufficient reason for them to be known apart from the perverse enjoyment which the group has in running down another's reputation.

The new Catechism also points out as wrong the encouragement of people in their wrongdoing by flattery or complacency (*CCC 2480*). It can require a great deal of courage in some circumstances to refuse to encourage such wrongdoing, particularly if such is being committed by someone who is more powerful than we are. Sometimes even our silence could imply consent, and so in such circumstances we would be compelled in conscience to speak out. This is part of everyone's obligation to help a fellow human being in our search for right action, in terms of our ultimate goal of life with God who is Truth.

We all realize that lying is wrong (*CCC 2482–2487*). But, as with all these instances, the gravity of the sin involved must depend upon many circumstances which common sense reveals to us. If lying would harm a person greatly, it could be a mortal sin; but the daily half-truths which we tell would normally come into the category of venial sin, or daily faults.

In this connection, it is often difficult to tell the difference objectively between lying and just withholding information which the person has no right to receive, or which would be harmful for that person to receive. Thus the new Catechism speaks of the right to receive information (*CCC 2488*), and also, paradoxically, of the obligation for priests to keep the seal of the confessional, which is absolute (*CCC 2490*), and the obligation of not revealing professional and state secrets. These can only be revealed under special circumstances (for instance a court case, or request from the highest state authority).

Thus parents will withhold information from children which they consider to be damaging for them at a tender age. A teacher might hold back a very bad mark so as not to hurt a weak pupil who is trying hard.

These methods of equivocation and concealment have to be watched. People can also become habitual deceivers. Doctors can so easily avoid telling awkward truths to a patient about the gravity of that person's illness when it is better for the patient to know the truth. In this matter of "telling the truth in love," each of us needs the help of God's grace to give us wisdom daily. How much more do those organizations involved in widespread dissemination

The new Catechism condemns temerarious judgment, which reveals the faults of another based upon insufficient evidence; backbiting, which reveals the faults of another which are true in fact, but without sufficient reason; and calumny, which tells falsehoods about another which damage that person's reputation (*CCC 2477*). The gravity of the sin will depend upon the gravity of the damage likely to be done to the victim.

Often, there is a very thin line between not revealing information to one who has no right to know, and a direct lie. A group of thugs searching for a victim might ask a helpless, frightened bystander to give them information about the victim's whereabouts: "Which way did he go?" The reply which deceives the thugs ("He went left" when really he went right) may be a concealed way of saying "You have no right to know." As also in business, where "He is at a meeting" sometimes means "He does not want to see you." (This latter example is certainly not a shining example of ethics at work.)

of information need God's grace and guidance in communicating truthfully and with love.

Potential for good

Many people criticize mass media. They allege sensationalism, distortion, bias, overemphasis of sex and violence. There is lively controversy over whether media reflect society or intensify its corruption. Much discussion ignores or takes for granted the immense enrichment that the media bring to our lives.

Never in history has such richness and diversity been available to every household in the country and so cheaply. Radio and the printed word combine with television to bring into our homes the greatest works of human genius and the current picture of the world.

Obviously there are silly, pernicious and brutalizing programs as well. The media can harm as well as help. We can be exposed to unhealthy and corrupting influences. There is constant need for discrimination on the part of the audience and reader and for a positive response to producers of programs and editors of newspapers. Passive silence signifies assent. Mass media are the nervous system of modern society. They are the means by which we speak and listen to each other. They bring us images of the world around us. The Christian has to take part in this ceaseless conversation.

Mass media and the Catholic Church

The Second Vatican Council is confident and enthusiastic about what the mass media can do for the world. In its document on social communications, it says that the media are there for the good of everyone, helping to bring people closer together and to understand each other by sharing knowledge and fears. They are seen to offer a "great round table" for humanity and "like salt and light add savor to the world."

The mass media are also presented as crucial to carrying out Christ's command to teach all nations. If the Church fails to use the media in this way she is accused of refusing to obey God and of "burying the talent" given by him.

The media have a threefold role – helping the Church reveal herself to the world, encouraging dialogue in the Church, and making current opinion clear to members of the Church. In many cases the media are the only communication between the Church and the world. In a country where few go to church, the only time the majority of people are in contact with religious teaching or news is through radio, television or newspapers. The media can also help Catholics to have a stronger experience of belonging to the universal Church.

How, for instance, do Catholics, even those who do attend church, know what the Pope is saying? It is mostly through Catholic newspapers. As the Pope travels more and more and as, partly because of this, interest increases in Catholic affairs, the national press, radio and television also report the Pope's words – though not always without bias or omission.

One of the greatest and most widely seen communications of forgiveness was surely the photograph of Pope John Paul II sitting closely and looking with compassion on the man who had tried to kill him in 1981.

Looking at other possibilities for good offered by the media, the Council suggests they could help overcome illiteracy, spread art and culture, further equality and help people to relax by "lightening burdens and filling leisure."

Among the very few negative comments that the Council makes is a warning that viewers, listeners and readers should be discriminating about the media and not allow them to waste time or damage their faith or dignity. Parents are reminded of their responsibility to keep dangerous material out of their homes, and priests are asked to help people to make the best use of the media.

Clergy or lay people taking part in programs must do so professionally and well because people have become used to high standards.

Most programs and articles contain a message whether the recipients realize it or not. They are often created with a motive. So many values and standards are constantly being preached. Objective programs or articles do not exist. The camera, tape recorder or typewriter is in the hands of one person. They only reveal as much as they decide, and this is not always the whole truth.

When Pope John Paul went to Poland in 1979, he celebrated Mass with some two million people at Auschwitz. Polish television cameramen were instructed to keep their cameras on a small side entrance to the camp which only relatively few people were using.

Information and freedom of opinion are important for the running of society, but as the Second Vatican Council points out, this must be "true and complete," not always easy when even the most responsible reporters involved have so little time to discover what has happened and to assess it.

Finally the new Catechism speaks of the importance of the beauty of art in leading us to God (*CCC 2500–2503*). Art shows something of the beauty of God in the beauty of his creation, revealed in Christ, the true form of God, the image of his substance (*Heb 1:3*). Following Christ leads us not only to the truth, but also to what is infinitely beautiful, the infinite love of God in the face of Jesus Christ.

Questions

1 Just how bad do you think are those "little white lies"?

2 To what extent do we now have a dishonest society?

38 The ninth and tenth commandments: a new heart

You shall not set your heart on your neighbor's house. You shall not set your heart on your neighbor's spouse, or servant, man or woman, or ox, or donkey, or any of your neighbor's possessions (*Ex 20:17; cf. Dt 5:21*).

You have heard how it was said, *You shall not commit adultery.* But I say this to you, if a man looks at a woman lustfully, he has already committed adultery with her in his heart (*Mt 5:27–28*).

For wherever your treasure is, there will your heart be too (*Mt 6:21*).

The usual Catholic numbering of the Ten Commandments separates out the commandment not to covet into two, as does the new Catechism. In the Catholic catechetical tradition, as the new Catechism states (*CCC 2514*), the ninth commandment forbids concupiscence of the flesh, and the tenth commandment proscribes coveting the goods of another person. In catechesis within the Protestant tradition, these two commandments are combined into one against coveting of all kinds.

This law against coveting was first promulgated at a time when a man's wife tended to be seen as a piece of his personal property like his house and his cattle. The way this commandment is framed could give that impression; thus the wisdom of tradition separating these two commandments into forbidding coveting people sexually and coveting property.

However, putting these two commandments together in a single chapter has the advantage of seeing the common root of covetousness, both of people and of their property. The root word is

The heart for the Hebrew symbolized more than romance ... It was the seat of human feelings and emotions.

180

concupiscence which means "strong desire or lust." Desires, whether of people or of things, are not in themselves wrong, but spring from our instincts. The problem is that concupiscence is the effect of original sin, where our instincts became disordered. Whereas baptism cleanses us from original sin by giving us the new life of God, and forgives us all our sins, our disordered nature still remains to haunt us – what St. Paul calls the "Old Adam."

Paul sees clearly that there is a battle daily going on within him, even as a committed Christian. This disordered nature inside him fights against the new life of Christ; and it is this which turns basically good desires into inordinate lust, whether of people or of things. This Paul often calls *sarx*, flesh in the sense of disordered physical desire.

Concupiscence turns true love, which is desiring the good of another person, into lust, which is the desire to possess either another person for one's own pleasure, or another person's goods. In either case, the good of that person whose person or goods are lusted after is swamped by overwhelming desire for sex with them, or avaricious desire for their property often expressing itself in envy.

What is the answer to concupiscence, this law of sin and death in us? Obviously, for St. Paul, it is to choose the other law, "the law of the Spirit which gives life in Christ Jesus," which has set us free from the law of sin and death (*Rm 8:1*). This daily struggle is an essential part of the Christian life, and we need the help of God and of other people, particularly spiritual directors and good confessors. It is a struggle essentially for our heart, the most important part of us according to Scripture.

> So I find this rule: that for me, where I want to do nothing but good, evil is close at my side. In my innermost self I dearly love God's law, but I see that acting on my body there is a different law which battles against the law in my mind. So I am brought to be a prisoner of the law of sin which lives inside my body (*Rm 7:21–23*).

The pure heart

The ninth and tenth commandments, against coveting, are unique among the Ten Commandments, in that the other commandments carry a legal penalty against their transgression. For instance, one who committed murder or adultery was put to death according to Old Testament law. But of course, there could be no legal penalty against an impure heart, since what goes on in our heart is secret and cannot be the object of sanctions by laws which can only punish external actions.

In this way, the Ten Commandments go beyond criminal laws, and touch the heart of the person. The heart, for the Hebrew, was not that of medical science, the pump which sends blood around the body. It was the seat of human feelings and emotions. Even today, we refer to a person having a

John the Baptist, who baptized Jesus, was also pure of heart.

God says, "I shall give you a new heart, and put a new spirit in you; I shall remove the heart of stone from your bodies and give you a heart of flesh instead. I shall put my spirit in you, and make you keep my laws, and respect and practice my judgments" (*Ezk 36:26-27*).

"big heart," meaning that they have courage and human vision. As a result of sin, the human race had a "wicked heart" (*Gn 6:5*); but the prophet Ezekiel promised that, in the new age, when the Holy Spirit came, the heart of everyone would be cleansed and purified.

Jesus, in his teaching, focused on the heart and its conversion as the very center of his message. He saw the heart as the principle of all sin, teaching that no one was defiled by disobeying external rituals of washing and so on. Rather,

> from the heart come evil intentions: murder, adultery, fornication, theft, perjury, slander. These are the things that make a person unclean (*Mt 15:19–20*).

For Jesus, the basis of all action pleasing to God was a pure heart. In the sixth beatitude, Jesus said,

> Blessed are the pure in heart: they shall see God (*Mt 5:8*).

How do we ourselves, then, acquire this pure heart?

One who has a pure heart will also, according to the new Catechism (*CCC 2518*), maintain orthodoxy of faith. This is hardly considered a virtue today, since there is a lot of encouragement of the freedom of the individual to believe what he or she wishes, without the constriction of dogma. While emphasizing the right of making the act of faith free and individual, the Church has always insisted that faith is essentially an act of obedience to God who reveals. This is not first and foremost an act of feeling or experience, but a reasonable act of the submission of the mind and will to the Word of God revealed to us in Scripture and in Tradition. Feeling and experience can and must play their part in the act of faith. But faith is not first and foremost the act of one who is on a "religious high." One who has a pure heart will believe because of what God has said and done in Christ, as testified in the Church, and not because of feelings that can be generated at a religious meeting. As St. Paul says,

> faith comes from hearing, and that means hearing the word of Christ (*Rm 10:17*).

Finally, says the Catechism (*CCC 2519*), purity of heart will enable us to see God, to see the other person as the Temple of the Holy Spirit, a manifestation of the divine beauty.

The battle for purity

Purity of heart will not be obtained without a long struggle, in fact the struggle of a lifetime. The new Catechism mentions purity of intention; purity of thought; the need for prayer (*CCC 2520*); the need for decency and modesty to protect chastity; the need for the purification of the social climate; the need to eradicate false views of freedom in permissiveness (*CCC 2523–2527*).

Avarice: the lust of the eyes

There is a distinction made between lusts of the flesh, which relate to sexual temptation, and the desire for other people's property.

Lust for goods or wealth is a much more subtle temptation of the heart than is lust of the flesh. This is so first of all because society approves those who are "go-getters." A salesman being interviewed for a job was told by a manager, "We want really greedy people for this job." Avarice often seems to serve the purposes of business, because it makes a person want to promote the good of the company by promoting his or her own interests.

Secondly, avarice can deeply affect our lives even more than problems of chastity. The boundless desire for wealth can destroy human relationships, because people totally devoted to making money put everything second to it, including marriage. It also leads to aggression, because anything or anyone who stands in the way must be removed. It will not always lead to penalties on this earth, because a clever person will often work within the law of the state in order to gain wealth; but in conscience, that person knows that, in the eyes of God, his or her true god is that of possessions. As Jesus said,

Wherever your treasure is, there will your heart be too (*Mt 6:21*).

The new Catechism defines those who are pure of heart as those who strive for holiness in their mind and in their will (*CCC 2518*), instead of being governed by concupiscence, their unruly instincts. The Catechism locates this purity in three areas:

Love or charity, that is, the theological virtue whereby we love God and our neighbor with the love of God. One with a pure heart, therefore, will eradicate selfishness and seek the genuine good of others, especially those in need.

Sexual chastity. One with a pure heart will not desire another's body for pleasure, or indeed their own body for pleasure, but will desire what is truly good for the other person. Of course, right sexual intercourse within marriage is itself an act of chastity, because it is an act of union where two genuinely become one flesh. But, even within marriage, the sexual act can become unchaste, where it is contraceptive, or where one partner is using the other purely for pleasure, and perhaps being inconsiderate to the other partner. It is not the pleasure of the sexual act which is wrong. That is good, and binds the marriage together. Rather, it is using the other person's body merely for pleasure which is an act of unchastity, for this does not proceed from a pure heart.

The love of the truth and rightness of faith. A person who strives for a pure heart will of necessity have a sincere mind; she will have integrity. That person will love the truth, not only in religious matters, but indeed in every area of life. A supreme example of a pure heart was John the Baptist, who denounced the people of his day for injustice and hypocrisy, and in the end was beheaded for telling King Herod unpopular home truths about his wrong relationships (*Mt 14:3–12*). In 1980 Archbishop Oscar Romero was shot dead in church for denouncing the injustices in his country, El Salvador. The Fathers of the Church insisted that anyone who died for justice died for Christ, because Christ is the justice of God revealed to us all.

Everything there is in the world – disordered bodily desires, disordered desires of the eyes, pride in possession – is not from the Father but is from the world. And the world, with all its disordered desires, is passing away. But whoever does the will of God remains for ever (*1 Jn 2:16–17*).

When the Law tells us: "You shall not covet," it tells us, in other words, to separate our desires from all that does not belong to us. For the lust for the goods of our neighbor is immense, infinite and never satisfied.

The old Roman Catechism, written more than four hundred years ago, is most perceptive about this. It says that avarice is not only a sin when we desire the goods of another in a way which breaks the law. It is also wrong for a businessman to be happy when his business rivals are in a state of bankruptcy when that means more for him (*CCC 2537*), or for doctors to desire people to become ill, particularly wealthy ones, in order for him or her to make a profit.

Avarice is the desire for what belongs to another; but this is not necessarily, in the legal sense, stealing. Taking this commandment in conjunction with what has been said about the seventh, against stealing, we steal whenever we acquire more than what we need, and what someone else needs. Thus, when we desire more than our needs, in that sense we desire what should belong to someone else. Needs, of course, differ, and are relative to many factors. St. Thomas Aquinas justified the accumulation of wealth in terms of social need. Some in positions of authority in business or in politics need greater personal resources than private individuals.

This raises the problem of mixed motives. A person has to ask, does my desire for more money arise because I need to develop myself and my dependents? Or is it pure avarice? In most of us, there are a mixture of reasons for our actions. What is important is that we examine our conscience honestly, with our spiritual director, to see whether we are being consumed by greed rather than being motivated by a just desire to better ourselves and our families.

The new Catechism underlines the importance of examining our consciences to find any trace of envy, referred to as a capital vice, that is a vice which is the root cause of other vices and sins. Envy can itself be a mortal sin, when it leads to us being happy when a serious misfortune comes to the person whom we envy (*CCC 2539*).

Life in the Spirit

How are we to conquer avarice and envy? The new Catechism gives us three ways.

First, to make a deliberate choice to follow the Spirit of God, by dying with Christ to all unruly passions of whatever kind (*CCC 2543*). The new Catechism reminds us that

The Catechism quotes what Gregory the Great, a pope in the sixth century, wrote about envy:

St. Augustine sees in envy "the devilish sin par excellence." "From envy is born hatred, slander, calumny, delight caused by the misfortune of one's neighbor and displeasure caused by his or her prosperity."

The Catechism further quotes John Chrysostom (*CCC 2540*) in encouraging us to be happy at the success of others, a happiness which envy will always deny to us.

All who belong to Christ Jesus have crucified self with all its passions and its desires (*Ga 5:24*).

Second, to acquire the gift of poverty of heart (*Mt 5:3*) which is the spirit of detachment from the things of this world (*CCC 2545*). This does not mean that we do not care for the things of this world, insofar as they are God's gift to us for our use, and for the use of others; rather, that we realize that whatever we possess is only for a time, whether wealth, position, or personal talent. A person who puts his or her trust in riches or power will ultimately always be disappointed (*Lk 6:24*).

Third, the new Catechism recommends that we focus our minds on the VISION OF GOD, which is our ultimate happiness in heaven. The new Catechism quotes Gregory of Nyssa:

> The promise to see God surpasses every happiness. In Scripture, to see is to possess. One who sees God has obtained all the good things which are possible to conceive (*CCC 2548*).

This last point is surely the most important in all the moral teaching of the Church. On this earth, we cannot see God, only the thing he has made. It is easy therefore to imagine that our happiness is to be found in the things we can see, whether possessions, power or people, for our own pleasure. But this happiness will never be complete, because there is always within us the desire for the Infinite, for God himself. This desire is perverted by concupiscence, the desire for God gone wrong in inordinate desire for possessions.

God wishes us to opt for happiness in him in this life, to the exclusion of everything opposed to this, in order to prepare for that final indescribable happiness with him in heaven. In Catholic teaching, this option is not made once for all, except insofar as our baptism is a once-for-all act on God's part which cleanses us from original sin and gives us the life of God. We have to make a daily decision to walk with Christ on the road to God, in company with fellow members of his Church.

Questions

1 How can we help each other to develop morally?

2 Do you think that a moral life is possible without Christian faith?

39 The Church: its life of prayer

Religion is the development of a personal relationship towards the mysterious Other: God, whom we do not see, but who we know is sometimes more present to us than we are to our own selves. The most important way to develop this is through prayer.

Why do we pray? People often pray for things. They also pray that God will heal them or make their life prosperous, or even end their life if they are suffering terribly. People who never go to church will often pray in times of need.

Some people think it selfish to pray for our own interests. If that is our only prayer, that is a fair criticism. But intercessory prayer is important, because it shows that we believe that this mysterious One, the creator of the universe, has our interests at heart, and can be "bothered" by our little concerns. Intercessory prayer is at least the beginning of the realization that God is our heavenly Father who loves us.

If this were the only kind of prayer we could say, it would still be worthwhile, because it expresses our relationship with God. Intercessory prayer is also based upon the realization that God actually answers our requests. How this happens, it is impossible to know. We only see the effects of God's plan in history. But it is important to realize that the ultimate cause is God. His answers are often surprising, sometimes shattering. But answers we do receive, if we are prepared to listen.

However, as we develop our relationship with God, we soon realize that it is selfish just to ask all the time. A baby begins by always crying for food or comfort. But soon, in a good parent-child relationship, genuine love develops.

So it is with God. The normal development of the life of prayer, in particular if we pray each day of our lives (which is the most recommended practice), leads to genuine love of God, with his help of course. We soon desire to be with God as much as we desire to be with a loved human being – even though, like human relationships, our love of God has its ups and downs.

The highest form of prayer is what is called the "mystical experience," the experience of being possessed by the love of God. This mysticism is sometimes accompanied by ecstasy.

These experiences occasionally happen because to grow in the love of God means that we can eventually love him totally. And, love can be crazy.

For most of us, prayer is basically a down-to-earth daily affair. Mystical experiences are rare, and they are not the most important thing. What matters is that our prayer life should lead to a union of heart and will with God. And this can happen to everyone. There is a simple aid to remembering the ideal order for prayer – the mnemonic "Acts." That is: adoration, contrition, thanksgiving, and supplication.

Prayer is not only a duty. It is our right as human beings to become lovers of the Lord of the universe.

Many people wonder, "What shall I say when I pray?" Sometimes, it is best to use your own words, to avoid repetition. But, for those who make prayer a daily practice, we soon find that we run out of words of our own.

Praying like the first Christians?

God created us to be holy. It sounds less alarming if we call it "wholeness," our whole being saying yes to God in love and joining into union with him. We cannot slice off a portion of ourselves or of our day and label that "spiritual." Our aim is to love God all day.

All the same, we will not recognize what God is asking unless we spend time looking at his Face.

The "Face" of God is Jesus. He alone has seen the Father, and he reflects him to us. We look at Jesus in two main ways. First, and most important, we see him and are drawn into his sacrifice in the Holy Mass. At Mass, Jesus gives himself, and though we may notice nothing, he slowly changes us into our true selves.

The more faithful we are to the Mass, the more we will understand that we must also pray alone if we want to know God intimately. When we are with other people, we are upheld by their faith and prayer, as well as by our own.

No one can tell us exactly what to do. An old man once said that he just sat in front of the tabernacle, where the Sacrament is reserved in church, and "I look at him, and he looks at me."

It is the real me who stands before the real God in all spirituality.

Catholic spirituality – past treasures

One of the greatest encouragements to prayer is "spiritual reading," either of Scripture or of one of the great mystics in the history of the Church. When we read one or other of the spiritual giants of the past, we begin to realize that prayer is a rich and varied subject.

Prayer should be the center of our whole day. We stand before God holding out our lives to his all-seeing but merciful gaze.

Two ways

Early on in the Church two different ways of integrating life and prayer became apparent. The first was for Christians to continue living in the secular world. The baptismal promises to renounce Satan and his works and to devote oneself to Christ express the seriousness with which this lay vocation

The new Catechism (CCC 2558) begins the section on prayer with a beautiful quotation from St. Thérèse of Lisieux:

For me, prayer is a bursting out of the heart; it is a simple look thrown up towards heaven; it is a cry of recognition and of love in the midst of temptation and in the midst of joy (*Autobiography, C.25r*).

All Christians are called to make their lives an extension of their prayer, so that we ourselves become "a living sacrifice, dedicated and acceptable to God" (*Rm 12:1*).

was taken. This was one reason why many were not baptized as children, but, like St. Ambrose, waited until they felt prepared to take on its commitments.

The second way was that of Christians who decided to cut themselves off from ordinary life in order to devote themselves exclusively to following Christ. At first this took the form of a life of solitude, such as that of St. Anthony, who seventeen hundred years ago retired into the Egyptian desert. Gradually similar hermits began to form groups which combined solitude with mutual support. A more common type of religious community was the monastery, in which monks prayed and worked together. St. Benedict's Rule in the sixth century provided the classical pattern for this kind of life.

New forms of religious orders developed in response to different needs of the Church. In the tenth century St. Bruno returned to the early pattern of the community of hermits when founding his order of Carthusians. In the next century the Cistercians (among whom St. Bernard is the best known) sought a stricter interpretation of St. Benedict's rule.

A new style of religious order, which aimed at a greater simplicity and mobility than was possible in the fixed life of the monastic orders, emerged in the thirteenth century. The two great examples were the Franciscan and Dominican friars, who provided a model which was subsequently adapted by the many active congregations which have been founded since. Each of the rules was followed by both women and men.

The expansion of religious orders had the unfortunate result that the pursuit of holiness could be seen as a specialist activity of monks and nuns which was beyond the aspirations of the laity. Vatican II firmly rejected this view, declaring that

> all Christians in any state or walk of life are called to the fullness of Christian life and to the perfection of love (*Church, no. 40*).

One of the most striking developments since Vatican II has been the flowering of many movements devoted to fostering

Some are called to dedicate their life to prayer.

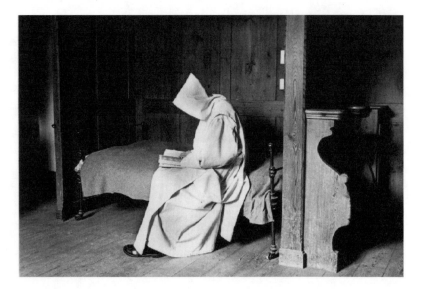

the holiness of the laity. Possibly more lay people than ever are devoting themselves today to serious prayer.

Place for prayer

There is a danger of becoming self-centered in prayer. Jesus illustrates this in the story of the publican and the Pharisee (*Lk 18:10–13*). If prayer is just us talking to God, it can become a cozy, private experience, leaving out the problems of the world.

The force of the great commandments is to love your neighbor as well as God and yourself. There must be balance. You can see balance in Jesus who is utterly given to people, yet always manages to slip away to pray. He links his work for others – miracles, preaching, calling apostles – with gaining renewed power through that time spent in prayer.

One yardstick for judging development in prayer is the depth of concern you have for the state of the world, for such issues as justice and peace.

This does not mean dashing out to join every group, never having a moment to yourself.

What it does mean is drawing closer to God in prayer, so that "the mind is in you which is in Jesus Christ." His concern is for all the world; yours becomes as wide. This concern shows in your life as your generosity and self-giving grow from your prayer. It is not easy to stand, sit or kneel before God humbly and openly, and then ignore the "cries of the prisoners."

Prayer and work

Once the sisters in one of St. Teresa of Avila's convents were complaining that there was so much work about the house that they had no time to pray. St. Teresa remarked firmly: "God moves among the pots and pans as well."

It seems to be difficult for people to allow prayer to be part of daily happenings. Time should certainly be set aside for God in prayer each day, but St. Paul's command was "Pray at all times."

Specifically here, we are considering what part prayer has in two ingredients of our daily living – work and leisure.

When working, we are supposed to be working. So prayer has to be introduced and become a habit by taking it as a natural part of life. This part needs sanctification as much as any other, and needs to recognize God's presence. Each individual should find a personal way. It may simply be a case of introducing God before and after work, on the way to work, an ejaculatory prayer and so on. These can be very short, a "glance at God" or a "hello."

Prayer

Lord, make me an instrument of your peace.
Where there is hatred let me sow love,
where there is injury let me sow pardon,
where there is doubt let me sow faith,
where there is despair let me give hope,
where there is darkness let me give light,
where there is sadness let me give joy.
O Divine Master, grant that I may not try to be comforted but to comfort
not try to be understood but to understand,
not try to be loved but to love.
Because it is in giving that we receive,
it is in forgiving that we are forgiven,
it is in dying that we are born to eternal life.
(St. Francis of Assisi)

In leisure, equally important to a balanced life, much depends upon how time is being spent. When one is involved in many leisure pursuits, God can be almost tangibly present in the scenery, in painting, in music, in personal contact with a friend. At other times we can be so taken up in a particular sport, family party at home, or any other activity, that God is forgotten. Here again, we must do what we can and remember that Jesus relaxed with his friends.

> Whatever you say or do, let it be in the name of the Lord Jesus, in thanksgiving to God the Father through him (*Col 3:17*).

An ancient practice in Christian prayer is to give some time each evening to an examination of the day gone by. This falls into a pattern of good and bad happenings, actions, words, thoughts and so on.

It is a review of the day in the presence of God. You open yourself so that the searchlight of his goodness and love lights up your personal human response to the day.

The object of the exercise is to reconcile your way of life during twenty-four hours with the will of God, his love and his service. This is not an exercise in guilt, but a genuine and positive assessment of your success or failure – or even indifference – as a follower of Jesus Christ.

Question

When and where in our lives do we feel God closest to us? What image of God do we have when we pray? Do we pray to one of the Persons of the Trinity (Father, Jesus, or Holy Spirit)? Is there a particular reason for this?

40 God's own prayers

Experiencing God – in prayer

Praying because we simply believe is essential. It does not deny but supplements the use of reason. For prayer experience we need Scriptural study, the use of theological insights, shared experience of Christian living, and practical involvement in loving God, self and neighbor.

In the Old Testament, God is so holy that his name is not to be used. Adonai was substituted. God is distant, the smiter of enemies, the judge. People reading and even teaching the Old Testament can miss the trust shown by Abraham in prayer, the close contact of Jacob wrestling with the angel, the forgiveness of David, the immense patience of God as he reclaims Israel again and again from idolatry.

Yet God is also portrayed more gently:

> I have loved you with an everlasting love (*Jr 31:3*).

> As a mother comforts a child, so shall I comfort you (*Is 66:13*).

Patriarchs, prophets and writers of the Psalms experienced his tenderness and closeness.

We share their experience when we read the Old Testament.

The new Catechism sums up its teaching on the Psalms by stating that the Psalter is the book where the Word of God becomes the prayer of humanity (*CCC 2587*). The Catechism quotes the words of St. Ambrose of Milan:

> What could there be better than a psalm? That is why David said very well: "Praise the Lord, for the psalm is a good thing; to our God, sweet and beautiful praise!" And that is true. For the psalm is a blessing pronounced by the people, praise of God by the assembly, applause by all, word spoken by the universe, melodious profession of faith ... (Ambrose, *On the First Psalm, 1,9*).

When reading or praying the Psalms we eavesdrop on the private prayer life of a people. The soul of Israel is exposed with an honesty and frankness which, to the modern Christian, can be disconcerting.

At the root of Israel's spirituality is faith in God's steadfast love and faithfulness. It is based on a "creed": the account of God's choice of Israel to be his special possession, and the history of the wonderful works that he performed in bringing the people out of Egypt and into the promised land (*Ps 105; 136*). Israel's destiny is to be the kingdom of God on earth.

Three main types of psalms have been identified: hymns, petitions, and thanksgiving.

Hymns are songs of praise (*Ps 100*). They begin with an invitation or statement of intent to praise God, followed by the reasons for such praise. Two reasons predominate: God's wonderful works in creation (*Ps 104*), and God's wonderful works in salvation (*Ps 135*). These include God's continued care for creation and constant care for his people, especially the humble and afflicted (*Ps 113*). God is the center of these psalms, and the person of the psalmist does not intrude or distract.

Petitions begin with a cry for help or with a statement of need (*Ps 5:2*). The plight of the petitioner forms the main interest. With frank simplicity the psalmist professes his own innocence and righteousness (*Ps 17*) while at the same time drawing attention to the malice and treachery of his enemy. He may suggest to God ways and means of dealing with his enemy (*Ps 109*). These are the "cursing" psalms. God is even reminded that it is to his advantage that one of his worshipers should be saved and not lost (*Ps 6:4f; 58:10*).

These psalms often end on a note of confidence, almost as though the prayer had been answered.

Thanksgiving psalms result from petitions that have been answered. They focus on the need of the psalmist who relates how God came to his aid in answer to his prayer. The occasion is sometimes used as a lesson for others and to that extent these psalms could be termed "didactic" or "teaching" (*Ps 34*). The language is often strongly figurative (*Ps 18:88*), and seldom can the precise situation be identified. This gives them a universal application.

The spirituality of the Psalms is influenced by the writers' view of life and death. There is some sort of existence in Sheol but no life after death. Reward for goodness, punishment for evil and the realization of God's kingdom are features of life on earth. Consequently, justice means the removal of those who cause injustice; peace means the end of war and the destruction of the enemy, who is also God's enemy.

There is also a strong sense of "balance": the lowly cannot be lifted up without the mighty being brought low; the hungry fed without the rich being sent away empty. This gives rise to what seems to be a vindictive streak. The psalmist prays for the destruction of enemies, in the most forthright language (*Ps 109; 137:8*). He is frank in protesting his own innocence and honesty. He also admits his own sinfulness and the disloyalty of his people (*Ps 51; 106*). He expresses his anger at God for the way he is treated (*Ps 44; 88*). He even tells God to get up and do something (*Ps 44:23*).

How many of the 150 Psalms David wrote or sang, it is impossible to say. Even those 73 psalms which are entitled "Of David" could have been dedicated "to" him, or written "for" him, rather than written "by" him. The Hebrew word used, *le*, can have all those meanings.

Themes may suggest when certain psalms were used. "Royal" psalms celebrate the kingship of God (*Ps 47; 96*). Others honor the human king and were probably used at his coronation (*Ps 110*), his wedding (*Ps 45*), his departure for war (*Ps 20*) and his return (*Ps 21*). The regal language of the ancient East makes these psalms exuberant. The king is God's son, "begotten by God." All the nations of the earth are to be subject to him (*Ps 2*). The reality was very different (*Ps 89*). This language allowed for a reinterpretation or "rereading" of these psalms, to refer to the King of the future (*Ps 72*), the Messiah. This is how they are quoted in the New Testament.

"Pilgrim" psalms recall the beginning (*Ps 112*), the journey and arrival at Jerusalem (*Ps 48; 84*). Jerusalem is the place of God's chosen dwelling (*Ps 46*). These psalms, too, take on a further meaning when given a messianic interpretation (*Ps 87*).

But David still more than merits the title "man of the Psalter." He inspired the worship and the music of God's people through centuries.

A shepherd boy in the fields of Bethlehem is summoned by the prophet Samuel, and is anointed future king. He slays a giant, Goliath, and enters the court of King Saul as a court musician, to soothe the king's frayed nerves.

Eventually, Saul is killed in battle, and David is crowned king. He captures Jerusalem and sets up his capital there, bringing in the Ark of the Covenant as the focus of regular worship, and celebrating the entry into the city with music and dancing. He destroys the Philistine armies.

David during his lifetime was already a national hero. But not all his actions were heroic; for example he sent one of his best soldiers, Uriah the Hittite, to certain death, in order to marry Uriah's beautiful wife Bathsheba.

And David was overindulgent with his son Absalom, who rebelled against him. Absalom was killed hanging from his hair caught in a tree and David was inconsolable.

David's spirituality and rich personality seem often to be reflected in the Psalms. His strong faith in Yahweh. His penitence. The way in which he speaks of God personally, even in anger. His suffering. His joy. His passion and his love.

A note on numbering

The numbering of the Psalms can be confusing. Older Catholic translations were one figure behind modern versions such as the Jerusalem Bible, for most of the Psalter. That is because the older Catholic translations followed the Greek and Latin

Wonder
Yahweh our Lord, how majestic is your name throughout the world! (*Ps 8:1*).

Joy
Acclaim Yahweh, all the earth, serve Yahweh with gladness, come into his presence with songs of joy! (*Ps 100:1-2*).

Desperation
My God, my God, why have you forsaken me? The words of my groaning do nothing to save me (*Ps 22:1*).

Faith
Yahweh is my shepherd, I lack nothing (*Ps 23:1*).

In old age
Now that I am old and grey-haired, God, do not desert me (*Ps 71:18*).

Thanks for forgiveness
How blessed are those whose offense is forgiven, whose sin is blotted out (*Ps 32:1*).

numbering making Psalms 9–10 one Psalm. The Douay translation joined 114 and 115 of the Hebrew Bible but divided both 116 and 147 into two. The Jerusalem Bible has gone back to the numbering of the Psalms as found in the official Hebrew texts.

Hallelui-jah!

"Hallelui-jah" means "praise Yahweh!" There is praise of God in all the Psalms. But the final twenty psalms have a particular emphasis on praise. Psalm 150 refers to praising God with a fanfare of trumpets, and with "tambourines and dancing." It is clear that praising Yahweh involves the whole person.

Frustration
Wake, Lord! Why are you asleep? Awake! Do not abandon us for good (*Ps 44:23*).

Sorrow for sin
For I am well aware of my offenses, my sin is constantly in mind. Against you, you alone, I have sinned, I have done what you see to be wrong (*Ps 51:3-4*).

Blessing
May he save your foot from stumbling; may he, your guardian, not fall asleep! You see – he neither sleeps nor slumbers, the guardian of Israel (*Ps 121:3-4*).

Questions

1 David was Israel's greatest king. He was also an adulterer and an accomplice in murder, yet Jesus accepted the title "son of David." What do we learn about a relationship with God from the life of David?

2 The "cursing" psalms sometimes cause problems for Christians today. Study these examples: Ps 58:6–11; 137:9; 139:19–20; 140:9–12.

Have you ever felt the emotions these writers express?

What advice can you offer to Christians trying to come to terms with them?

41 Suffering

The new Catechism (*CCC 2742*) offers prayer "constantly" (*1 Th 5:17*) as the way in which we will get through and conquer all our suffering. This prayer can be informal as well as formal:

> It is possible, even if going on a solitary walk, to make a frequent and fervent prayer. Sitting down in your shop, whether about to buy or to sell or to cook the dinner (*St. John Chrysostom, Eclogue on Prayer 2*).

St. Alphonsus Liguori (*CCC 2744*) says bluntly:

> The one who prays is certainly saved; the one who does not pray is certainly damned (*St. Alphonsus, The Great Medium of Prayer*).

Some people argue that the existence of so much suffering is a reason to believe that God does not exist.

"If an infinitely good God exists," the argument runs, "why does he allow such horrible things to happen such as the Nazi holocaust?"

For Aquinas, God in creating the world with finite creatures had to allow for the possibility of evil. Only God himself is infinitely good, with no possibility of evil. That possibility of evil becomes even greater with created beings such as us humans, with free will.

The goodness of God, therefore, consists of God's being able to organize a world in which, whatever evil choices are made by human beings, and whatever natural disasters occur (disasters, that is, for some people. Disasters for some may be lucky for others), all will in the end come to good. That is why our faith in the resurrection of Jesus is so vital in order to understand suffering in the world; because that is the final part of "the plan."

One problem, however, with St. Thomas Aquinas's explanation is that it cannot explain why a particular form of suffering afflicts one person and not another. Why do some become rich, while others starve to death? Why do some have good health all their lives, while others have long and crippling illnesses? Why do some people die immediately without suffering, while others hang on for years in pain and loneliness?

With our limited knowledge, we cannot explain this. What we can say is that God loves each of us personally, and gives us the cross that is right for us.

As Paul, who suffered greatly in many ways – physically, psychologically and spiritually – said, "We are well aware that God works with those who love him, those who have been called in accordance with his purpose, and turns everything to their good" (*Rm 8:28*).

St. Thomas Aquinas, in the thirteenth century, asked "If God existed, surely no evil would be found?"; and came up with this answer: "It relates to the infinite goodness of God, that he permits evil to exist, and from it brings forth good" (*Summa Theologiae, Q.2., A.3., ad 1*).

There is a story of a man having a dream going to Joseph the carpenter to change his cross, which he thought was too heavy to bear. Joseph took his cross, and asked the man to choose another. The man searched through all the other crosses and, after a long time, finally took one. "That is just right for me," he said. Joseph replied with a smile, "That is the one you brought in."

Contrary to legend, Job did not have much patience. But he did have a lot of courage and faith.

The patience of Job

The story of Job, included among the "Wisdom" books of the Old Testament (*see ch. 7*), probably written about the fifth century B.C., proves that very point.

Why should my baby be born with a disability? Why should my child be killed or maimed in a motor accident? Why should my wife die of cancer? Why should my parents become senile and need constant care when so many others live unscathed and happy?

The misery of such tragedies makes a test of faith. Can a loving God really permit such agony? Is not the world in fact ruled by unreasoning chance and marauding forces of evil?

Job, lost in the darkness of misery – made worse by its suddenness – is at grips with just such a doubt, and yet he clings firmly to trust in God.

42 Catholic prayers in common use

Why three times

The disciples asked Jesus to teach them to pray

> as John taught his disciples (*Lk 11:1*).

Jesus gave them a prayer that summed up all we need to ask God. We know this prayer as the Lord's Prayer or the "Our Father." It is such an all-encompassing prayer that the early Christians felt it could replace the Jewish prayer texts entirely. So the early Christians said it three times daily – replacing the three times appointed for Jewish prayer.

Is the "Our Father" a "blank check" kind of prayer? Can anybody who feels that there is one creator and that the human race is one family pray it adequately? The Christian community has never thought like that. We do not deny that God is Father of all and loves all. But the Lord's Prayer can be prayed with full meaning only by those who try to live the life of Jesus and embody his attitudes.

Admittedly – and this is often a puzzle – there is no reference to the passion and resurrection of Jesus. But the passion and resurrection were possible because Jesus lived his prayer. His relationship with God and towards us is shown in it.

The secret is one word: Abba! Jesus called the awesome and omnipotent Lord by a familiar word for father. Christians were so stunned by this that they kept the word, even in other languages.

God is Abba. He is Jesus' full horizon and endless sustainer. He is to be hallowed and obeyed. He will give what is needed and preserve his loved ones in the evil hour. In Gethsemane Jesus was still saying Abba, and on Easter morning he told Mary that he was going "to my Abba and your Abba." The Lord's Prayer is the Lord's relationship with the Father. When we pray it we enter into this most sacred mystery.

The new Catechism quotes the Church Father Tertullian in saying that the Lord's Prayer is truly the résumé of the whole Gospel. Tertullian insists that

> Everyone can therefore address to heaven different prayers according to need, but in beginning always with the Prayer of the Lord which remains the basic prayer (*CCC 2761*).

We should pray the "Our Father" slowly and reflectively every day of our lives. It is the pattern of prayer. No matter how "holy" we become, we can never outgrow the "Our Father." And no matter how ignorant we might think we are of theology or religion, we can still say the "Our Father," with meaning, as our Lord's own prayer.

Each petition of the "Our Father" introduces us to an essential aspect of prayer:

Our Father, who art in heaven

We call God "Our Father," because he loves us as our creator, and he sent his Son Jesus Christ on earth to be our brother, and to lead us back to the Father. "Who art in heaven" defines

God, not in terms of space "up there," but as greater than any notion we can have of him. This thought raises up our minds and hearts to the infinite God.

Hallowed be thy name

Literally "May your name be made holy." We need in particular to recover the sense of the holiness, the "otherness" of God. Whenever we utter his "name" with reverence, we "make holy his name." All prayer should begin with reflection on the powerful truth of the unbounded presence of the all-holy God.

Thy kingdom come

Our first prayer is not for ourselves, but for God's kingdom. "Set your hearts on his kingdom first, and on God's saving justice, and all these other things will be given to you as well" said Jesus, "So do not worry about tomorrow: tomorrow will take care of itself " (*Mt 6:33-34*). It is daily an act of faith to put God's kingdom first in our lives, and to believe that God will look after our needs.

Thy will be done on earth as it is in heaven

Having addressed the prayer to God the Father in heaven, we now pray we may be able to carry out God's will on earth. We have so much evidence of God's love. But sometimes it is very hard to do his will. At such times, we remember the words of Jesus just before he was arrested in the garden of Gethsemane: "My Father, if it is possible, let this cup pass me by. Nevertheless, let it be as you, not I, would have it" (*Mt 26:39*).

Give us this day our daily bread

Having set our minds to seek God's kingdom, and to do his will, we are prepared to ask for our daily physical and spiritual needs. In asking for daily bread, that does not mean that we are not asking for butter and jam as well. God knows that we need the sweet things in life, in every sense of that word, to make life more enjoyable. But in asking for daily bread, rather than for riches, we are focusing on what we *need* for this life, rather than for always what we *want*.

Christ warned continually against avarice, the desire for possessions for their own sake, which causes inequality and injustice and destroys us.

Note also that the prayer says "Give US our daily bread," not "Give ME my daily bread." Because God made us all one people we pray for others also to have what they need. This implies that we will try to make that happen.

And forgive us our trespasses, as we forgive those who trespass against us

Christ gave one condition for forgiveness, that we forgive others their wrongs against us. See the parable he told of the unforgiving debtor (*Mt 18:23–35*). Often when we pray, we remember we need forgiveness from our heavenly Father; and we remember people who have offended us, and who need our forgiveness. It is only in daily prayer that we form the right attitudes, to ask forgiveness from God, and to become forgiving people like Jesus our Lord.

And lead us not into temptation, but deliver us from evil

To be tested is a necessary part of everything in life: business, family, school, sport, art. So also in the spiritual life. What we pray in this petition is that God will not allow us to be tempted beyond our strength, and that he will deliver us "from the Evil One," that is from Satan the adversary.

St. Paul assures us: "You can trust that God will not let you be put to the test beyond your strength, but with any trial will also provide a way out by enabling you to put up with it" (*1 Co 10:13*).

God will not desert us in our trials; what this petition secures is that we are aware of possible tests to come, and that we form attitudes of dependence on God, who alone can bring us through.

Amen!

This is a Hebrew word, used continually in our prayers, and often on the lips of Jesus himself and his people the Jews. It means "trustworthy, reliable, secure." At the end of our prayer, by saying *Amen*, we say to God, "I believe that what I have just said and done is right and true. I believe that with your help, I can now put it into practice in life."

Each one of us has access to the love of the Father through prayer and worship. This is the constant witness of millions of people, young and old, of all classes and colors and centuries. In prayer, events of life, the wonder of nature, and personal relationships, we experience the presence, power, compassion and love of Abba, who is the tenderness of mother and the strength of father.

The "Hail Mary"

Second only in popularity to the "Our Father" as a prayer among Catholics is the "Hail Mary." This prayer is often said after the Our Father, to remind us that worship is given only to God, not even to a human being as holy as Mary; and that our devotion to Mary is to our spiritual mother in heaven, part of the "communion of saints" which we will join one day by the grace of God at the end of our journey on this earth. The "Hail Mary" is divided into three parts.

The first part,

HAIL MARY, FULL OF GRACE, THE LORD IS WITH THEE,

is a direct quotation of Luke 1:28, when the angel Gabriel appeared to Mary to tell her that she was to bear a son Jesus (we call this event the "Annunciation"). We share Mary's joy at the news that she is to become the mother of our Savior Jesus Christ, and ask for the same faith that she showed when she replied simply to the angel.

The second part,

BLESSED ART THOU AMONG WOMEN, AND BLESSED IS THE FRUIT OF THY WOMB, JESUS,

is a direct quotation (apart from the last word "Jesus") of Luke 1:42. This was said to Mary by her cousin Elizabeth, when Mary went to visit Elizabeth. (We call that event the "Visitation.") Elizabeth was also pregnant, due to give birth to John the Baptist; and so they rejoiced together as proud mothers. But Elizabeth recognizes that Mary's son-to-be is to surpass even John the Baptist in God's plan. So she blessed Mary as the "Mother of my Lord" (*Lk 1:42*); and we join Elizabeth

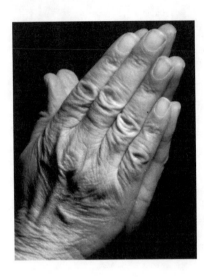

in that blessing, recognizing Mary as the Mother of God.

The third part,

HOLY MARY, MOTHER OF GOD, PRAY FOR US SIN-NERS, NOW AND AT THE HOUR OF OUR DEATH,

has been added by the devotional tradition of the Church. By this, we turn a Scripture meditation on the Annunciation and the Visitation into a prayer, a personal address to our spiritual mother. Just as we ask other Christians on this earth to pray for us, so now we join the "communion of saints" in heaven by faith, asking the "Queen of Saints and Angels" to pray for us. Note that the prayer is going back even-tually to God. It does not stop at Mary. She prays for us to God. We ask her, the sinless one, to pray "for us sinners" especially "at the hour of our death," because we remember that she suffered a mother's agony, as her divine Son was dying on the cross (*Jn 19:25–27*). She remembers her sufferings, and shares in ours.

Glory to the Father ...

The third element in what we might call the Catholic "Trilogy" of prayer is the "Glory to the Father":

GLORY TO THE FATHER, AND TO THE SON, AND TO THE HOLY SPIRIT: AS IT WAS IN THE BEGINNING, IS NOW, AND WILL BE FOR EVER. *AMEN.*

Catholics very often say these prayers one after the other.

They go well in sequence, because together they express the whole of the mysterious and wonderful relationship between ourselves and God in the Christian revelation.

First, the "Our Father" makes us realize that all prayer is to the one God, our Father, who loves us and wants to give us all that is good.

The "Hail Mary" makes us realize that we never pray alone, even if we are physically alone; because we pray in union with other Christians on earth and in heaven, meditating on the Gospel with the one who first said yes to the Good News, Mary the Mother of God.

The "Glory to the Father" makes us realize that in our prayer, we are caught up in the life of the Trinity, a life which begins on earth, but will con-tinue for ever. Prayer is never just personal reflec-tion. It is giving praise and glory to the Trinity.

It is important to try to understand the words of the "Our Father," the "Hail Mary," and the "Glory to the Father." Otherwise, the saying of these prayers could become a routine, a vain repetition, against which our Lord warned (*Mt 6:7*).

With care and reflection, the daily recitation of these prayers is a tried way of personal communion with God for anyone who wishes to deepen their relationship with him.

Place for prayer

If we look at Jesus in the Gospels, we find one outstanding fact about his relationship with his Father – he gives him lots of time!

The key factor in prayer is giving time regularly to God. We often speak of this as "wasting time with God." We decide to pray and immediately there are a hundred and one things claiming our attention – a person to see, a letter to write, the potatoes to be peeled. But unless we follow Jesus in making ourselves available for God, we will never know him more clearly, love him more dearly. Look at Jesus! No matter how busy he was, he went off to pray:

> Large crowds would gather to hear him and to have their illnesses cured, but he would go off to some deserted place and pray (*Lk 5:15-16*).

Prayer is about our loving relationship with God. Love is not simply an emotion, a falling in love. Love has to be worked at.

The mirror of this love is God's love in sending his Son. Jesus says:

> My food is to do the will of the one who sent me (*Jn 4:34*).

He had to work hard at this as he brought his human will into line with God's will. The cost we can see at the garden of Gethsemane.

This means in our daily life Jesus expects us to work out our salvation. We need to take on some form of discipline which can help us to center on God in the midst of our ordinary busyness and distractions. So, for instance, we must exert our will out of our love for God, regularly each day, whether we feel like praying or not. It is the test of the seriousness of our love that we set aside time daily.

Morning and night prayers are an obvious example. Ejaculatory prayers during the day or a mantra are also excellent.

It is also important not only to "say" prayers, but to follow Jesus' word and shut yourself in "your private room," praying to God in secret. As an expression of love – stop – think – love. Only regularity, perseverance, and generosity will deepen your relationship of love. If you are doing your part, God will show you his everlasting love in return.

Prayer

Come, Holy Spirit, fill the hearts of your faithful, and enkindle in them the fire of your love. Send forth your Spirit and they shall be created. And you shall renew the face of the earth.

Questions

1 In the Old Testament, God is sometimes portrayed as being distant and remote and at other times he is seen as being very close to his people. How do you imagine God? Make a list of qualities and characteristics you think he has.

2 Some people see the "Our Father" as containing a list of all the elements we should include in prayer. Using the text of this greatest of all prayers, discuss how these essential elements are present in the "Our Father."

Prayers

The Our Father

Our Father, who art in heaven,
hallowed be thy name;
thy kingdom come;
thy will be done on earth
    as it is in heaven.
Give us this day our daily bread;
and forgive us our trespasses
as we forgive those who trespass
    against us;
and lead us not into temptation,
but deliver us from evil.

For the kingdom,
    and the power, and the
    glory are yours,
    now and for ever.
    Amen.

(This ending is not in the original
prayer taught by Christ; but it
has been added by ancient tradition, is used by many Christians
today, and is included in the
Catholic Vatican II liturgy almost
immediately after the Our
Father, as part of the Communion.)

The Hail Mary

Hail Mary, full of grace,
the Lord is with thee;
blessed art thou among women,
and blessed is the fruit of thy
    womb, Jesus.
Holy Mary, Mother of God,
pray for us sinners,
now and at the hour of our
    death.
Amen.

The Glory to the Father

Glory to the Father,
and to the Son,
and to the Holy Spirit:
as it was in the beginning,
is now, and will be for ever.
Amen.

The Rosary

This is an ancient prayer of devotion, using the repetition of the
Our Father, the Hail Mary, and
the Glory to the Father, as a
means of meditating on the mysteries of the Gospel. It will be
useful to find a set of rosary
beads, which serve as a means of
counting the prayers, not as a
"vain repetition" which our Lord
condemned, but rather as an aid
to concentration; Mary, as it
were, takes us around the "rose-
garden" (hence rosary) of the
Good News of her Son's life,
death and resurrection:

The joyful mysteries

1. The Annunciation
    (Our Father once, Hail Mary
    ten times, Glory to the
    Father once, after each of the
    fifteen mysteries).
2. The Visitation
3. The Birth of Christ
4. The Presentation
5. The Finding in the Temple

The sorrowful mysteries

1. The Agony in the Garden
2. The Scourging at the Pillar
3. The Crowning with Thorns
4. The Carrying of the Cross
5. The Crucifixion

The glorious mysteries

1. The Resurrection
2. The Ascension
3. The Descent of the Spirit
4. The Assumption
5. The Coronation of Mary

At the end of the rosary, we say this prayer:

O God, whose only-begotten Son by his life, death, and resurrection, has purchased for us the rewards of eternal life. Grant we beseech thee, that meditating upon these mysteries in the most holy rosary of the Blessed Virgin Mary, we may both imitate what they contain, and obtain what they promise. Through the same Christ our Lord. *Amen.*

N.B. Before beginning to use this wonderful meditation, it would perhaps be helpful to find a priest or lay person who can set you on the road to praying the rosary. Many Christians have found this prayer a great strength, so easy is it to use, no books being required.

The Angelus

This prayer is said at 6 a.m., 12 midday, and at 6 p.m. by many people, in order to remember the stupendous fact that God became man in Jesus, and that Mary said yes in faith to the angel (hence "angelus" in Latin). Perhaps you might begin by just reciting it each midday:

The angel of the Lord declared unto Mary:
and she conceived by the Holy Spirit.
Hail Mary, etc...

Behold the handmaid of the Lord.
Be it done unto me according to thy word.
Hail Mary, etc.

And the Word was made flesh,
and dwelt among us.
Hail Mary, etc.

Pray for us, O holy Mother of God;
that we may be made worthy of the promises of Christ.

Pour forth, we beseech thee O Lord, thy grace into our hearts; that we to whom the Incarnation of Christ thy Son was made known by the message of an angel, may by his passion and cross be brought to the glory of his resurrection. Through the same Christ our Lord. *Amen.*

There are many other Catholic prayers, some of which you will find in *Faith Alive*, and some you will find as you look through various prayer books. But the above represent the "basics."

Prayer for those who have died

Eternal rest grant to (him, her, them), O Lord.
And let perpetual light shine upon (him, her, them).
May (he, she, they) rest in peace. *Amen.*

The Creed

For the text of the Apostles' Creed and the Nicene Creed see chapter 5.

The Rite of Christian Initiation of Adults (RCIA)

Faith Alive will be of great help to those involved with the process of the instruction and initiation of those who wish to become members of the Church.

The Vatican (the central organization of the Catholic Church in Rome) issued in 1972 a new Rite of Christian Initiation of Adults, which revives the ancient practice of the formation of initiates by stages.

Stage one: evangelization

At this stage, the person wishing to become a member of the Church makes preliminary inquiries as to whether he or she accepts the Good News of Christ. When the inquirer is able to make an act of faith in the Gospel, the service of enrollment takes place, and the period of formal instruction commences.

Stage two: the catechumenate

At this stage, the new "catechumen," the person now committed to learning about life in the Church, is introduced into doctrine, morals, spirituality, and above all the community life of God's people, as a preparation for full initiation. At a suitable time, the candidate is "elected," and a final period of spiritual prepara-tion ends with the wonderful liturgy of baptism and welcoming into full communion by receiving the Body and Blood of Christ in the Eucharist.

Stage three: post-baptismal catechesis

The Church does not wish the learning process begun during the catechumenate to finish after the candidate is made a full member of the Church. In fact, in the early days of the Church, it was only after initiation that the central mysteries of the Christian faith were disclosed to the candidate, these doctrines being kept secret from all those except full members of the Church. That is why this period is sometimes called "mystagogical catechesis," because it was instruction about mysteries undisclosed to unbelievers. In *Faith Alive*, however, we have simply used this period of post-baptismal catechesis in order to reflect more about the mission and ministry of the church, and the Christian's role in it.

N.B. For teachers, catechists, and group leaders, it will be most useful to look more closely at the RCIA, in order to relate the material in *Faith Alive* to the whole process of Christian initiation.

Contributors

The editors and publishers of *Faith Alive: New Catechism Edition*, would like to thank all those who originally contributed to *Faith Alive*, especially Fr. Austin Flannery and Fr. Michael Hollings.

Mrs. Helen Alvare
Fr. Ninian Arbuckle OFM
Wendy Mary Beckett
Sir John Betjemen
Fr. Steve Bevan SVD
Rabbi Lionel Blue
Sr. Cecily Boulding
Fr. Frederick Broomfield
Prof. F. F. Bruce
Archbishop George Carey
Dennis Chiles
Fr. Tony Churchill
Dr. Francis Clark
Fr. Hubert Condron
Msgr. Michael Connelly
Dr. John Coulson
Tom Coyle
Fr. Gabriel Daly OSA
Fr. Robin Duckworth
Michael Emms
Fr. Michael Evans
Dr. Rachel Evans
Fr. Sean Fagan SM
Br. Daniel Faivre
Fr. W. Fearon
Julian Filochowski CAFOD
Dr. Anna Flynn
Dr. John Goodwill
Dr. James Hanratty
John Harriot
James Hastings
Sr. Martina Hayden OP
Sr. Perpetua Healy
Peter Hebblethwaite
Dr. Ian Jessiman
Msgr. James Joyce
Fr. Ignatius Kelly
Mr. John Kelly FRCOG
Fr. Dermot Lane

Fr. Tom Lane CM
Fr. Rene Laurentin
Msgr. George Leonard
Br. Damien Lundy
Rabbi Magonet
Fr. Thomas Marsh
Fr. Edward Matthews
Dr. Enda McDonagh
Fr. James McManus CSsR
Prof. Peter Millard
Canon Edward Mitchison
Msgr. Martin Molyneux
Bishop Donal Murray
Gertrude Mueller Nelson
Gloria and Laurie Nobbs
Fr. Gerald O'Collins SJ
Fr. Sean O'Collins
Bishop C. Murphy O'Connor
Fr. Christopher O'Donnell
Fr. Paul O'Leary
Fr. John O'Toole
Fr. Robert Ombres OP
Vicy and Sandra Pajak
Sr. Maria Parcher
Fr. Michael Prior
Fr. Pius Smart OFMCAP
Fr. Michael Smith
Msgr. Peter Smith
Rabbi Norman Solomon
Cardinal Suenens
Bishop Frank Thomas
Fr. Hugh Thwaites
Fr. Simon Tugwell
Fr. Henry Wansborough
Archbishop D. Worlock
Anne White
Fr. David Williamson
Fr. Edward Yarnold SJ

Picture Credits

Pages 36, 64, 69, 87, 100, 103, 115, 119, 133, 159, 165, 173, 188: Barnabys Picture Library

Pages 33, 39, 41, 45, 78, 108, 111, 125, 129, 146, 182, 192, 193: Sonia Halliday Photographs

Pages 9, 11, 47, 90, 92, 96, 126, 135, 196: Gabriel Communications Ltd.

Pages 17, 30, 86, 142, 156: Illustrations by Annie Valloton from the *Good News Bible*, © American Bible Society 1976, used with permission

Pages 131, 148, 200: John Howard

Pages 57, 136, 153: Illustrations taken from *The Adventure Bible: A Study Bible for Kids*, copyright © 1989 by The Zondervan Corporation. All rights reserved, used by permission of Zondervan Publishing House.

Page 4: Laurie Burn

Page 12: Reproduced by courtesy of the Director and University Librarian, the John Rylands University Library of Manchester

Page 23: Reproduced by courtesy of the Trustees, The National Gallery, London

Page 116: National Portrait Gallery

Page 163: Joanne O'Brien

Index